PARENT-TEACHER
INTERVIEWS

A Modern Concept
of
Oral Reporting

R.C. Bradley, Ed. D.
North Texas State University

International Standard Book Number 0-8418-4561-1
Library of Congress Catalog Card Number 77-148556
Copyright © 1971, The University Press

Printed in the United States of America
THE UNIVERSITY PRESS
Wolfe City, Texas 75496

Why this work is important.

PREFACE

The Problem: All teachers confer with parents. Many teachers are beginning to confer on a scheduled basis. That is, personal conferences are being scheduled with elementary school parents as often as two times a school year. It can be demonstrated that teachers receive less professional training in the area which is perhaps of greater importance than any of their other many faceted school tasks— communication with the parents of the children they teach. Though this is the major reason for this book, it is also needed for the following significant reasons:

> 1) Instruction is becoming more highly *personalized*. Teachers are striving to meet the needs of various pupils in small-group and private instructional fashion. This necessitates keeping more records of a subjective nature on individual pupils.

2) There is much discussion among prominent educators of the possibility that gradecards will soon be abandoned from our educational system. The National ASCD has already gone on record for this statement; so has the National DESP.

3) Traditional classroom organization is being modified. Many school systems are adopting non-graded systems at their elementary levels or modified versions of the self-contained classroom plan. Hence, the traditional progress reports are no longer satisfactory ways of communicating pupil progress to parents.

4) The school is a communications center. Parents want to know more than what grade-cards can show in the first place. They want to talk with a qualified listener who is familiar with their child's development.

5) Schools have employed more specialized personnel. With the growing numbers of special school staff personnel (speech therapists, remedial teachers, school psychologists, school nurses) the need for conferring with parents is gaining momentum.

6) More public schools are turning to their own inservice training programs for upgrading the performances of their staff members. This book will provide them with the latest research and periodical literature which is sometimes non-accessible in public school areas. Moreover, the "how to" do it style of writing will show personnel actual ways of improving their conference techniques.

7) With the growing number of university teachers, it is believed that this book will be a valuable aid to those instructors who have not had experiences in conference methods themselves. Particularly it is believed that many methods teachers at the university level will find uses for this book as a supplementary aid to their coursework.

8) There is a growing interest in many school districts for the elementary principal to be responsible for instructional problems in his building. Most principals are aware of the need of their teachers becoming more adept in visiting with parents. Hence, one of the first programs principals seek to attack is the one dealing with how to increase the effectiveness with which their staff reports progress of pupils to parents.

9) At one time in history schools served small communities and parents attended school meetings and activities regularly. Now schools are larger and serve many patrons since they even have their own bus transportation and the like. Some parents might not come to visit the school if it were not for parent teacher interviews. Portions of this book deal with what the parent needs to know about his school and what it is doing for his child.

The Audience:

This book is written for those who have any part in conferring with parents about their child's school progress. This group includes: College and University professors, school administrators, teachers, and special school service personnel. Primarily it is aimed at administrators and teachers since it contains an abundance of rich information for teachers who direct conferences with parents; describes an ideal set of conference tools for administrators and teachers to initiate in the local school setting; suggests kinds of information that should be reported to parents through the conference procedure and ways of imparting that information; gives the most current research dedicated to the purpose of upgrading conference procedures; and provides samples of guidelines for teachers to use in conducting conferences with parents.

The Benefits:

For the most part reports to parents have been too general. Even when the teacher tried to be specific he found it difficult because of failure to have at hand a book of ideas, tools, and techniques which would make his conference penetrating, informative, and purposeful. Moreover, there has been little if any uniformity to conference reporting whatsoever. There is a need for every parent to have certain types of information about a child's school progress at each and every regularly scheduled conference. Special conferences should be called when needed rather than to use scheduled school conferences for the major purpose of discussing poor conduct, discipline, or the like. In other words, there are some things which a parent should be told about his child at each conference before going into specific problems unique to that given child.

Every teacher needs a conference guidesheet to take with him to his conferences with parents. Sometimes teachers have an idea about what to report but haven't given much thought to what parents may want to know. The guidesheets have combined within them what parents want to know as well as what they need to know.

Principals will find copies of this book helpful in that they can use it in their in-service training programs, can recommend it to beginning teachers who are in their buildings for the first time, or hand it to the established teacher who needs to be more specific in his reports to parents.

Professors in higher education will find the book most helpful in that it will contain the recommended procedures necessary to effective conferencing. Moreover they will find the conference guidesheets thorough and complete. This book will aid them in their college teaching plus its serving as a valuable resource and guide in their personal conduct of in-service training programs.

All senior student teachers will find this book a valuable aid to both their instructional and professional activities in course work on the college campus but will particularly find it valuable when they go out into the field to do their practicum.

Those who use this book should find it to be truly a guide toward more effective conferences with parents. The end result being of course, an enhancement of the educative welfare of the child.

ACKNOWLEDGMENT

Acknowledgment is gratefully made to each copyright holder who granted permission to reprint from previously published materials.

This book is dedicated to my boys, Danny Ray and R. C., Jr., and their fine teachers who take their valuable professional time to confer with parents. Particularly mention is made of Mr. Olan Ford, elementary principal, Eula Mae Lyle, first-grade teacher, Mrs. Pat Raney, teacher of second grade, and all other teachers of Sam Houston Elementary School, Denton, Texas, who, by their example have impressed the author of a genuine interest in children and who, additionally, hold the type of private conferences that parents should receive.

*　　*　　*　　*　　*　　*

AN INTERVIEW MUST BE JUDGED NOT SO MUCH BY WHAT IT MEANS TO A PARENT AS BY WHAT IT DOES FOR THE CHILD

FOREWORD

This book for teachers and administrators is based upon published and unpublished research concerned with the parent-teacher conference method of reporting pupil progress. The published research appeared originally in various professional books and journals; the unpublished material, which makes up the major portion of this publication, comes from studies conducted by the writer.

It is believed that the contents of this book will be useful to administrators who organize conferences, teachers who practice conferring with parents, and both junior and senior student teachers interested in learning about the conference method of reporting.

Although the conference method is not a panacea for all ills encountered in the many practices used for reporting, it may be viewed as one of the better methods of imparting information to parents who have children attending the modern elementary school.

The Department of Elementary School Principals, NEA, has recommended through their associational resolutions that reporting practices presently employed in many elementary schools are inconsistent with our knowledge about children and how they learn. Consequently, on the basis of available evidence, educators are urged to discard the traditional report card in favor of a more effective procedure; namely, THE PARENT—TEACHER CONFERENCE.

Author

North Texas State University
Denton, Texas

INTRODUCTION

For several significant reasons many elementary schools across the country are turning to Parent-Teacher Conferences as a method of reporting. Certainly this is in keeping with current investigations in individualizing instruction as well as providing a basis for more effective teaching and learning. Several of the schools are adopting the conference procedure as a supplement to their present method of reporting at the elementary school levels.

The *conference procedure* not only provides for two way communication between the parents and the school but it permits individualizing reports for each and every child. Moreover, parents should be guided to understand the interrelation of significant aspects of their child's growth. To this end the individual conference provides the opportunity for the teacher to discuss all phases of the child's development with the parent.

The kinds of information that teachers should report to parents is one of the major contributions of this book. Dr. Bradley's professional experience in conferencing, original research, and survey of materials coming from major school systems using the conference method of reporting makes this book a very practical, thorough, and creative approach to the improvement of conference procedures.

School people who want to keep in harmony with the changing times and who hold the better interests of children in high regard will profit much from the information contained herein. The move to conferences receives much of its impetus from the (1) individualization of instruction, (2) non-graded elementary organization, (3) dissatisfaction with traditional report cards, (4) need for modern day parents to become more thoroughly acquainted with the function of the schools, (5) demand for children to be more respectful to law and authority of which this burden of responsibility is mutually shared by both parent and schools, and (6) professional educators themselves who are seeking to evaluate the learning of children by measuring their "behavioral changes" academically, physically, socially, emotionally, mentally, and aesthetically.

For the most part school people are least trained in the major school function for which they serve the most—communication with parents. Certainly Dr. Bradley does more in this book than bridge the gap between what is actually being done and what should be done in reporting. His work contains a practical and functional philosophy toward reporting which should be of great interest, value, and help to administrators, supervisors, counselors, and classroom teachers.

B. Dwane Kingery, Dean
College of Education
North Texas State University
Denton, Texas

Contents

II Critical Issues Meriting Special Handling By Teachers in the Inter-View Situation

*Evaluative Criteria
Against Which to Judge One's
Current Parent-Teacher Interview Plan*

12

304

With Respect to the Nature of the Conference Procedure, 305 With Respect to the Essential Features of the PTC Procedure, 306 With Respect to Materials and Equipment, 307 With Respect to Evaluation of the Conference Program and Its Contribution to Pupil Achievement, 307 Summary, 308

Epilogue 309

Appendices 312

Subject Index 319

Why Confer?

New ideas can be good or bad, just the same as old ones.
—F. D. Roosevelt

Introduction

Of all areas of school business, the area of reporting pupil information to parents is the one in which educators have been most insistent on the need for re-examination. If a school system does examine its method of reporting to parents, usually a revision results. This area is one where innovations, more likely than not, have collided violently with established educational ideas and evaluation standards. The result has been changes, experimentation, and much controversy.

Teachers, principals, and counselors are going to have to conduct interviews with parents for a number of reasons. Specifically, (1) parents are eager to learn from school personnel about the school program, (2) educators will want to secure parental help in guiding their children, and (3) regular interviewing will not only help secure much parental participation, but of the right kind in school and classroom activities.

What Makes a Good Report System?

Most of the literature discussion about systems of reporting focuses on forms, marking techniques, and periodic distribution of cummulative findings. But it will be putting the cart before the horse if one tries to judge a system by starting there. Instead, start by looking for standards that can be used to measure the effectiveness of "report systems" in general, whatever form they happen to take.

The following criteria are not necessarily universally agreed upon, but all widely enough accepted to provide a reasonable basis for investigation and comparative purposes. These are some significant hallmarks of a good system:

1) *All parents can easily understand it.* Since parents come from all sorts of backgrounds, have varying viewpoints, and show vested interests in their own children, a report to them must be highly personalized. If the system is too complex, it can easily be misinterpreted. The advantages of reporting student progress by interview are readily apparent on this point. If the interview is managed correctly, unfamiliar professional terms are ruled out and a simplified language is selected to meet the varying needs of parents (e. g., ghetto areas).

2) *It has been worked out through mutual cooperation.* Teachers, counselors, principals, and parents view progress reports from several vantage points. When they work together and share in developing the system, it reflects what each group seeks to learn. Interviews keep open these channels of communciation in that parents continue to feel free to request, and teachers free to offer.

3) *It agrees with preconceived policies, practices, and behavioral objectives formulated by school personnel.* If educational theories represented by the system of reporting do not "square" with the theories upon which the school operates, confusion and dissatisfaction can result. In a chapter section that follows evidence will be cited of the close relationship of the interview practice of reporting to a method of learning entitled, the "normal progress" theory.

4) *It reports on the student as one member of a group.* Letter grades, for example, show how much a student deviates from the average of the class. The student who stands far above the average also stands high in relation to the attainment of his classmates. His progress and achievements are discussed in interviews in terms of what is expected of his

age and grade. A teacher does not rate him only in comparison with himself.

5) *A child, as an individual, is considered.* A student should not have his work compared only to an exterior standard nor with only the average achievement of his class. His progress should be described in terms of his own ability and personality. The teacher asks the question, "Is this pupil working and achieving in accordance with his known capacity?" He is not rated only in comparison with marks, norms, or his class group.

6) *The concentration is upon evaluating areas of behavior and learning considered as attributes of an active community citizen.* Traditional reports have attempted to measure the child's performance with a specific, objective standard. Character development was seldom analyzed except in broad, generalized terms. One of the major purposes of the conference is to convey an accurate picture of the performance and behavior of the child at this moment in time.

7) *It is fair and accurate.* If parents and children are to respect and believe in the report coming from the school, then the system selected must provide the structure which promotes that confidence, accuracy, and fairness for all concerned. For example, a low score on a report card usually invokes a "cold" feeling with both the parent and the child. While on this same issue an interview provides the setting in which a low academic score can be discussed with respect to its several ramifications.

8) *It tells not only what but how and why.* A good report is somewhat diagnostic in nature. It pinpoints specific types of progress, probes underlying causes of behavior, and makes some projections as to possible outcomes. Interview systems seek to analyze the "whole child."

9) *It has degrees of flexibility.* Much can be determined from marks, numbers, and symbols, but to adhere only to this type of reporting leaves much to be desired. Reporting a child's academic performance is essential, but it is only one part of a good report system. The letter system of grading, for example, does not consider the limited capacities of the poor student. If he is continually compared with his mentally superior classmates, he may soon cease to put forth any extra effort. Feelings of inferiority may be fostered. An interview system can be organized to allow for the degrees of flexibility necessary for the giving of a comprehensive report.

10) *It is efficient.* A teacher can become burdened with clerical duties under some systems of reporting. Moreover, a

system could require more skill, training, or ability than a teacher has at his command. In schools where multiple systems of reporting are used in traditional fashion, record keeping becomes unwieldy. In a twenty minute conference there is an exchange of nearly 4000 words; hence letter marks and grade scores can be kept to a minimum. With respect to the time involved in implementing an interview system as compared to grade card methods, and considering the multiplicity of rewards coming from it, interviews are not only more effective but thorough.

11) *It should fit with the system of record keeping.* Teachers keep a record of the pupil's achievement in a class record book. Observations of pupil behavior are kept in written form as an anecdotal record, while sociometric data is compiled on a sociogram. These data plus other forms of information can be adapted to the interview report. Much of the data coming from the devices above are placed on cumulative record sheets for file purposes. There is no unnecessary duplication, no inconsistency.

12) *All participants directly affected are helped to understand and use the reports.* Teachers, parents and children are provided those school services which implement the conference report. That is, if the child has a health problem the school nurse can be sought. If the child has a major academic problem, he may be referred to the school guidance specialist. Special school services are more apt to be used in the interview technique than any other single method of reporting.

Education is a co-operative venture in which school and home are active participants. In order to play its role in education more effectively the school must make a special attempt to make periodic reports to parents. The method to be followed for report purposes, should meet each of the twelve criteria presented above.

What is the Function of a Report?

All too often the report card has served as an end in itself. It was a goal toward which all children worked. Children viewed it as a periodic reward or punishment. Parents viewed it as the major goal for which their child should seek to achieve. Teachers used it as a basis for a definitive judgment of a given child's progress. Neither of these points of view satisfy the criteria of a functional report.

Report cards, then and now, merely represent only one of many measurements for determining the extent of a pupil's progress, or lack of it. It is an aid to a report, not *the* report.

Reporting systems that fail to convey to parents information they understand about their children's progress which goes beyond the traditional grade card report, invite trouble. A functional report includes information from grade cards, test measurements, health data, daily class records, anecdotal records, family information, special school services, teacher recommendations, and the like. All of which are collected and analyzed to evaluate thoroughly a pupil's development.

More specifically what are the functions of reports? The following factors must be considered. Which do you consider of greater importance? Which does your school system seem to stress? What method of reporting best achieves these goals? An effective report system:

a. Provides guidelines to help teachers reach conclusions about their students, to make instructional plans for reaching desirable goals, and to judge the effectiveness of their own work.

b. Encourages the student to do better work by indicating to him what progress he has made, where it was made, and what he must do to increase his skills and abilities in the future.

c. Provides an incentive for the pupil to work up to his native ability with due consideration for his strengths and weaknesses, balance of successes and failures, and in accordance with desirable attitudes and values.

d. Promotes appraisal by school officials of the effectiveness of their counseling and guidance program, planning for the future, and general over-all success of their students.

e. Informs parents on their children's academic, social, emotional, physical, and mental progress. It should suggest the kind of guidance their children need with respect to the nature, aims and direction of any personal educational programing.

f. Assimilates appropriate information required by most schools, colleges, the military, or prospective employers.

Thus, it can be seen that principals and their staffs have the responsibility for communication with parents at four major levels of increasing generality: (1) information *about* the learner himself; (2) information *from* the learner; (3) the relating of these findings to the parents' understanding of the local school; and (4) the more general educational picture concerning a child's attributes for a vocational, academic, and professional career.

Why Other Methods Fail

In the light of afore-mentioned criteria, one can see that any one of the following methods would be inadequate to adopt as an only method of reporting. Moreover, it is doubtful as to their effectiveness were they to be used in combinations. Though each of these methods could be used for the supplementation of the interview system, certainly it is important that their inadequacies be remembered or they will tend to minimize interview efficiency.

Narrative reports. Letters are time consuming and the skill of writing them is difficult to acquire. One tends to pull his punches when a permanent record is established which can be shown visually to others. For the most part, letters are: (1) easy to misinterpret, (2) hard to understand, (3) compared among certain parental clicques, and (4) have limited academic coverage.

Progress reports. These evaluate progress made in terms of the child's own individual ability, but they offer no "hows and whys." Check marks, symbols or letters (E, S, M, I, F) may be used to indicate whether or not a child is doing his best; however, pupils are conditioned to think that "average" or "satisfactory" is good enough. Top-quality students get no reward or recognition for their work, while slow ones are led to think that poor achievement is acceptable. Seldom is achievement data available for use in choosing courses, appraising aptitudes, measuring vocational skills, or the like. Under this method there are very few incentives, if any, to do better. The child accepts "status quo."

Letter grades. In using the "E, S, M, I, F," system of marking, the pupil's performance is compared with a norm (usually a minimum standard for the grade). Since teachers differ in applying letter marks to papers, it is doubtful as to the objectiveness of grades assigned at the end of a quarter or semester. Pupils are urged to work for grades, and grades *per se* are not effective incentives for learning. Below average pupils are discouraged by them, while bright children tend to be satisfied with any good mark as long as little effort has to go into obtaining it.

Some teachers give only a grade for what has actually been achieved on pencil-paper tests, while others grade primarily upon the amount of effort that a child portrays in his achievement of a set standard. Through the use of letter grades one tries to isolate academic progress. Certainly this is not in keeping with what is known about principles dealing with child growth and development.

Combinations. To offset some of the pitfalls of report systems mentioned above, some schools have developed cards that combine the features from several marking systems. Although one can give dual ratings, one set on achievement and one on progress, usually emotional and social development are not seen in positive relationships. Even if one utilizes the space provided for "teacher comment" on report cards, seldom is there room for writing more than trite and inadequate phrases such as, "Jimmy is immature," "Bobby is working hard," or "room for improvement." Succinctly, combinations have one tremendous disadvantage: They are too complicated.

Emergent Philosophies.

The above facts reflect three varying viewpoints about reporting. One view emphasizes standards of achievement (letter grades). Those who use this standard believe that schools are not intended to serve as baby-sitting institutions merely to raise children for parents but to equip them with selected skills and knowledges. The need is stressed to measure actual achievement against set minimums or standards.

The second view emphasizes progress measurement according to individual ability (progress reports, letters to parents). Those who use these methods say that education is to develop the fullest capacity of the individual. However, the fact is that pupils are measured by standards which most of them cannot meet. If any given child cannot be fairly measured and marked in accordance with the system adopted, it to him is useless and even dangerous. The incentive value of rating effort over rigid performance levels, however, is generally considered by those who use progress reports. The basic premise of this belief is that students learn best if allowed to progress at their own rates.

And, of course, there is the eclectic approach for those who cannot ally themselves with one camp but find valid arguments in all approaches. This belief results in combination approaches to reporting. In the last five years many school systems have turned to combination methods of reporting. However, the current trend is a movement away from the use of only written procedures for reporting information to parents and a movement toward the full or part-time use of interviews. It is to the discussion of the interview system that the remainder of this book will be confined.

The Current Viewpoint That Really Counts

In elementary education, particularly, there is a fourth viewpoint rapidly gaining the support of those actively involved in reporting to parents. It emphasizes the diagnostic type of report. Persons who hold this view believe that schools are designed purposefully to lead children into socially desirable skills and behavior. This philosophy recognizes that a child must be considered in his completeness. Academic growth is believed inseparable from other kinds of developmental growth. Curiosity, creativity, and imagination are engendered through the use of this method. The child's "wanting to learn" is the major workable incentive. Educators who wisely advocate the individualization of instruction hold the belief that each student must be analyzed and described, not just marked and rated. Those who hold this viewpoint that each child must be considered as a separate entity, ascribe to the interview system of reporting.

Why Conference Contact is Imperative

Parents are also teachers. They were the child's first teacher. They influence their children in the community as a citizen and in their school as pupils. As educators, we rely heavily upon parents to do things thought best for the child. When parents cannot do these tasks, the child's life is affected. The suggestions that follow, then, in this section and throughout the entire book, are based upon the following beliefs:

1. Parents can help the school program. Ultimately, the information obtained through interviews will help or hinder the child in school success.

2. Parents usually know what makes their child react effectively. The teacher can use this knowledge to promote the educational welfare of the child.

3. Most children strive to please their parents; they need parental support and assistance. Educators will want to secure parental help in guiding their children.

4. Some children will have serious types of educational

problems. Some will be more severely handicapped than others. Without parent-teacher teamwork, their success will be unnecessarily limited.

5. Teachers should be the first persons to whom parents might feel they could turn when questions arise concerning their children. Thus, parents are eager to learn from school personnel about their children and the school program. If the school program is directed toward making useful citizens out of boys and girls, most parents are usually willing to follow the advice of educators.

Of the various and frequently conflicting purposes of report systems, the five factors mentioned above seem clear-cut and justifiable. A parent should be given the best available information about his child's progress and standing in school. This information should be placed in proper perspective according to life's purposes. When this is done, then systematic interviewing will not only help secure *more* parental participation, but of the *right kind* and in the right quantity in school and community activities.

Parent-Teacher Conferences—An Overview

The parent-teacher interview as a report of pupil progress to parents is growing in practice throughout the schools of this nation. Its growth seems to be a result of dissatisfaction with the traditional report card. Grade cards, letter systems, and progress reports at one time served an important function in the educative process, but they have been outgrown with respect to modern educational purposes. Each of these systems have presented a limited amount of coded information to parents with no provision for the return of information which the parent might possess. In summary, the interview method for reporting pupil progress is the single most effective medium of reporting because:

a. Face-to-face communication seems to be as effective in reporting to parents as in other matters.

b. Interviewers clearly distinguish between marks and comments related to a pupil's present standing and those related to his recent progress.

c. Goals such as subject-matter achievement, work habits, behavior traits, character development, and the like can be established for each child through verbal communication.

d. Some knowledge of what parents are like inside, and why, is certainly a necessary aspect of planning an educational program for their children.

e. A primary step to successful consultation with parents is to organize what one knows about the child and to take account of oneself relative to his own personal abilities and limitations as an educator, as well as those of the parent he is about to see.

The perplexity of parents and others (teachers, parents, citizens) which more often than not comes to a climax at report intervals, is a direct result of misunderstandings growing out of multiple report systems. The parent's confusion about how his child is doing in school is real and must be fully recognized. Just as real is the classroom teacher's desire for better ways of helping his individual learners. Conferring with parents will assure the teacher that appropriate steps are being taken to personalize and humanize the educational program of each pupil to the extent that the student can take it and use it, and his mental health will be better because his educational program and the method of reporting it is tailored to his needs.

How to Organize an Interview Program

If we know not what harbor we are making for, no wind is the right wind.

—Seneca

Introduction

The parent-teacher interview represents one of education's greatest hopes and efforts in determining the extent to which a child has achieved academic and social success. The role of the interviewer in assessing the competencies of children cannot be easily overestimated. Regardless of years of conference experience, the fact remains that even successful interviewers can be hampered by the structure of the system in which they must operate. Moreover, as a vital procedure in relating pupil success or lack of it, the conference cannot be a haphazard process subject to the unjustified whims of a selected few. It must represent a program intelligently conceived and based upon wise analysis of experience viewed in the light of new demands and discoveries. The ultimate success of conferences is determined very largely by the inclination, wisdom, and clarity

2

with which school personnel utilize and organize the resources which can be welded into a program of educational
interviews.

Principles Underlying the Formulation of the Interview Program

The presence of a scheme which represents the studied
attempt to develop a situation in which an interviewer can do
his best, does not necessarily involve rigidity and reduce
creativity. It merely serves as a method for assuring flexibility
and establishing some feelings of security. Since Boards of
Education, superintendents, principals, counselors, supervisors, teachers, and parents must have a meeting of the
minds as to what constitutes a well-organized interview
program, it seems advisable to suggest a few basic principles
which underlie the development of any effective interview
system.

1. *An interview program is based on a "normal progress" philosophy of education.* Most of the planned activities
of people are based on a set of beliefs or assumptions. It
would be possible, therefore, for interviewers to proceed
without an expressed philosophy. Actually, they are operating upon a philosophy acquired from their own prior
training. The practices of a large number of American schools
may be categorized as "grade standards" or "normal progress" in theory. If this be a plausible assumption, then it
seems reasonable to assume that the reporting practices of
schools will express one or the other of the theories.

Elsbree[1] has pointed out two assumptions that are made
by those who advocate the "grade standards" theory of pupil
progress. His first assumption was that "a basic body of
essential knowledge exists for all children in the elementary
school and that this knowledge can and should be arranged
and learned in some kind of orderly sequence." The second
assumption[2] was that "norms or standards of achievement
can be readily established for each of the six elementary

---

1. Willard S. Elsbree, *Pupil Progress in the Elementary School,* New York:
Teachers College, Columbia University, 1943, p. 2.

2. *Ibid,* pp. 2-3.

grades and that the teachers and administrators can parcel out the particular knowledge and skills in harmony with the grade norms thus set up."

The "continuous progress" theory and the "child growth" theory are philosophically very close to the "normal progress" theory advocated by those who interview. Caswell and Foshay[3] aptly contrasted the "grade standards" theory with the "normal progress" theory when they stated: "The former implies a minimum grade standard achievement for all children if they are to pass to the next grade while the latter imposes maximum individual standards of achievement."

Succinctly, there are several significant differences between the "grade standards" theory of pupil progress and the "normal progress" theory. Advocates of grade standards seem to be ignoring important facts of individual differences. Furthermore, when viewed in light of a democratic philsophy of education, the grade standards group seems to militate against equal educational opportunity for all children when one prescribed standard of educational achievement is established for all pupils.

When the role of the parent is considered, there are implications in the normal progress theory that are not evident in the grade standards theory. In the former, parental cooperation and understanding is of utmost importance; in the latter there is little the parent is asked to do beyond sending the child to school, enforcing good conduct, and supervising homework. It may be seen that the classroom program based on the "normal progress" theory will be a broader, more inclusive educational opportunity than was formerly known. The major emphasis is on maximum child growth in many areas. Subject matter mastery is important only to the extent that it serves the total growth of the child in terms of educational experience.

The fact that a marking system of "E, S, M, I, F," is used does not always mean that the philosophy of the school is "grade standard." The important consideration has to do with the inclusion or omission of the child's abilities, interests, and other personal factors in the evaluation process. Teachers may use the letter system of marking and yet base

3. Hollis L. Caswell and A. W. Foshay. *Education in the Elementary School,* New York: American Book Co., 1942 2nd ed.) p. 335.

those marks on non-competitive, child centered tasks. The marking system used for the purpose of obtaining information for parent-teacher interviews, however, should draw information from many areas of the child's school life.

In the final analysis, the individual teacher and the school as administrative unit must attach to one theory or the other. A basic requirement for effective and adequate interview programs is that the term "normal progress" be thoroughly understood and a functional philosophy be formulated concerning it. Parent interviews should be so designed that they are capable of maintaining effective communication between parents and teachers about all areas of child growth resulting from school experience. This is essential in a "normal progress" interview system.

2. *An interview program should be directed toward known purposes.* Out of a philosophy of reporting one formulates his purposes and goals of the interview. Reporting a child's academic performance is essential, but it is only one part of an adequate interview program. The interview should reflect some scheme of evaluation that is not totally based on classroom competition, but rather on the child's mental, educational, emotional, and social readiness and ability to achieve in the school program.

It seems sufficient to suggest here that the nature and success of the interview program must be determined in the light of what it sets out to do—its purposes. One may assume further that the interview system is effective to the extent that the purposes are known and understood by all who should contribute to their realization. When any one of the three groups (educators, parents, students) fail to fulfill their obligations to the respective purposes, an important link vital to the reporting process has been lost.

3. *The interview program depends upon appropriate methods for achieving its purposes.* Purposes are of little value until they are activated by some method for achieving them. The methods must not only be directed toward the accomplishment of the goals of reporting, but must also be consistent with the philosophy underlying the whole process.

The method of the interview program is considered to be the total machinery necessary to ensure its conception and it also includes the processes used to guarantee its continued success. It involves record keeping, motivation, group planning, mock conferences, in-service training, development of conference forms, scheduling, and many other phases of the reporting process.

4. *The ultimate effectiveness of the interview program depends heavily upon the quality of personnel responsible for its continued operation.* The kind of interview that parents receive can be little, if any better than the understanding of the professional staff who implement it. Those who formulate and implement the interview program should know fully its purposes and be highly skilled in its methods. It is conceivable that a salesman may experience reasonable success selling a given product in which he has little interest, but it is usually conceded that one of the basic factors in sales success is the enthusiasm of the seller for his product. By the same token, it is nearly inconceivable that one engaged in the process of interviewing will experience any degree of success without a strong belief in the purposes to which his time and talents are dedicated.

5. *The interview program must be realistically related to the basic functions of the teacher as he conducts daily teaching experiences and activities.* Theoretically, it would be quite possible for the teacher to teach in ways sufficient to meet the demands of the conference report, but still be somewhat below the quality of work expected of those who meet parents face to face in interview situations. Most teachers will accept the challenge of the new system of reporting as they probably already have learned that education is not made easier under the "normal progress" theory. Accepting and using the facts of individual differences requires high competence. Planning activities to challenge the very bright youngsters as well as directing the experiences of the slower pupils so that they progress at their levels of performance, is time consuming and difficult. Inasmuch as some teachers will find it difficult to prepare themselves for the teaching role which must accompany the modern approach of conferring personally with parents, it would seem that they might have some difficulty seeing the relationships between what has been taught and what ought to be reported.

6. *The interview program, to be successful, must have the faith and support of the parents and school community.* Since parents are expected to play a most active role in the interview program, they should have some part in its formulation. Their contributions should have some part in its formulation. Their contributions should be made mainly in the realm of what the interview program is to do rather than in the area of how it is to be done, which is more appropriately considered a professional function in nature.

The real obligation of the administration and staff in this regard is to develop conditions for balanced contributions from all persons and agencies, professional and lay, who have a genuine stake and part in the interview system.

Reporting a child's academic performance is essential, but it is only one part of an adequate interview. Therefore, the teacher must provide a learner with types of experiences that provide opportunity to secure information about his intellectual, emotional, social, and physical maturity. Certainly one of the prime jobs of the teacher is to offer opportunities for children to perform those tasks about which he is going to report during parent interviews. The omission or inclusion of information in conferences must be the result of a conscious effort to teach the child those understandings in daily life situations, rather than to rely on reporting information that comes through happenstance or feelings of the moment.

Simply stated, before educators can have a sound interview program, they must seek appropriate answers to the following questions as they relate to their particular school system:

1. What is important, and educationally vital, to those who are going to operate and support this interview program?
2. What are the specific purposes of the interview procedure for this school system?
3. By what processes and methods does this school expect to achieve each of its purposes and goals?
4. To what extent do members of the school staff understand the objectives and to what extent are they skilled and qualified in sound procedures for achieving them?
5. Once the interview system is inaugurated, how will a teacher's daily planning differ from that which was once his general procedure of teaching?
6. To what extent will the support of parents and local citizens be sought in planning and initiating action for the interview system?

ELEMENTS ESSENTIAL TO THE ORGANIZATION OF THE INTERVIEW PROGRAM

The interview program is really the means by which a school attempts to accomplish its tasks of reporting;—it includes the steps through which the administration and its staff must go in order to transform its objectives of reporting into actual outcomes during conference. If such a program is to be conceived wisely, several factors must be considered with some degree of rank order and uniformity. Three of these basic factors are: (1) to develop a consciousness within the staff and with the school patrons of the purposes for which the interview program should be attempted, (2) to prepare a plan for enlisting the aid and gaining the support of parents, pupils, and teachers in accepting this new system of reporting, and (3) to establish a written policy upon which the interim system will be based. Each of these will be treated in some detail in the following sections of this chapter as well as in subsequent chapters which are concerned with related duties and responsibilities of the principal and his staff.

Steps the Principal Should Take in Organizing An Effective Interim Program

School systems, like business enterprises, have their own individualities. But usually it is the principal who is expected to exercise leadership in the formulation of new school programs and policies. The interview program is no exception. The effectiveness of an individual conference report is in large measure determined by the basic groundwork laid by the principal as he strives to structure the total interview program. It is safe to assume that once all of the following steps have been followed, a very sound structure will be laid to which new ideas can be anchored as they arise.

STEP ONE: PREPARE THE AUDIENCES

Meet with Teachers. There will need to be several meetings with teachers before seeking a vote as to whether or not the conference method of reporting will be adopted. The principal will need to hold both group meetings and private sessions. After conference ideas are presented to the whole staff in group settings, quite likely some private meetings will be needed for those who suffer misunderstandings or for those teachers who simply want additional information. Factors such as these often necessitate the conduct of small group meetings or special private conferences.

The principal will need to seek three levels of committee action from among his staff: (1) a temporary committee must be appointed to study whether or not there is enough interest and need for the establishment of a conference system, (2) a second committee of temporary standing is necessary whose purpose it is to determine the depth and breadth of faculty qualifications for implementing such an interview system, and (3) a standing committee is needed to sit in on general meetings, planning sessions, and policy making of the administration whenever certain facets of the conference program are subject to review.

The committees mentioned above serve three separate, distinct purposes. The first committee studies the value that conferences hold for that specific school area. If the system is adopted, then the second committee is appointed to determine the qualifications of the staff for implementing the interview program. Their findings should suggest the type of inservice training that would be necessary to qualify the staff for an efficient execution of the several conference duties. The third committee is selected to serve as a liaison between the administration and staff. Their purpose is to offer "feedback" to the building staff with respect to what transpired in general administrative sessions. Several administrative meetings will be held to deal with the various stages of study of conference problems which ultimately will lead to the adoption or rejection of the conference plan. Committee groups are essential. If one has a part in the planning of the program, he will participate in it with much more interest and enthusiasm.

Meet with the Superintendent. While a principal may believe that conferences are essential to good education, he cannot operate a sound conference program unless his immediate superiors share this belief. Before the principal seeks to win the approval of others who should be interested in interview sessions, he should exercise his administrative function necessary to the establishment of any new program. He must discuss the matter with his superintendent and together they should recommend the strategy that should be used to initiate moves for adoption of an interview system.

After gaining the support of the superintendent and securing the approval of the board of education for exploring the possibilities of an interview system, the principal can begin more specific movements to expedite action. He is authorized to (1) organize parent committees through the auspices of the PTA Executive Board so that all parents can be reached for the purpose of understanding the nature and scope of conferences, (2) go to each grade level in his building and discuss the purposes of conferences which may soon be held with school parents, (3) secure resource persons who can help his teachers learn how to handle conference information and to manage special problems, (4) study the best means (brochures, TV, telephone, radio, newspapers) that are at his disposal for informing his many publics who must be sold on the idea of this new method of reporting; and, (5) personally furnish leadership and advisement as policies are discussed and formed within faculty and parent groups.

Meet with Parents. Since school parents will be actively involved in interviews, then they need to know what conferences are all about. Not all parents can be reached during PTA meetings, therefore it is mandatory that special sessions similar to "back to school night" be conducted with them. As parents come to this night conference to learn about school activities, an opportunity is provided for the principal to meet with them in a large group setting. It is recommended that all parents first meet in the auditorium on "parent's night" so that the principal can indicate in general terms the need for an effective plan for reporting in a better way their children's progress.

During this evening session with parents, the principal should discuss how interviewing would: (1) enable the teacher to know more about the child from the home viewpoint, (2) increase the probability of the teacher making an early focus upon the causes of problems, rather than expending effort upon symptoms of problems, (3) provide the teacher with information as to how parents deal with their children on behavioral problems arising in the home, (4) give them, as parents, an opportunity to know their child in the light of his native potential, and (7) give them opportunity to participate in the program of evaluation of their child.

When the parents are dismissed from the audience situation to go to their respective rooms as a group, then each homeroom teacher needs to further explain the possibilities of the interview system. The principal should instruct his teachers to elaborate upon what conferences contribute to the reporting practice. Some suggested topics include how conference settings provide opportunities for: (1) talking about a child's progress as compared to his own potential, class norms, school norms, and national norms, (2) interpreting school policies, (3) planning his educational program cooperatively, (4) talking about samples of work that can be shown at that time, (5) analyzing the child's behavior from both teacher and parental viewpoints, and (6) sharing subjective information about a child that cannot be obtained from achievement tests nor be reported on grade cards in the form of traditional marks or grades.

A brief session like the meetings mentioned above, gives the parent a feeling that he does have something to offer to his child's educational experience and that he is an important link in the total school program. Perhaps as an outgrowth of this meeting, a panel composed of parents can be scheduled for a later date whose purpose will be to indicate the kind of conference they would appreciate most and the role they believe a parent should play in actual interview sessions.

Meet with Pupils. The principal should explain to the pupils in his school the reasons why conferences will be forthcoming for them. Some children prior to this time, have had only sad experiences with conferences. For the most part conferences were called for them only because something was out of order. Some parents have only been at school when their children were in trouble. The pupils will appreciate knowing that current interviews will be mainly for the purpose of reporting the extent of their academic progress. Certainly they should also be told that comments will be made in private interviews about their own social, emotional, physical, and intellectual growth and development. In addition, pupils should be told that some of their conference time will be allotted to a discussion of the values they seemingly hold as active American citizens.

STEP TWO: DETERMINE THE EXTENT OF INTEREST

Although many people should be involved in the planning stage and teachers will actually implement many of the specific changes, it is the principal who is accountable for the establishment of an interview system. After having informed his several audiences of the importance of conference procedures, he must then assume the responsibility of identifying and determining the extent of interest of his staff and school patrons for establishing a personalized procedure of progress reporting.

Seeking Staff Approval. To move from traditional forms of reporting to interview procedures may take a year or two of planning. This move from grade card methods of reporting to conferring with parents in private sessions calls for "reconditioning" of all adults involved. The tendency may be to draw up the organizational pattern, cite a few examples of possible implementation, and say "We're ready!" The principal should want to move as rapidly as possible in obtaining staff consent, but to make changes without careful meditation is usually wasted effort. One of the lessons to be learned in conferring with parents is that interviews imply an ongoing, constantly evolving process. An appropriate analogy is comparing interviewing with climbing a mountain. The higher one climbs, the broader the horizons. The more one interviews, the broader the the coverage during an interview session.

Much information can be given to groups of teachers by utilizing demonstrations, recordings, lectures, films, and discussions. Like parents, teachers need to gain more understanding of the purpose and procedures of the parent interviews and the interpretation of test results. After they gain confidence in what would be expected of them, they will more likely vote affirmatively for the interview system. A meeting should be called at the discretion of the principal to determine the extent to which his staff agrees as to the adoption of the newer method of reporting. Even though the staff may not be ready to make a decision, it is to their advantage to learn what ideas have accrued since the original planning sessions, what tools and techniques have been acquired for implementation, or what obstacles seem to be forming. If he gains the apparent support of his faculty, the principal is ready to begin the implementation of the change process.

Obtaining Detailed Responses from Parents. After securing the support of teachers and after having held "back to school night" with parents, the principal should prepare a questionnaire to be sent to the parents for the purpose of obtaining their responses to pertinent details of the interview program as they perceive it. A sample of what should go into this questionnaire is provided below:

QUESTIONNAIRE TO PARENTS

At the recent meeting ("back to school night") held in our school, both parents and teachers have expressed a wish for a closer working relationship between school and home on the subject of *the pupil progress report.* We all agree that a conference between a child's teacher and his parents is one means of strengthening our school and home relationship. Because several have expressed an interest in parent-teacher interviews, we are using this questionnaire as a means of finding out the exact extent of this interest and what you believe constitutes a satisfactory parent-teacher conference report. Therefore, will you please respond to the following questions by placing a check mark (✔) in the blank which best answers what you believe?

Please sign your sheet and return it by your child
before_____, 19_____ . THANK YOU.

_____
Principal

1. Would you like to have a time reserved for a conference
   with your child's teacher?____YES____NO

2. As our future reporting system which of the following do
   you prefer (check one)?

   Conference only____ Grade Card only____ Conference &
   Grade Card____

   Other, please list

3. How many conferences a year would you prefer?
   One____Two____As many as needed____

4. Would you like for your child to attend a portion of this
   conference also? ____YES ____NO

5. How many minutes long would you like for your
   conference to be?
   ____15____20____25____30____Other

6. Should the majority of teachers and parents indicate that
   they prefer conferences for our school, what would you
   specificially like to know about your child during the
   interview with his teacher? List your suggestions below.
   Use the back of this sheet if you need additional space.

After the questionnaires are received, then tallies can be made and judgments can be formed as to the interest that parents hold in initiating an interview system. Helpful information may also be contained in question six which is geared to find out what parents would like to know during interview sessions.

If the responses are favorable, then a short note from the principal is in order to indicate that plans are being made for inaugurating interviews into the educational policy of the school. Should there be a limited number of affirmative responses, and his staff is still much in favor of continuing plans for obtaining a conference system, then the principal knows with what group he needs to do additional selling activities. For example, wider newspaper and television coverage may need to be sought. Possibly a few teachers will want to invite some parents for a brief interview in hopes that those same parents will tell others of the rewards that come from having conversed with their child's teacher. An important point to remember here is that though the majority of parents may not have voted for the interview system, the school staff must continue to hold communication lines open with all parents. Particularly, it is important to maintain contact with other supportive parents. Sometimes the minority group can be used to influence positively those who need additional time and experience in which to formulate a more desirable response.

STEP THREE: ESTABLISH WRITTEN POLICY

There is a point at which philosophical orientation, educational objectives, and possible alternatives meet, and it is toward this point that the school principal who is sensitive to his faculty and community now moves. This is the art of the educational process in the making. After interview acceptance, what is the next move? The principal needs to establish policy with his staff. These policies will serve as guidelines for all of the staff to follow in the interview system. School policies may be considered as broad agreements which guide decisions to be made by school personnel. Interview policy needs to be established concerning the following factors:

1. *What is our philosophy of what a report to parents should contain?* One of the satisfying things that comes out of writing a philosophy of why one reports is the fact that the ones who do it learn more about why reporting is practical and important. Principals and teachers will feel better about conferencing when it is discovered that neither group wants children to fail; neither wants children caught between pressures of the home or school; neither believes the school curriculum contains all that is significant for children to learn, nor do either of the groups want pupils pushed faster than would be good for them. Therefore, the philosophy of reporting should deal with what is reasonable to expect in achievement from each child; something of the working knowledge the teacher must have of child development and psychology; and the degree to which reporting assists the child in becoming a more capable pupil and citizen.

2. *What is to be reported about each and every child?* Parents are going to talk things over with each other after conferences. They should learn some common things about their children. This policy should include the progress expected of every child with respect to each of his school activities and content subjects.

3. *What kinds of information are going to be retained in confidence?* Not all information about children should be reported to parents. For example, it is questionable as to whether or not a parent would need his child's I. Q. score. Some parents will push for this score. However, if the teacher is able to say, "I understand that you may have some need of John's I. Q. score, but our school policy is such that I can't release it. You may visit with my Principal and he may see need of deviating from written policy in your case." For the most part, parents will not seek out this information from the principal if there is a policy on it. The teacher avoids an awkward position because he has a rule to which he can refer which illustrates to parents that if it has been discussed by the professional group, then there must be sound reasons as to why such information is not to be released. Moreover, if information is not going to help the child, it is doubtful as to its importance. For example, if for minor infractions of behavior that would serve only to get the child in trouble at home and ultimately make him "hate the teacher."

4. *What sources are to be tapped in obtaining the information that has been agreed upon as being pertinent to report?* Unless this is determined beforehand, some teachers will use primarily their own observations as the major source for obtaining information to report to parents. Others will use only test data and objective devices. Still another group may report ideas coming largely from guidance specialists, the school psychologist, or other special service personnel. What one should strive for is a composite report which includes information from each of these sources. The written policy prevents some child from having a limited report since the request will carry with it an indication of the teacher's responsibility in seeking out information from the several specific sources within his jurisdiction.

5. *What should transpire if a parent is scheduled but does not attend?* Some parents will not be able to meet their scheduled conference because of illness, emergencies, and the like. These parents can be easily scheduled at a later time. The major problem, however, stems from those very few parents who find it hard to make it to the first conference perhaps because of lack of interest. An effort should be made to contact each parent who for any reason did not maintain his previous conference commitment. This contact should be made by the principal and teacher immediately after all regular appointments have been met with those persons who were able to fulfill their commitments.

6. *Are children to attend any portion or all of the interview?* There may be times when the three-way conference (teacher-parent-pupil) would be of much value. For example, a teacher may wish to demonstrate a technique of working with the child in order that the parent can offer some remedial services at home. Possibly some child is giving a different story to his parents regarding his school work than is the actual case. If he must tell the story in his teacher's presence, more likely he will tell the truth of the matter. Then too, there will be children who seem to be stimulated by the fact that they are asked to participate in the interview. On the other hand there will be children who are sheepish and shy. Probably each case will need to be considered in the light of the conditions of the given moment, but certainly there should be some policy regarding whether or not a three-way conference can be held. If three-way conferences are to be permitted, then some sample conditions should be listed within the written policy.

7. *Will gradecards be discussed in the interviews?* The interview could be used as a supplement to the gradecard system. One major pitfall of discussing gradecards in interviews is that often the conversation oscillates to how grades are determined. This usually leads to a dead-end street since teachers score differently and parents have been educated in still a different method. It is important here that the written policy indicate the number of minutes that will be spent on explaining gradecard marks so that ample time is reserved to discuss more significant matters.

8. *Will a limit be enforced on the number of teacher-initiated conferences per school year?* At times it will be impossible to do an adequate job of interviewing with only two conferences per year. It is next to impossible to do an average job of interviewing with parents whose children have unique or serious problems. Several conferences may be needed for them. Moreover, there are a few parents who would like to meet more than twice a year to hear how their children are doing even though there is no special problem involved. A few of this group simply fail to realize how busy the teacher is with the daily routine of classroom teaching. These types of individuals should not be allowed to incessantly infringe upon the teacher's valuable free time.

9. *How frequently will conferences be scheduled?* If conferences are worth having at all, then there should be time for at least two conferences per school year. One conference should be held in the Fall; the other in early Spring. October

and April are excellent interview months. If one attempts to confer too early in the Fall, he will not know as many problems about his pupils as might be necessary. If he waits until May in the Spring, there may not be ample time to correct those things which might be solved as a result of having talked to the parent.

10. *How much time should a teacher reserve for each interview?* The minimum time allotted to each conference should not be less than fifteen or twenty minutes with the ideal time being at least thirty minutes spent in actual word exchange with each child's parents.

11. *Will Conferences be on school time or the teacher's personal time after the school day ends?* Teachers should be released from teaching responsibilities to hold these conferences. It would be good to have a written policy which allows them some time free to prepare and assemble data concerning their children prior to the initial conference sessions.

12. *Should all of a child's work be shown in the initial conference?* Although the teacher should seek to report certain types of information about every child, at times individual differences and parental inquiry should take precedence. For example, if a child is capable, but not doing satisfactory work at all, the teacher should collect a variety of material to back up his comments regarding that child. Some agreement must be sought as to the extent to which work samples will be shown for each child. The time factor itself prevents the showing of all of a child's class papers to his parents. Most experienced interviewers show some of the child's work selected at random from each of the subject matter areas. Sometimes specific worksheets and personal classroom papers are selected because they can most beautifully illustrate what otherwise might take many words to say.

13. *Is every teacher expected to follow a conference guidesheet?* Guidesheets are mandatory tools of the interviewers. All scheduled interviews should have some structure. Even master teachers find it difficult to remember all of the things that need to go into a single parent-teacher interview. Guidesheets should be used along with the folders of work and academic scores collected for showing at conference time.

SUMMARY

Twenty minute conferences held twice a year during October and April on a school scheduled basis are to be greatly respected.

Interview programs should not be adopted at the administrative level and imposed upon the instructional staff. While there is a greater amount of time usurped in democratic planning, it is time well spent for much less time will be needed for explaining interview policies since all major decisions have previously been reviewed.

Teachers who use the interview system become better teachers. Planning, accepting, and using the facts associated with individual differences of pupils, as well as impartation of these facts to parents, requires high competence. It is a challenge which most teachers in a system can learn to fulfill.

How to Operate an Interview Program

Without going one can get nowhere.
—Chinese Proverb

Introduction

3 There are principles of operation to be considered after having organized the interview program which, while they may not be set down with complete exactness and finality, seem to be logical, which have been justified in business and personnel administration, and which should be kept in mind as good general rules to guide the operation of the principal and his staff. Among these are certain more clear-cut ones which may be referred to as the principles of:

1. co-ordination of authority and responsibility.
2. preparation and procurement of materials and information determined as a prerequisite to an effective interview program.
3. recognition of basic human psychological factors: tradition, attitudes, sharing of experiences, the right of creative expression.
4. relative values.
5. adaptation of responsibility to staff personnel.
6. encouragement and inspiration.

Co-ordination of Authority and Responsibility. Once a program has been organized, those who implement it must be given adequate authority and opportunity commensurate with the responsibility. This principle aptly applies to the implementation of the interview program, yet it comes from the business world: "Employ the best person you can for the job, turn the job over to him, and hold him for results."

An application of the principle may be seen in the relationship of the principal to his staff. If the teacher in a given school is to be held responsible for improving the quality of his interviews with parents, he should have opportunities and working conditions appropriate to the development of this degree of his responsibility. For example, if teachers are expected to take a large measure of their interview material from cummulative records, then they should have some part in selecting the types of records that best fulfill these needs.

The efficient principal provides his staff with adequate "professional backing" when they must take a stand on a decision, belief, or recommendation. Some parents cannot accept the fact that their child is retarded, is not accepted by his peers, needs psychiatric help, is dishonest and so on. Thus if it is believed that the interview program is dedicated to the philosophy that parents should be given a tactful, but truthful report about a child's progress, then in operating the report program a principal must expect some conference situations wherein the teacher will need the official administrative support that his title affords. The interviewer should be supported by the principal and superintendent for maintaining his professional prestige. Moreover, the administration should see that all teacher recommendations are carried through when a child's welfare is affected. Some parents need to be prodded by an administrator or they will not do what is best for their children.

Although the superintendent must be in on the planning and organizing of the interview program, in its operation the principal becomes the professional leader of the teaching staff, working scientifically, considerately, and democratically.

Preparation and Procurement of Adequate Interview Materials. The efficient principal formulates a definite, well-organized plan of interview activities. This principle of operation indicates that before a comprehensive program of reporting can be installed, teachers must have the tools and materials with which to work. These materials should be prepared for the sole purpose of improving the teachers preliminary preparation for interview work and increasing the efficiency of the actual parent teacher conference.

The advantages of teacher participation in constructing or selecting interview materials are varied and rewarding. Not only is the experience and judgment of these persons made available to the administration, but these future interviewers become much better informed. They become more sensitive to the philosophy, objectives, problems, and points of view of the administration and of their fellow teachers who must also deal with certain aspects of the interview program. Thus, the selection of interview material becomes a means to an end, not an end in itself.

Recognition of Basic Human Factors. Although it is desirable to have people participate in policy making, selection of materials, and the like this is no assurance that they will continue to plan their work carefully in the implementation of objectives, content, and procedure. The feeling that he has had a share in determining the policies of the scope and sequence of the interview program operates advantageously to give the teacher a general concern for the success of the procedures which can hardly be expected when the plans are handed down by authority of their professional superiors. Nevertheless, it is true that the fruits of participation are not always what might have been desired. Participation may lead to undesirable conclusions, to controversy and disagreement. The extent to which these things come out into the open, or are avoided, depends largely upon the skill and wisdom of the leader. Generally, however, a recognition of the desire for expression of *self* is universal. A policy of participation coupled with a reasonable degree of ability is likely to produce results quite superior to those typical of a completely autocratic policy.

Relative Values. Frequently occasions will arise in the operation of an interview program wherein the teachers or principal will need to assume responsibility of making decisions that have not been covered in conference policy. Occasionally, not often, the interviewer may have to deviate from interview policy to meet the needs of individual parents. Under ordinary conditions the judgment of what to do in such instances would be left to co-operative consideration or to a committee. But the true test of the extent of the staff's ability to operate effectively comes when they are able to decide if *in the long run* one objective of the interview program must be sacrificed in the light of the priority of objectives. For example, the school policy may be to report similar facts about each and every child. But in the case of a particular parent, whose point of view seems lodged upon an issue of major concern to him, the interviewer may find it wise to resolve this problem so that they might get through to the parent on subsequent conferences. Thus, he waives several of his prepared comments and seeks to adapt the interview to specific problems of current concern to the parent.

Adaptation of Responsibility to Staff Personnel. The place of any teacher in the interview program must be determined in part by his individual talents, training, character, and experience. For example, some teachers like to talk freely with parents; others would just as soon never talk with a parent. Persons who have the natural talent for conversing will see their responsibility as being easily transferred to interview situations. On the other hand, the less verbal individual may look upon interviewing as a responsibility beyond the scope of his interests and abilities. In still another instance, individuals may have the talent for interviewing, but fail to have adequate training to assume conference responsibilities. It follows that an effective interview operation must make provisions for an inservice training program which will help all types of teachers adapt to conference procedures.

Encouragement and Inspiration. The principal, more than anyone else, must see that all persons are given the right kind of encouragement as they experience personal visits with parents. Nearly all human beings respond to persons who exhibit kindliness, sympathetic understanding, and an earnest desire to be helpful—democratically and constructively. Open-mindedness, professional frankness, and genuine co-operation of both the parent and interviewer promote good working relations. The degree to which they are evident in interview situations is due in large measure to the work of the principal. If the principal does not exhibit the fine personal qualities he expects his teachers to personify in their interviews with parents, it is doubtful whether or not he will make much progress in making them sensitive to those needs through workshop experiences and faculty meetings.

The Role of the Principal in Bringing About
An Effective Interview Operation

One organizes his interview program in order that it can be administered, and it is administered so that it operates effectively. An interview program is likely to fail if (1) the conference materials are inadequate, (2) teachers neglect to use the materials that are available, (3) the principal does not analyze the current qualifications of his staff for the new task of conferring verbally with parents, or (4) if there is no systematic plan which provides for a continuous evaluation of the interview system in terms of its value in meeting educational needs of pupils. It is to identify the significant steps necessary to effective operation of the interview program that this section is dedicated. These are responsibilities which principals must assume.

STEP ONE: PREPARE IN QUANTITY, WITH QUALITY, ALL INTERVIEW MATERIALS

Someone in the central office area must assume the responsibility for developing the forms and letters which are a significant part of the overall plan of operation. If teachers are expected to supply their own forms and the like, it is probable there would be as many variations in structure as there would be teachers. Therefore, it is the principal who must prepare and provide at the appointed time those materials which have their place in the conference system. He must. . .

a) *Prepare Materials for Parents.* The success of the interview program depends in large measure upon the whole-hearted support and participation by the parent. The communications sent to the home should have a friendly tone about them rather than appear too directive. All forms should be sent several days in advance of the date expected for their return.

A duplicating machine can be used for the preparation of letters to parents but the material should be in good form and without typographical error and ink blotches. Each classroom teacher should be held responsible for sending out the letters and for recording the information for his classroom when data is received. It is wise to follow the alphabetical list of names in the room register when addressing envelopes to parents, and to check each one off as the name of the parent is written on the letter. This eliminates the possibility of overlooking some parent and creating a somewhat embarrassing situation. In recording names of parents on the blanks going out to the respective homes, one should carefully note from room register evidence with whom the child is currently residing. For example, some children live with only one parent, some have guardians, others live with grandparents.

The reader will note some major differences in the two sample letters which follow. These letters might be varied to meet the needs of local neighborhoods and school communities. Sample A is more of an informal approach used by the teacher who is seeking out a conference appointment with the parent, while Sample B is quite formal and commands the respect associated with a principal's office. Each sample, however, seeks the same information. If stencils are used for these letters it does seem easier to type in, DEAR PARENTS, as the greeting. However, it takes only a few seconds to write in the appropriate name. This provides the letter with a personal touch and warmth that is not found in most form letters.

Letter Sample A

IDEAL PUBLIC SCHOOL
Ideal, Texas

October___, 197___

Dear_____:

WHAT?

Parent-Teacher Conferences for grades Kindergarten through Grade Level Six.

WHEN?

Thursday and Friday, October___ and___, 19___. Our school will not be in session Thursday afternoon after 2:00 p.m., nor all day on Friday.

WHY?

1. To get better acquainted.
2. To let you know how well your child is doing in the fundamental subjects.
3. To discuss results of the special standardized tests.
4. To show you some samples of work of your child.
5. To exchange ideas which might contribute to the increased educational growth of your child.
6. To obtain the first quarter progress report for your child.
7. To be provided with an elementary handbook of information about your school.

WHO?
Not just Mother, but Dad, too, if possible.

TIME?
It takes only thirty minutes. The exact time is indicated below. If the hour is not satisfactory, please indicate a more acceptable time. Please sign and return this blank tomorrow. You may detach the form and keep this letter for future reference.

Cordially yours,

APPROVED BY:
John Doe
Principal, Ideal Public
          School   _____
                                        ____Grade Teacher

(Parent's record)

Conference scheduled for _____ to _____ on _____.
------------------Detach and Return to me------------------------
Conference scheduled for_____ to ____ on _____.
(School Record)

_____
Signature of Parent

REMEMBER: YOUR CHILD WILL BE GLAD TO SEE YOU AND HIS TEACHER PLANNING TO-GETHER FOR HIS BETTER INTERESTS.

* *

Although letter Sample A comes directly out of the classroom, it should be prepared in the quantities needed for each teacher by central office personnel.

Letter Sample B

IDEAL ELEMENTARY SCHOOL
Ideal, Texas
October____, 19____

Dear_____ :

We are writing this letter to ask for your cooperation in reporting the progress of your children. We want to arrange a series of conferences between parents and teacher. We believe education is a cooperative enterprise between teachers and parents, and that neither group can do the most effective work without the assistance of the other. It is our opinion that these two groups, working together, can best help the child to progress. That is the reason we are asking for your assistance.

We are very much interested in the child as an individual, and in trying to determine if he is making the progress of which he is capable. We also believe that such a conference gives you a better knowledge of our schools and the work they are trying to accomplish for your children and our community. These conferences will last approximately thirty minutes. If some special problem arises, another meeting can be arranged. Only the parents (guardians) of a child and the teacher will be present in the room. Additional conferences can be scheduled with teachers of special classes (speech therapists, remedial teachers, guidance personnel, etc.) at your request.

Will you please fill out the blanks below, and return it to your child's teacher.

Very truly yours,

John Doe
Principal

Will you be able to meet with your child's teacher for a visit about the progress of your child? YES____NO_____

Which grades are your children in?___ ___ ___ ___ ___

Three conference sessions will be held on the___and___of October: Thursday evening from 7:00 p.m. to 9:00 p.m.; Friday morning from 9:00 to 12:00 a.m.; and, Friday afternoon from 1:00 to 4:00 p.m.

Which sessions mentioned above do you prefer?

First choice:_____Second choice:_____
    (The exact time of your conference will be given later)

Name of child_____, Grade _____ School_____

Name of parent _____

* *

It should be noted that Letter A includes the set time of the interview, but Letter B gives the parent an opportunity to choose when he would like to come to the conference. If Letter B is used, then the teacher must send another note indicating the exact time and date that the conference has been scheduled (see Letter Sample C). Letter B provides the teacher with the advantage of knowing when a parent would like to come. This offsets the possibility of scheduling a parent for a conference on a day which they already know must be allocated to another purpose.

In addition, Letter B is more helpful in that the parent is

requested to identify all grade levels in which their children are currently enrolled. This saves school personnel from having to pull each enrollment card to determine which teachers have children coming from the same family. Unless this information is sought out, it is conceivable that some families would be given interview appointments by the several classroom teachers on different days, or with too much time elapse between appointments with teachers of different grade levels.

Letter Sample C

Dear _____ :

    Your appointment with your child's teacher,___ Room___, was scheduled for (Thursday morning, October 29, at___a.m.)

    We hope that you will find this time convenient. As you well know scheduling several parents for conferences is a rather difficult task. Therefore, if we have imposed seriously upon your home schedule, let us know so that we may set up another appointment for you.

Principal, IDEAL ELE SCH

Although the parents will already have the appointment schedule coming from the principal's office, some teachers like to send "friendly reminders" home by the children the day before conference sessions are to begin (see Letter Sample D). Phone calls could be made to some of the parents for these same purposes.

Letter Sample D

Dear_____:

Just a reminder that I am looking forward to seeing you on (Thursday morning, October 29, at 10:15 a.m.) for your conference regarding (Judy's) progress.

Sincerely,

Teacher, Grade III

    b) *Prepare Materials for Teachers.* Although conference guidesheets are a major part of the teacher's tools for interviewing, they will not be included here since discussion is given to them in Chapter 7. But there are two additional forms which should be prepared for teachers to use before conferences begin. Form No. 1 is a handy sheet for the classroom teacher as it reveals at a moment's glance not only who is in line for a conference but the teacher's insert reveals to what professional group they belong. All too often teachers go into the conference without a thorough knowledge of the educational background of the parent. For example, the teacher must be highly selective in the vocabulary that he uses to explain the progress of a child whose parent has not been beyond elementary school training. He must keep the vocabulary simple; use several concrete examples and illustrations to get his points across. On the other hand, there are parents who will have more college background than the teacher himself. In these cases, the teacher will want to keep on his "educational toes" and seek to deliver as high level a conference as possible.

PARENT-TEACHER INTERVIEW SCHEDULE FOR GRADE _____ , _____ , 19_____

MORNING (October 22)

	Name	Occupation		Name	Occupation
9:00- 9:30	Mrs. John Doe	Housewife	1:00-1:30		
9:30-10:00	Mrs. Tague	Farmer's wife	1:30-2:00		
10:00-10:30	Mr. Jones.	in private business	2:00-2:30		
10:30-11:00	Mr. Green Mrs. Green	Florist Tax Scry	2:30-3:00		
11:00-11:30	Mr. Smith	College G. Engineer	3:00-3:30		
11:30-12:00	Dr. Brown	College G. Dentist	3:30-4:00		

NIGHT (October 22)

	Name	Occupation
7:00-7:30		
7:30-8:00		
8:00-8:30		
8:30-9:00		

MORNING   **AFTERNOON**

	Name	Occupation		Name	Occupation
9:00- 9:30			1:00-1:30		
9:30-10:00			1:30-2:00		
10:00-10:30			2:00-2:30		
10:30-11:00			2:30-3:00		
11:00-11:30			3:00-3:30		
11:30-12:00			3:30-4:00		

NIGHT

	Name	Occupation
7:00-7:30		
7:30-8:00		
8:00-8:30		
8:30-9:00		

Form 1

Form No. 2 deals with the written record that should be completed as soon after an individual conference as possible. Any unique cases or problems should be discussed with the principal after the block session of conferences has been completed. For example, if a child has been referred at the parent's request for additional therapy under the realm of the school psychologist, then the principal needs to be aware of this referral. Moreover, these interview summaries can be pulled out of the record for review as needed between conference sessions. Lastly, it would be good if the interviewer would read each of these summary sheets immediately prior to his next regularly scheduled conferences. This would refresh his memory as to the major purpose of the last conference, the general discussion that took place, and the extent to which the suggestions made in that conference were or were not achieved.

A PRACTICAL REPORT TO BE COMPLETED AFTER THE INITIAL PARENT-TEACHER CONFERENCE

Form 2

Name of parent (s) . . . _____

Name of child . . . . _____

Name of teacher . . . . . _____

Date of conference . . . _____

PURPOSE: (General problem _____ ; Specific problem* _____)

No notable problem, typical report _____

DISCUSSION:

SUGGESTIONS FOR ACTION:

_____
Signature of Principal

_____
Date of reading

---

*All unique or specific problems such as possible failures, discipline cases, gifted children, under-achievers, and the like, are to be referred to the principal who will then sign this sheet, after his records have been brought up-to-date.

STEP TWO: PLAN AND CONDUCT INSERVICE
TRAINING EXPERIENCES FOR INTERVIEW PERSONNEL

*Types of In-Service Experiences to be Conducted Prior
to the First Block of Interview Sessions.* Both beginning and
experienced teachers need an appropriate mind - set toward
getting ready for the forthcoming conferences. One way to
achieve this goal is to have a panel of experienced interviewers tell how they prepare and conduct interviews.
Another way to improve the efficiency of interviews is by
helping teachers discover possible psychological blocks which
may be hindering interviews. Listening to actual tape-
recorded conferences and analyzing the results aids this
purpose.[1] The development of the ability to diagnose and
interpret data and child behavior will improve interviews
particularly if resource persons are available to assist teachers
in handling this information.

In the early Fall the principal should devote at least one
faculty meeting to showing his teachers what materials
should be accumulated and studied for interview purposes.
These include samples of the child's work, health reports,
achievement test data, anecdotal records, personal data
sheets, results of sociometric tests, summaries of progress
reports, teacher interview guidesheets, and additionally
teacher-prepared questions geared to the needs of the given
individual for whom the conference is being conducted. At
this same meeting, the principal should give some current,
helpful hints toward making conferences more effective.
Such information might include:

1. keeping a child's paper work in chronological order.
   Papers filed with the date recorded on them can be
   found readily if they are needed to illustrate a point
   which arises when the conference is underway.

2. establishing a more cooperative relationship with parents
   through moving from behind the teacher's desk to sitting
   nearer the parent with no obstacles in between. If the
   interviewer stays behind the desk, this dominating
   position may keep the parent on the defensive as he sees

---

1. Wallace R. Johnson and Pauline Chamberlain. *The Principal Prepares His
Staff.* Anoka, Minn.: Anoka-Hennepin District 11 Press 1963. A program
consisting of slides, tapes, a script, and transparencies designed to equip
teachers to prepare and conduct effective parent-teacher conferences.

the teacher always in the position of authority not on a common par with his own ideas.

3. urging teachers to invite the guidance specialist in to confer with certain parents for a few minutes on selected technical points. He has been trained to discuss problems which are somewhat beyond the capabilities and jurisdiction of the generalists. For example, the counselor can give extended coverage of why a child may be stealing, has certain phobias, or is continually using offensive language.

4. helping a parent feel at ease in the interviewer's presence. For example, in the early moments of the conference, the teacher might walk about the room with a parent, pointing out the displays of classroom papers posted on the wall, while at the same time drawing the parent's attention to a discussion of the merits of their child's progress.

The interview program will only be as effective as the teachers are efficient who operate it. To improve this efficiency the principal can turn to role playing, demonstrations, and case study techniques. A group of the experienced interviewers within a school should be selected to give a mock conference of some typical problem which will be encountered by most of the staff members in the forthcoming interview session. A group discussion of the "pros and cons" of the mock conference is an efficient, economical means of bringing the standards of interview operation to a higher level.

Demonstrations are also valuable techniques to employ in the inservice program. Key problems which often arise in conference situations can be outlined, and staff personnel can show how they would go about explaining the problem to parents. For instance, if a child is having trouble with his handwriting, one teacher might illustrate how she would show his papers that were collected from the beginning of the year to the current date for the purpose of illustrating progress (or lack of it), while another teacher who was asked to report on this same problem, extends the idea to include showing a transparency on an over-head projector which depicts what a company author recommends and what the child actually has been able to achieve. Essentially, the child's handwriting is being compared to what is recommended for his grade level.

Case studies should be duplicated and given to the faculty for attracting increased interest and attention on some problem the principal has noted to be an oversight by most interviewers. The elementary supervisor can use these case studies to elicit responses from the teachers about the case in question. This allows one to find out what approach is most effective.

A check list can be used for the purpose of giving all teachers the opportunity to indicate which method they might have used if it were their conference and why they would have selected the approach mentioned. In using role playing, demonstration, and case study techniques, a good follow-up procedure entails teacher participation in evaluating each activity immediately after it is conducted. The evaluation may be written or oral in nature. In some cases perhaps both procedures will be necessary.

The aforementioned procedures can also be used to help teachers identify more specifically: (1) the vocabulary load and technical terms used by fellow teachers in interview situations; (2) the timing with which certain ideas should be injected into the interview; (3) the way that the interview guide can be used in the conference; (4) how an expert interviewer gets the parent back on the subject; (5) the types of questions that some teachers seek answers to in the conference; and, (6) how children who are selected to participate in certain conferences are worked into the interview currently in progress.

STEP THREE: KEEP TO A MINIMUM THOSE ROUTINES THAT CONSUME A TEACHER'S VALUABLE TIME AND EFFORTS

Schedule "School Families" First. Some parents will have 3 to 5 children in the same school. It is conceivable that if each teacher schedules them on his own, the parent might have to make the same number of trips to school that he has children. Therefore, to offset this problem, the principal should supply the teachers with names of those parents who have 2 or more youngsters in school and the grades or rooms in which these children are located. In small group settings, teachers can meet and determine when it would be more convenient to schedule these school families so that they can come on the same morning or afternoon. This eliminates a long wait between conferences since there may be as many as three different teachers seeking interview appointments with them. In large school settings it may be possible to schedule school families by the administrative personnel.

Arrange Schedule for Non-Attenders. Since it will be

impossible for some parents to meet their appointment with their homeroom teacher, then it is the principal's responsibility to provide that teacher opportunity to meet with them as soon after the regular schedule as possible. For a faculty of 30 or more members, it may be necessary to devote an additional half day to "make-up" conferences. The principal should work out a routine of team teaching among his faculty members for that afternoon so teachers who need to confer can be released to do so. In smaller faculties, probably one substitute teacher can move from room to room as needed for one day while the teachers finish conference appointments. Simply because a parent missed his appointment is not reason enough to eliminate him from his deserved conference time. Nor should it be expected of the teacher to make his own conference arrangements. It is the duty of the principal to check with his teachers to determine the day which would be better for them to work in those conferences, and to provide them with substitutes while the make-up conferences are being conducted.

STEP FOUR: MAKE YOURSELF AVAILABLE
DURING CONFERENCE SESSIONS

Tour Your Building at Planned Intervals. The days that conferences are held in a principal's building is not the day for him to tie himself to his office. A good secretary or parent should be assigned to take messages and phone calls for him. He should not schedule routine conferences on this day either. His responsibility is to make himself available to teachers when they think they need him, and to be ready to avail himself when he thinks his assistance will be of aid to the parent, teacher, or child. Therefore, on any day of scheduled conferences a principal is providing a very satisfactory service when he tours the auditorium to meet the new group of parents that are arriving for conferences, or is found walking down the hall speaking with those coming out of conferences. This is not only good public relations, but it also gives him opportunity to find out whether or not the majority of parents are pleased with what they are learning from interview sessions. Moreover, as the alert principal passes by rooms he can usually tell at a moment's glance whether or not the conference being conducted within is moving as it should be.

Don't Allow an Irate Parent to Confer Alone with a

Teacher. Unpleasant results are likely to occur if an angry parent is allowed to confer alone with any teacher, particularly a young inexperienced one. The principal is responsible to his staff. Therefore, in an effective conference operation he should always make himself available to protect the teacher from verbal abuse and ridicule.

A quick check with teachers prior to conference sessions will no doubt reveal the names of some parents who were difficult to interview during previous conference sessions. Teachers should not hesitate to invite the principal in for a brief explanation of policy or the like, or simply to be present throughout the complete interview. He can offer guidance and comments at random during the interview. The parent will not even know that he is there for any other purpose. His help may not be needed; however, his very presence often tempers the climate of the interview to the extent that his interjections of an authoritative nature can be kept to a minimum. This kind of help from a principal keeps the interview session operating smoothly and successfully.

STEP FIVE: RESPECT THE TEACHER'S POINT OF VIEW

Support the Teacher's Conference Report. Occasionally there are parents who refuse to believe the frank report of the teacher. It is difficult for them to face the situation realistically. These parents may seek the counsel of their principal with respect to the authenticity of the teacher's report. The principal often shows people where he stands on issues by the type of response he gives to their opening comments. For instance, if a parent "feels him out" regarding a teacher's comments by saying, "I want to talk to you about Mrs. Smith's report." If he replies, "I'll be glad to explain further. Isn't Mrs. Smith a fine teacher?" The parent who aimed to maneuver him into an awkward position, upon finding that he respects this teacher may forget the whole idea, or will be more likely to yield on debate and get down to the fact which they must·squarely face.

Remember that the parent's ego is so involved with the success of his child that being realistic in regard to his child's unsatisfactory progress, is hard for him. Nevertheless, all parents must be brought to realize that all interviews won't be rosy and bright. Their child probably, like most individuals, has his strengths and weaknesses. Therefore, a principal's job is to support the teacher in what has been told to parents in the interview. When there is doubt as to what was actually said, if it is believed comments have been misconstrued by parents, the teacher should be allowed to clarify these points himself in the presence of the parents and under the auspices and jurisdiction of his building principal.

STEP SIX: PROVIDE SCHOOL TIME FOR INTERVIEWS

Seek Released Time for Teachers Who Conduct Interviews. Conferences take time, but it is time well spent. There are several good methods which might be used to provide time for interviewing parents. For example, if school could be dismissed at two o'clock for one week for the purpose of scheduling interviews until 5:30 p.m., then several twenty minute interviews could be conducted on school time. Two evenings of that same conference week should be used in holding conferences for parents who work and cannot come to school during the day.

Some districts may prefer to keep children actively engaged in school while conferences are going on; therefore, conferences could be arranged on a "staggard" basis. That is, one week can be devoted to primary level interviews with the following week being used for intermediate grade reports. In this case, principal, substitute teachers, and special supervisors command classes for a period or two a day during a designated period of time, thus releasing primary teachers for interviews with parents. The next week this same plan should be extended into intermediate grades.

The author urges the use of the following plan as the major method for releasing the teacher for his interviews. The superintendent, principals, and Board of Education should agree to add six days to the school term, with salary adjustments for the extra days, for the purpose of conducting interview sessions. Three full days can then be devoted to each Fall and Spring conference session with two nights of conferencing coming from the teacher's own time. This plan is most satisfactory because: (1) the elementary principal is also left free from outside duties, and can then make himself available to meet in conferences with the teacher and parents on unique problems or situations; (2) teachers approach their work with more enthusiasm knowing that they are being paid for their efforts; (3) teachers are more at ease knowing that their children are not involved in some other activity in which their services might also be needed at any given moment; and, (4) with all parents coming in a three day period it gives the teachers and their principal opportunity to do something special in the school for the parents who are waiting for their interview (e.g., displays to look at; coffee breaks; special films; discussions with special supervisors; meeting the principal; and the like.).

The teacher will never be able to have all of his conferences on school time; neither should he expect this. But "block sessions" of conferences should come on school time, and teachers should be paid for these services.

STEP SEVEN: CONTINUALLY EVALUATE THE BUILDING STAFF'S QUALIFICATIONS FOR INTERVIEWING, BUT PARTICULARLY PLAN INTERVIEW TRAINING FOR THE NEW TEACHER.

Faculties are so large today that it is difficult for the elementary principal to keep attuned to the many individual abilities of his staff. However, it is most detrimental to both the conference program and the individual teacher if the neophyte is allowed to conference without first having the necessary background experiences and information about successful interviewing. If an established teacher comes to a system without conference experience, or a beginning teacher isn't ready for interviewing with parents, what is to be done?

Since some conferences of the non-scheduled variety are going on nearly all of the time somewhere in the school, then these inexperienced teachers should be invited to sit in on and listen to several actual conferences. Several articles, such as the ones appearing in the selected bibliography of this book, should be zeroxed and placed in the school mailboxes of those who may need information about conference procedures, techniques, and values. The teacher's professional reputation is at stake if he is allowed to go into interview experiences without adequate background experiences. The teacher, who has not had previous conference experiences, would benefit considerably if the principal or his assistant would personally conduct five or six of the conferences for him during his first interview session. As the inexperienced interviewer observes the principal's techniques of interviewing, he will gain much confidence in his own ability and feel more secure as he completes the remainder of the conferences on his own.

The Personal Role of the Teacher in Maintenance of an Effective Interview Operation

Though there are certain responsibilities that a teacher

has to fulfill for his principal, and a number of additional activities that should be done cooperatively in group meetings with contemporaries, he has a personal role to play in making his own interview sessions more effective. He must establish personal guidelines for interview conduct, prepare data and information before actual interview sessions are to begin, and continually strive for the development and establishment of effective interview habits. Any teacher who wants to do interviewing can learn to do it effectively. The steps that follow are designed to help along the learning.

STEP ONE: ESTABLISH PERSONAL GUIDELINES

The principal usually gives some instructions to his teachers as to how they might follow and use the guidesheet which has been designed to give some structure to conferences. But each teacher is expected to find for himself his own private, personalized way of going about the initial presentation to parents. The effectiveness with which the total conference program operates is tremendously increased when each teacher directs adequate attention to his own strategies of dealing with parents. Some factors that should be considered by all teachers who interview, follow below:

a) *Keep adequate records.* Though the type of record one keeps may differ in constituency from grade level to grade level, it is the classroom teacher who is responsible for seeing that parents learn of both objective and subjective information during the interview settings. Tests of basic skills should be given in the Fall in order to determine as early as possible the academic strengths and weaknesses of individual pupils. By the same token, follow-up forms of these same tests should be given in late Spring. The results obtained from these two test settings can be compared with special attention being given to "degrees of progress" noted.

Some standardized tests should also be selected and given for the purpose of identifying specific learning difficulties of children. If an achievement test with diagnostic features is administered, then appropriate remedial activities can be initiated and the purpose of this work can be discussed with the pupil's parents. These tests might well include several major content areas.

Records should be compiled on the personal and social development of pupils. Along with astute teacher observations, such records as those dealing with results of personality tests, interest inventories, and socio-metric instruments are a part of the teacher's source materials.

In addition the teacher must maintain records with respect to the child's progress on "teacher-made tests." These tests should include the measurement of a pupil's ability in three significant areas of thinking: (1) knowledge (information), (2) comprehension (understanding), and (3) application (including transfer abilities). In order to explore the depth and breadth of a child's experiences on the three categories mentioned, evidences must be obtained from true-false tests, multiple-choice, essay, matching, complete the blanks, and other significant methods of measurements which may be required by the school. All of these tests offer some picture of scholarship which can be related to a child's ability to think and perform.

The interview program that is "pupil-centered" is of little value if there are no systematic plans followed in recording test data on a cumulative basis. The more individualized the instructional program, the greater the number of records that should be kept. Hence, the collection of cumulative data by all teachers on all pupils is essential.

b) *Seek to give a tactful, but truthful report.* Some feel that being truthful means that you simply tell the facts no matter what they may be and no matter who they may hurt. But there are many ways of giving facts that parents should know about their child without putting either the parents or the child on the defensive. By the same token there are some facts which need not be given to make a point clear regarding the position of the child in his school work. The teacher must learn to hold some facts in reserve, particularly if the parents' knowledge of them would in no way assist the child to do better.

If the parents ask questions which a teacher may not be able to answer, there is no reason he may not respond with "I don't know." Perhaps an opinion from the teacher is justified. Then he might state, "I don't have sufficient objective evidence to validate this point, but my own opinion is. . ."

The teacher who seeks to be truthful and honest with parents is the one who strives to be supportive of the child, yet as frank and straightforward as necessary. If Johnny is noted for his mathematical ability, his accuracy in computation, speed of comprehension, and thoroughness in covering his material, then this information should be revealed to his parents. However, it is doubtful that such statements as the following are helpful: "Johnny isn't doing well in music. He doesn't like it; he puts little effort into it; he isn't earning a passing grade."

Though the aforementioned statements about his music work are true, it is not reasonable to assume that they make any significant contribution to upgrading his efforts and achievements. Therefore, being honest with parents about their child's work means that the interviewer will try to make a point with them about those things that are going to be of major help to the child.

The cultivation of such qualities of tactfulness and sensitivity to people as people cannot be over-stressed. Webster has defined tact as "sensitive mental perception; nice discernment of what is appropriate to do or say in dealing with others without giving offense." This definition might well be adopted as exemplifying the relationship desired between teacher and parents.

c) *Be serious in the verbal approach.* Parents are very serious when they discuss the problems of their children. The teacher, too, must treat their "anxieties" with respectful attention. One is making a grave mistake if he seeks to turn a parent's questions aside no matter how simple or complicated they are. It is not uncommon to find that some interviewers offer significant answers to the problem but follow up immediately with such statements as "Though there is room for concern, I don't think I'd get too worried about it." As interviewer, it is important to remember that the parent is concerned or the question would not have been posed. If an acceptable answer to the question is given, why ruin the essence of a remark by saying, ". . . I wouldn't get too worried about it." Although one would not want this comment to be taken in the wrong way, more often than not, the parent thinks, "If my child were really his, he would be concerned about it."

Interviewers who treat parental comments lightly may be cultivating the feeling within the parent that he neither understands his position on the matter nor does he understand fully what is best for his child. Of course, the interviewer must not treat every small problem as if it were a crucial issue, but the wise teacher will consider all problems respectfully and dwell a few moments upon the pertinent aspects that may be really troublesome to the anxious parent.

d) *Decide the vocabulary to use with specific parents.* The interviewer should not talk down to parents, neither should he talk in "teacherish" language or "educational jargon."

An interviewer should be certain to complete the professional categories shown in Form 1 (see p. 37) of this chapter. An understanding of the professional backgrounds of parents will, for the most part, provide a teacher with some idea of their educational experiences. This information helps one to select the words and ideas in accordance with what parents are more likely to comprehend. In any case, however, the teacher should try to consult with the parent in terms of layman's language without using words that might serve to confuse the issue rather than to enlighten the parent's understanding of the problem.

STEP TWO: PREPARE YOURSELF BEFORE
INTERVIEW SESSIONS BEGIN

Review Conference Techniques. No doubt each teacher will find it necessary to vary the approach to interviewing in the light of the wide range of personalities with whom and about whom he will visit. For example, the interview technique used in conferring with parents in a Harlem Ghetto area would be somewhat different from that used with professional people who should be much more sensitive to academic and social problems. Nevertheless, there are some general techniques he will want to employ in each of the conferences. For example, it is the teacher's responsibility to select a point of attention and to keep conversation focused upon it. When the parent digresses from the business at hand, then it is the teacher who must seek to regain the point that was lost. To return to the point, he could say, "You mentioned something earlier in which I was interested. Let's go back to that point for a minute."

Parents quite often find themselves at a loss when it comes to dealing with certain phases of their child's growth and development. When the teacher observes this fact, more can be accomplished if he indicates that "parents traditionally have this difficulty with twelve-year-olds." Hence, universalization is an effective technique of approaching some problems encountered in conferences.

Every conference should have woven into it a technique for obtaining additional information from parents. For example, the teacher can often gain much more information by simply stating, "I wonder if you would be willing to tell me more about that last point." Most parents are happy to aid the teacher in any way they can.

Finally, the teacher should be prepared to give information in such a way that the parent is willing to accept it. The less directive a teacher is in his statement, the more likely the parent will use it. A statement such as the following is usually well received and accomplishes its purpose: "Some parents find this helpful. Perhaps you might want to try it." In the long run, parents are more apt to be receptive to what teachers have to say if what must be said is imparted in a tactful, kind, and considerate manner.

Collect and Prepare "Hand-Outs" for Parents. At the close of each interview, some purposes are served by giving materials to parents for study at their leisure. Particular emphasis should be given to the use of the material in the light of the needs of that parent's child. He will more likely read and study it if the purpose is directly tied to his child's specific needs. The materials to be collected for distribution to each parent during the interview include a (1) reading list; (2) school handbook; (3) pamphlet for parents of nursery, kindergarten, adolescent, or teenage groups; (4) school newsletter; (5) PTA booklet; (6) Emergency (health & accident) Almanac; and, (7) a copy of the "disaster plan" if in the case of national emergency the parents are expected to call for their children at another location. In some instances it may be necessary to make comments regarding these materials by summarizing the purposes for which the items are being distributed for their perusal.

STEP THREE: BE ALERT TO CORRECT INTERVIEW HABITS

Have Data and Information at Finger-Tips. The effective interviewer is an organized individual. He will place his materials (folders of work, achievement test data, workbooks, and the like) in an order which corresponds to the names of those who are expected to come for interview purposes. As an interview is completed, a pupil's paperwork should be replaced in his file folders or the like so that it is available for future reference.

In addition to the regular cumulative records, class papers and the like, one must anticipate what he believes parents will want to know and have these materials available, too. Nothing is more embarrassing to an interviewer, nor reduces parental confidence in his classroom organization, than to make a comment in the interview which should be supported by appropriate material, yet the material is seemingly misplaced. The parent may wonder if it were available in the first place.

Any data or information (IQ scores, standardized test data, etc.) which the teacher wants to refresh his memory with during the interview, but does not want the parent to see, should not be left on the top or corner of his desk. Some parents, knowingly or unknowingly, are bound to pick it up and it is somewhat awkward to reach out for these confidential materials or to suggest that they are items of information which cannot be verbally discussed with or shown to parents. If such materials are kept in the center desk drawer, the teacher is in position to look for his own purposes and upon finding at a glance what is needed for discussion purposes, return them to this seclusive storage place.

Let Parents Talk Some, Too. Parents play two important roles in the operation of the conference program. They not only come to the interview to *receive* information, but to *give* it. Therefore, the teacher should not spend all of the interview time imparting his ideas to the parents. Parents have their own beliefs about, "how Bill is doing" from the home viewpoint. A teacher needs to know their point of view.

The following statements are representative of what teachers have found out through listening to parents. One intermediate grade teacher wondered why a child always acted too sleepy of a morning and the parent revealed that their boy had a paper route and was up at 4:30 a.m. every morning. After listening to a child's parents, one second grade interviewer became less disturbed about the child's completion of his homework when he found that they lived in a very small apartment and there were four other younger children in the home. Seldom was there opportunity for him to settle down to extra-class duties or homework assignments.

Another teacher in a departmentalized system discovered that a parent was much concerned about his child's "over-load" of homework. It seemed that each of his three teachers in a departmentalized program were simultaneously assigning as much as 30 to 40 minutes of homework each evening. To complete these assignments to the satisfaction of "self" and his teachers, of course, was getting beyond the child's emotional, mental, and physical endurance. Still another teacher was amazed to find that all one child did after school was to watch television. Yet neither the child nor his parents could find time for his needed study practice at home. All of the above mentioned facts came from the parents involved as volunteer information. If those teachers would have dominated the interviews to the extent that only information coming from them was imparted, then these problems may have gone on some time undetected.

Parents really want and need to know the answers to many other types of questions. These are discussed in a later chapter of this book. However, at this point the author wishes to point out that the teacher must plan to operate his conference in at least one of two ways; either guide the parent into conversation throughout the conference, or set aside a few minutes in the middle or near the end of the interview for questions coming strictly from the parents. Obviously, some of the questions the parent really wants to inquire about and needs to know the answers to, are loaded questions. The skilled interviewer will supply several basic answers to which the parent can apply his own judgment as to which is the more effective advice to follow.

Stick to Time Limits. Some parents will want more than their share of conference time. To reduce such infringement upon another parent's conference, one can reset the school bells for ringing at twenty-five minute intervals. This would include two to three minute period for interview summation if needed. A very satisfactory arrangement is to have a pupil assigned to each classroom whose duty it is to go to a central location, such as the school lunchroom or auditorium, ask for a certain parent, take them to their conference room, and if need be, introduce them to the teacher. This procedure prevents parents from becoming confused about where they should be in large schools with several levels and classrooms, or visiting with each other past their appointed time schedule and throwing off all other schedules which follow, and so forth. Moreover, if the child is taught to knock softly at the door before entering, and then courteously states: "Miss Smith, Dr. and Mrs. Jones, Mary's parents, are here to see you." This oftentimes makes the lingering parent more aware that others must have their conference time, too. The teacher who rises when the child enters will find that the parent, also, rises and begins to walk toward the door.

Suggest a Follow-Up Procedure. Conferences really open

up new avenues that other systems of reporting seem to close. When grades are placed on report cards, they carry with them a message of "finality." These are the facts (school-marks) and this is the way it stands (final grades). But interviews are usually considered as a key for unlocking new ways of dealing with a child and his school achievement. For example, after a child's problem is discussed in the interview and a mode of attack is cooperatively planned to solve it, then the teacher should plan to phone the parent in two or three weeks to inform them as to the extent of the progress made by their child. Perhaps a new approach will be needed, or the plan agreed upon in the past conference, now needs revision. Therefore, an effective interview operation goes a step beyond the present conference. Before the conference terminates, plans should be made with the parents as to when additional communication should be expected from the teacher.

Summary

The principal and his staff must prepare themselves for the interview program. Teachers will need to ready materials for interview use and must think deliberately about what they intend to bring about through interview services.

A principal must survey the needs of his staff and from these results offer an in-service training program for his whole staff. It is his responsibility to offer leadership in the study of techniques, procedures, and tools necessary to effective interviewing.

Although preliminary preparation of conference materials was of necessity stressed in this chapter, and they do contribute considerably to the efficiency of the operation of the interview system, these are only a means to an end. They must be worked out in the light of the use to be made of them. An effective interview operation depends as much on the material available as it does on the user and the methods of its use. No doubt as new possibilities are envisioned, the greater the effect these materials will have upon the total operation of the interview program.

Standardized Test Information-- What to Report and How to Report It

A teacher's program of evaluation should not be limited to those facts and skills which are measurable by standardized tests, but should be designed to provide evidence of pupil growth toward all the major goals of instruction.
—Torgerson and Adams

Introduction

4
Is my child academically talented enough to be a college graduate? Is his I.Q. high enough? Will he make good scores this year? Will he pass? All of these questions plus many more of similar category will be asked of the teacher. That is why it is necessary for the teacher to talk about the area to which many parents are already supersensitive—standardized tests.

The teacher should talk to a parent about those tests his child has taken, is currently taking, and will be expected to take as the school year progresses. Particularly tests that measure his child's academic talents and mental ability need to be discussed.

The information given parents and students by teachers about tests can have an enormous influence on a child's progress in school and perhaps even a greater impact upon a school's public relations. The best approach in handling parental questions about testing is to answer them as fully and as understandably as one possibly can. The interview is an excellent place to clear up "misnomers" about tests arising from faulty information in newspapers or periodical literature, or coming from points of view derived from the parent's limited experiences with them when they were in school.

MENTAL APTITUDE

Parents are often confused about intelligence tests and the meaning of intelligence quotients. Thus they desire some explanation of what the "I. Q." means in the educational program of their youngsters. When parents learn that the intelligence quotient constitutes one additional, significant measure of a set of qualities possessed in varying degrees by all people, then they will more likely plan intelligently for their child's future. A major cardinal principle of mental health is to "know thyself." By the same token if both parents know something of the major strengths and weaknesses of their child's intellectual abilities, more likely they can govern themselves and their child's actions accordingly.

I. Q.—General Ability or Specific Ability? The intelligence quotient does not represent total general ability, but relates to special abilities derived from manipulation of abstract symbols. The I. Q. one possesses should not cause one to presume the extent of scholastic achievement, only that intelligence in some measure is contributing to it. At least equally significant in achievement is one's seriousness of purpose, mechanical aptitude, social insight, and will to succeed to mention only a few. Therefore, parents should learn from the interview that at best, an I. Q. score represents only a sampling of an individual's abilities.

What Should a Report About I. Q. Contain? Parents should be told that the I. Q. is a measure established by commercial paper-and-pencil tests which more often than not have been administered in group settings. In special cases, of course, an individual intelligence test may be given wherein the examiner reads the test items to the child thus elimi-nating the reading factor. They should learn that in spite of the general constancy of the I. Q. some fluctuation over the developmental years may be noticed. Great fluctuations, however, occur only in rare instances. Appreciable changes in I. Q. come about when there seems to be "interference" with intellectual functioning as might appear with physical illness or handicap, impoverished environment, or emotional illness. A report of this type reduces the probability of a parent seeking to raise his child's I. Q. by special tutoring, or through purchasing inappropriate commercial products, devices, and the like.

The I. Q. Itself is Confidential. Teachers are advised against revealing raw I. Q. scores to parents (i.e. "Your child's I. Q. score was 97."). One may feel that he can reduce undue parental pressure on his pupil if he lets a parent know their child is not very bright. Although parents do find out that their child is working up to capacity, one cannot be assured that they will not use the information to coerce the child to study harder. Moreover, if there are two or more children in a family, the child who receives the lower score may be looked upon as being much duller than he really is. Parents, who have obtained raw I. Q. scores, have been known to make such comparisons repugnant to common sense.

How to Report Information Derived from Intelligence Tests

Present a Sample Problem. Parents can be directed in their thinking to see that an intelligence test is a carefully selected set of tasks for the solution of which varying amounts of mental ability and skill are required. The score obtained on a test of intelligence can be interpreted by referring to a sample problem which illustrates its utility. Although one may want to point out that the I. Q. is really a measure of brightness, he should stress the idea that mental age is of greater educational value to educators.

The I. Q. score is a ratio of mental age to the mental age normal for a given chronological age ($\frac{MA}{CA}$ x 100). For example, a child seven years of age chronologically would be expected to also have a mental age of seven if he were to be of average intelligence (100 I.Q.). A parent can understand the significance of mental age when it is shown that pupils can have the same I. Q. but different mental ages as the following illustrates:

	CA	IQ	MA
Joe	7-9	75	5-10
Jim	11-3	75	8-5

By applying the mathematical formulae of "IQ times CA gives MA," it can be seen that Joe is probably a candidate for reading readiness while Jim might be guided into a first-level reader.

Use Conversion Techniques. There are many good ways of revealing information about intelligence test scores in interviews. The following procedure is recommended because it allows the teacher to indicate the level at which a child's actual I. Q. score is located without the necessity of revealing the exact score. For example, if the interviewer knows that Mary's obtained I. Q. score was 112, a generalized comment can be made to the parent, "Mary has above average intelligence." The next step should include a discussion of the meaning of this generalization. An appropriate classification chart such as the one which follows can then be shown to the parent.

Classification	IQ	Percents of all persons
Near genius or genius	140 and above	1
Very superior	130-139	2.5
Superior	120-129	8
Above average	110-119	16
Normal or average	90-109	45
Below average	80-89	16
Dull or borderline	70-79	8
Feeble-minded: moron, imbecile, idiot	60-79 59 and below	2.5 1

From charts of the type pictured above the parent learns how Mary compares with the percent of all persons who obtain scores at this level. The teacher might further impart, . . .

"This table shows the classification of IQ's offered by Terman and Merrill who developed the Stanford-Binet Test. It indicates the percent of persons in a normal population who fall in each classification. One should bear in mind that any such table is arbitrary since there is no flexible line of demarcation between 'superior' and 'above average', and the like."

After the parent completes his analysis of the chart, the interviewer might draw one further generalization, "We can expect Mary to make above average marks in some school subjects." On the other hand if a child has a borderline I. Q. the teacher might comment, "In view of the I. Q. score obtained by your child, he should earn average grades in some subjects, but let's not expect him to be in the top group on tests." Charts of this type serve to supplement in a rather concrete way the verbal comments made by an interviewer.

Admit its Limitations. The I. Q. test does not measure some of the qualities that teachers have found necessary in the well-rounded development of an individual. For example, one's character is extremely important to his success on the job. He must show the willingness to assume personal and social obligations. After their assumption, he must set himself to the task and persevere in that work until it is completed. Intelligence tests do not measure the individual's ability to use his creative potential, imagination, or depth of curiosity. Neither are they measures of "social adjustment." Certainly one's readiness and willingness to meet people, to guide and direct them, comes as a result of intelligent action but these factors have not been measured on the I. Q. test.

TEACHER INTERVIEW CAUTION. The wise interviewer will study his parents and children well before he discusses a child's intelligence in great detail in the first place. Parents of bright children have been known to push their offsprings into aspirations to be doctors, lawyers, and school teachers. Even parents of dull children have forced their youngsters to work longer and more strenuous hours thinking that this will enable them to fulfill their professional promise. In either case, there is no need for an interviewer to release that information which can only lead to frustrations and eventual mental ill health for a child.

ACADEMIC ACHIEVEMENT

Through a testing program, the teacher evaluates the child's instructional level of each skill area, establishes the skill area that appears to be most basic to a child's efficiency and by analyzing the results pinpoints more precisely the nature of the difficulty. During the time allotted to the academic portion of the conference the parent's attention can be captured by having them look at charts, graphs, tables, and drawings devised for interpretative purposes. Usually the typical parent can tell at a glance what his child is doing when he notes the peaks and falls that have been registered on a line or bar graph.

What to Report About Standardized Achievement Tests

Since tests serve in giving a more critical account of the pupil's achievement, then raw scores from standardized tests should be interpreted to parents. Information selected should have uniform meaning to parent and educator. It should have demonstrated relevance for the purpose of the discussion (i.e. aid parental understanding of grouping, promotion, and guidance practices.) Moreover, the information presented should be understandable, dependable, valid, and note-worthy.

The kind of information to report will vary for each child. In one instance the teacher may see the need of reporting the raw scores from a test as a child's parents can understand them, while in another instance it would be wiser to show samples of test items that a child consistently seemed to be missing. In the former case it is assumed that a child is doing quite well with no evident problem, while in the latter the pupil is in need of special help and specific areas of difficulty must be identified so that educational therapy might be administered.

How to Report Data From Standardized Tests

Achievement test scores should be explained to parents in terms of "converted scores." Grade equivalents, percentile ranks, and norms are among the forms most widely used for interpretation of test scores.

Grade equivalents. A child, who makes a grade equivalent of 6.3 on a given test, has made the same as that made by the typical pupil in the sixth grade at the end of the third month in that grade. One must be certain that a parent follows this line of interpretation. Parents often believe that a child's high score enables him to do work at a grade level substantially higher than the one in which he is currently assigned. To have scored above his actual grade placement simply indicates that he has earned a score equal to the average score earned by pupils in some subsequent grade and this is all that one should infer. Obviously, the child has not had all of the skills necessary to do the work at some subsequent grade level.

Percentile ranks. Some educators prefer to use percentile ranks in reporting test results. Though percentile ranks are not equivalent units, they can be used for showing the percent of scores in a distribution equal to or lower than the score corresponding to the given rank. To interpret test scores through a percentile technique, one might say:

> "Imagine that your child has a position in a hypothetical group of 100 pupils arranged in rank order of their scores. If in this group of 100 pupils your child stood 80th from the bottom, he would have a percentile rank of eighty. This would mean that he had surpassed 79 percent of the group. If his standing in the group was 20th from the bottom, he would have a percentile rank of 20 which in turn indicates that 19 percent of the group exceeded his performance."

It must be remembered that percentile ranks are not equivalent units and this limits their value as a means of reporting about test data. For example, it takes a wide range of scores to move from one percentile rank to another at the ends of the distribution. On the other hand, it only takes a single score point at times to jump the percentile rank values in the middle of the distribution by several points.

Measures of central tendency. Frequently teachers need a measure that best represents a whole series of scores. For this purpose, the mode, median, or mean is figured. They are points at or near which the scores from a test tend to cluster. These points give the teacher and the parent a quick and meaningful way of talking about a large number of scores. The parent may think of a mean, median, or mode as a score that best represents a group of scores. In this system a student is marked according to his deviation from the class average. If his score is far above average, he is given an E, and if far below the average, an F. Smaller deviations receive marks of S or I; scores clustering near the average are given an M.

Combining Data for Reporting Purposes

Data to be used in the parent-teacher interview of necessity comes from many sources other than standardized tests. Grades are assigned to teacher-made tests, daily recitations, essay reports, and the like. Even art products and physical education power tests are assigned marks and ratings. All of these items are discussed at one time or another in parent interviews. Therefore a common system is needed for quantifying all such information. Hence, *the Stanine System* is an excellent operational tool of the classroom teacher. By the use of "stanines" an interviewer is permitted to compare both individual and group performances in all phases of the educational program.

What are Stanines? The word *stanine* received its derivation from "STAndard NINE-point scale." The stanine scale is a nine-point scale of standard scores. In this scale the raw scores are converted to scores which range from 1 (low) to 9 (high) with a mean of 5 and a standard deviation of two. This allows a means of grouping scores and similar measures into intervals which are crude enough to permit use of a single digit to represent each class. Yet it is precise enough for many practical, simple statistical purposes.

How Can One Effectively Use Stanines for Reporting Purposes?

A useful feature of stanines is that they are equally spaced steps in a scale (see Table I). For example, a stanine 9 is as much better than a stanine 7 as a stanine 6 is better than a 4. Therefore it is easy for parents to look at the scale and see the relative strengths and weaknesses in the several subjects that their children may have. The parent also knows at once that their child who has a stanine of 8 or 9 in a subject is well above the typical pupil in the same grade in the subject reviewed. By the same token, the child who has a stanine of 3 or 4 is well below average.

TABLE I

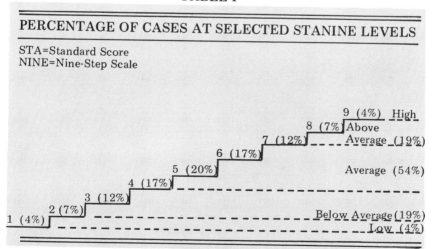

PERCENTAGE OF CASES AT SELECTED STANINE LEVELS

STA=Standard Score
NINE=Nine-Step Scale

9 (4%) High
8 (7%) Above
7 (12%) ____ Average (19%)
6 (17%)
5 (20%) Average (54%)
4 (17%)
3 (12%)
2 (7%)
1 (4%) Below Average (19%)
Low (4%)

How are Stanines Computed? Since almost any current book on statistics gives several samples regarding the assigning of stanines to scores, the author will deal only with informative steps of how to arrange scores coming from a set of classroom papers. However, themes, drawings, speech performance check-lists, and art projects can be sorted into the respective categories described for the very same purposes. The following steps should be suggestive of an acceptable approach to computing stanines:

1. Assume that "Superior," "Excellent," "Very Good," "Fair," and "Poor," are the ratings to assign to the pupils' papers. These words should be written on 4x5 cards and placed on the teacher's desk, allowing room for the papers to be placed under the appropriate titles with respect to the teacher's choice of rating.

2. After all of the papers have been categorized, those papers within the middle group ("very good") should be arranged in order of judged excellence (from the best to the poorest). No restriction should be placed on the number of papers that may be put in any one category.

3. All papers within each category should be processed in the fashion mentioned above. The result will be a total rank order comprising all of the papers from the "Excellent" top rating to the downward rating of "Poor."

4. After ranking all of the papers in this way, it is a relatively simple matter to determine the number of cases at each stanine level by referring to a Stanine Table.[1] The number of cases will coincide precisely with the numbers in the table because the papers are arranged in rank order.

Should the Teacher Tell Parents How Stanines are Used? Where homogeneous grouping is a policy, it might be explained that children in stanine levels 1, 2, and 3 go into a low group; 4, 5, and 6 into an average group; with 7, 8, and 9 being placed in an advanced or accelerated group. Stress the fact that these "groups" are flexible ones with no child staying in the same group all year long. Assuming heterogeneous grouping, suggest that instruction is differentiated within class in order that every child may be challenged at his level of learning ability no matter the instructional group in which he might be found.

What if Parents Seek Information About the Relation-

---

1. Henry E. Garrett. *Statistics in Psychology and Education.* New York: Longmans, Green and Co., 1959. P. 318-319.

ship Between Stanines and the Grades Given by the Teacher? Clarify this relationship by explaining that stanines are entirely objective and refer only to the test from which they were derived, but the teacher's system of grading contains a large subjective element and is more broadly based. Although there is generally a high degree of agreement between school marks and achievement test scores, any wide divergence indicates the need for teacher and parents to investigate possible reasons for the inconsistencies. The use of graphs such as those shown in Figure No. 1 and Figure No. 2 oftentimes makes it much more clear to parents where imbalances in learning have occurred for certain individuals, groups, or classes.

TEACHER INTERVIEW CAUTION: Information regarding standardized test results should be given to parents as long as they recognize that these data contributed to the cumulative evaluation of the child's performance, and that the score their child obtained was not the sole criterion upon which his achievement was based. Furthermore, the test scores of a pupil should not be considered by teachers or parents as infallible. No matter the preference that a teacher may have for a certain method of reporting test data, the efficient reporter will need to have at hand several means for interpreting test results to parents.

FIGURE 1. Stanine Distribution for a Single Class.

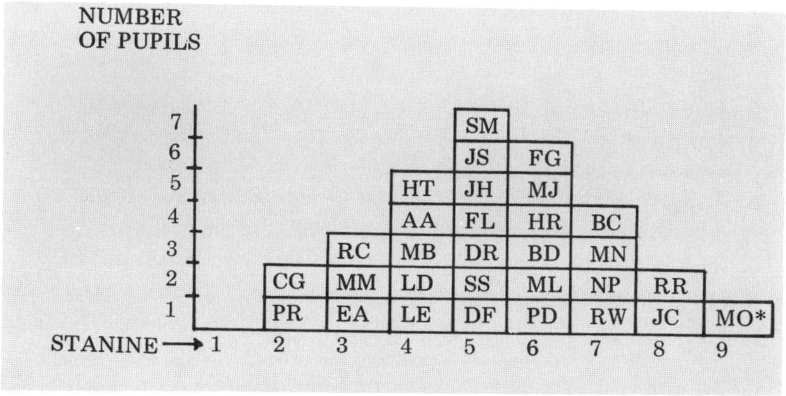

*Initials of each pupil are used to identify their position corresponding to each stanine.

FIGURE 2. Bar Graph Depicting Two Stanine Distributions.

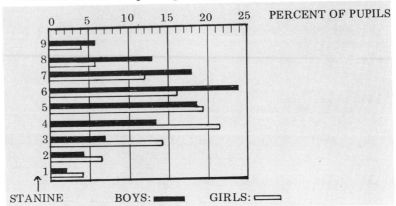

This type of bar graph is useful in contrasting achievements on two testings with equivalent forms of the same test or subtest when a period of instruction has intervened.

Summary

In view of the changing nature of a child, the tests that the school provides for him to take should be administered throughout every stage of his school experience. These test settings should include systematic intelligence testing, the regular use of standardized tests of achievement, specialized tests in reading, arithmetic, and the like, plus teacher-made tests.

Parents should be interested in the school testing program for two major reasons: (1) They provided the money as citizens and taxpayers for the total educational program in their school district, and, (2) as parents they have much to do with the guidance of their children when test results point given directions. Hence, teachers have the responsibility to keep parents informed about tests given to their children. The interview program provides the setting in which parents can also learn to understand and to learn to use the results of their local testing program for child guidance purposes.

Personal and Social Aspects of Child Development-- What to Report and How to Report It

Every child is distinctly different from every other child in most aspects of his growth and development. The elimination of these differences is neither desirable nor feasible.
—John I. Goodlad

Introduction

Everything in a pupil's development is a product of an interplay between his heredity and his environment. Each pupil's growth is indeed determined to an important degree by the heredity from which he comes. Although parents are powerful figures in the child's environment, a child's inborn qualities make a difference in what adults can and cannot do for him.

The child who grows in a physical and psychological sense takes on his own signs of individuality. However, his growth patterns can be compared to those principles of child growth and development that normally occur in a healthy child with the passage of time. As a child grows physically

5

with respect to increase in height, weight, and changes in body structure, he also changes for the most part in the thinking power generated in his central nervous system. That is, there is a modification of behavior that has been brought about by virtue of experience, both public and private in nature. He *maturates*.

As children maturate, they make physical changes which should result in functional changes, too. These graduations of growth are gradual and judgments can be made about them. Parents need to learn of the extent to which their child is adapting to his growing abilities. Although one cannot change the child from one pattern of growth to another, many experiences can be planned to promote his fuller and richer development. The purpose of the interviewer who reports information about child growth patterns is to attempt to adapt a child's formal school training and home guidance to his growing abilities. It is to this end that the comments in this chapter are dedicated.

Social Growth and Development

Social Growth, What Is It? An important aspect of a child's development is wrapped up in his ability to fulfill personal social needs. These needs include (a) self-control, (b) independence, (c) social conformance, (d) human interest and adjustment, and, (e) the desire to belong and to identify with a segment of society. As he seeks to satisfy his own social needs, he will show social maturity or lack of it in his growing perception or awareness of the feelings, moods, and intentions expressed by others. In the close associations of life itself, the learning of appropriate social skills is of great importance. A child who has a pleasant disposition, considerate manners, tactful speech, and a mutual respect for his neighbor's feelings should be able to maintain a strong regard from his fellow schoolmates. Moreover, these traits of social competence may place him in a position of leadership when he takes his place as a contributor to societies' needs.

Measuring Social Adjustment. Since children have few fixed social patterns and often display vague understandings of social concepts, attempts to measure social adjustment have not been as thorough as most educators would like. In many cases it would be advantageous to the child and his parents if the interviewer would report the social acceptability of his endeavors from the standpoint of his acceptance or rejection as implied in comments from classmates. This may give a more accurate picture of his social acceptability as an exhaustive study indicates that teachers' observational estimates of social acceptance of various children by their associates are notably unreliable.[1]

Sociometry. One of the most helpful techniques developed for observing and recording the social appeal children have one for another is *sociometry*. This technique was developed on the hypothesis that the individual pupil can be understood only in the light of the group, and that the group can be understood only by knowing something of the individuals who comprise it. Through the study of interpersonal relationships of his pupils, the interviewer can obtain much information that will help him understand the social needs of individual children. A simple chart can be used as the form upon which sociometric data might be recorded (see Figure No. 1). There are several advantages to the use of this type of device, namely: (a) a parent can tell where his child stands with respect to the total class (e.g. "has few friends," "star," "isolate"); (b) numbers may be used to designate who the children are, thereby eliminating parental embarrassment and keeping all other names confidential; and (c) parents tend to accept the feelings expressed by a whole class than they would honor comments of a select few, including those of the teacher.

Social Development Scales. There has been a tendency for educators to follow the false assumption that a child's social development will be commensurate with his mental ability. High or low test scores have been viewed as indicators of a child's social success. Therefore, to offset this problem educators should seek to ascertain social adaptation of the child without regard to his personality, intellectual status, or reference to his noticeable degrees of social success.

The *Vineland Social Maturity Scale*[2] is one of the better-known scales of social measure. It is a standardized instrument patterned somewhat like the Stanford-Binet mental scale. There are 117 items in the scale which represent progressive development. The Vineland Scale is designed in

1. Marion Vere DeVault. *Relationship of Sociometric Status to Selected Factors in Grades One Through Twelve.* Bloomington: Indiana University, Doctoral Dissertation, 1953.
2. E. A. Doll. *The Vineland Social Maturity Scale.* Minneapolis: Education Test Bureau, 1946.

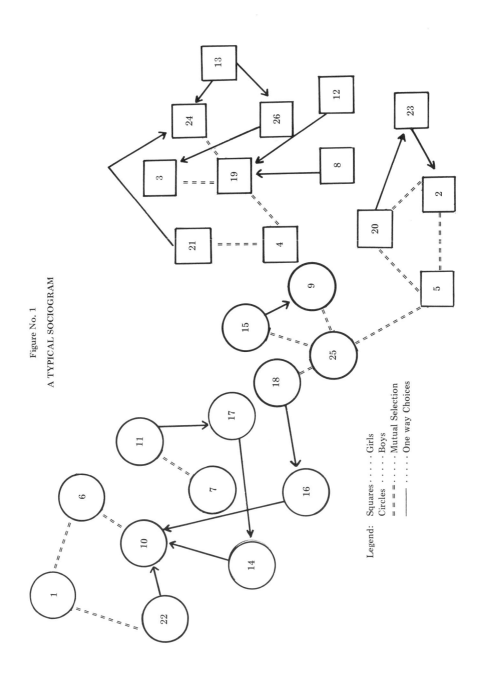

Figure No. 1

A TYPICAL SOCIOGRAM

Legend: Squares· · · · · Girls
Circles · · · · · · Boys
= = = = · · Mutual Selection
————— · · · · · One way Choices

such a way that detailed performances for each age are given to show progressive capacity on the child's ability to look after himself and to accept responsibilities leading to eventual social maturity. This scale reveals a social quotient which could be used to determine the probable social competence of the child at a given intellectual level. If a child's sense of social responsibility is not somewhat commensurate with his intellectual status, the interviewer may want to obtain parental help in guiding a child toward a better pattern of self-adjustment.

Social Distance Scales and Related Sociometric Instruments. Some indirect approaches have been used to give the teacher insight into the social attitudes of children. For example, Roger's *Personality Schedule*[3] consists of items such as, "Who is the smartest girl in school?" The pupil thinks about who he believes to be the smartest girl. The examiner follows up with, "Are you just like her?" And, "Would you like to be just like her?" Questioning of this type gives the teacher information of a quantitative nature about the child's social attitudes, his adjustments to his parents, his feelings of inferiority, and his tendency to day-dream.

Another good device, the "Guess Who" test,[4] allows one to obtain a composite picture of the kind of person other children see a given child to be. In this test, children are given word pictures or verbal portraits. They are asked to write down the names of any boys or girls who might fit that portrait. For example, "Here is someone who is always ready to play or work with the rest of the group even when he or she can't have his or her own way?" In tests of this type one can see the frequency of acceptance or rejection by the children would be rather revealing; knowledge that parents should have.

Inter-Personal Relations and Personal Adjustments— What to Report and How to Report it

Probably the most ill-used term in educational jargon is

---

3. C. R. Rogers. "Measuring Personality Adjustment in Children, Nine to Thirteen Years of Age." *Teachers College Contributions to Education,* New York, No. 458, 1931.

4. *The Guess-Who Test.* Institute of Educational Research, New York, Teachers College, Columbia University.

"Your child seems immature." Rarely do teachers or parents sense the true meaning of this statement. When it is used, the parent is likely left with a false or undesirable impression. Therefore, if the topic of social maturity is brought up at conference time a specific social skill should be identified and compared to known social characteristics of children of that respective grade level.

Social maturity is best understood when samples of behavior are identified. For example, these would include such statements as "Your child takes personal initiative in winning friends; recently he invited some fifth grade children to join in our sixth grade games." Or, "You will recall that one general characteristic of seven-year-olds is that they are beginning to be concerned with doing right and wrong, but, very often, have a tendency to steal small things. I don't believe we will need to worry about Suzy taking Bob's pencil unless this becomes a habitual case. I will keep you informed of her actions hereafter."

In another instance if the problem be of a negative nature one might report, "The general characteristics of pre-adolescents suggest there will be some teasing and antagonism between girl and boy groups, but I do believe Joe's problem is getting somewhat beyond what is normally acceptable for his age level. Would you like for me to call him in for a personal visit with us on this matter?"

It will be noted in the above discussion that knowing the background of the parents is imperative. On the one hand some parents can infer from examples the extent to which their child is measuring up in his social attributes, while in other cases it may be necessary to explain what is commonly accepted as appropriate forms of behavior for the given grade level. In either case, the parent is more able to compare what his child is actually doing with what has been previously outlined by the interviewer. He should leave the conference much more informed about the generally acceptable traits or standards for which his child should strive.

Children tend to reflect the social background of their parents in language, manners, beliefs, customs, and human traits. The teacher must proceed with caution in the way he reports information about the child who is "shy." The parents may also display timid, self-conscious personalities. Likely it would be just as critical to report directly any information about the child who displays extreme shyness if the parents display bold, outward examples of self

Figure No. 2

A SOCIAL DISTANCE SCALE

SOCIAL ACCEPTANCE AS DETERMINED THROUGH "FREE RESPONSE" OF CLASSMATES

Names

1. . . . . Is one of my close friends.

2. . . . . Would like to have (him, her) as one of my close friends.

3. . . . . Would like to be with (him, her) once in a while, but not very often.

4. . . . . Doesn't bother me, but seems to bother other people.

5. . . . . Don't mind (his, her) being in class but I don't want much to do with (him, her).

6. . . . . Wish (she, he) weren't in our room at all.

confidence in social settings. Undoubtedly, out-going parents will let it be known in one way or another that this is what they expect of their child.

The sociometric method is not only simple to apply, but the information it yields is quite reliable and significant. Children's choices show a high degree of stability when a sociometric test is administered and then given again after a few months. Consequently, an interviewer may want to show two or three of his completed sociograms to the parents. By utilizing numbers in lieu of names (as in Figure No. 2), the interviewer can point to a number and describe the type of social attributes that its owner personifies.

Although there will be notable exceptions, parents should gain at least two general ideas from their conference about children's social acceptance or non-acceptance: (1) children who win a high degree of acceptance are active, alert, interested, cheerful, and friendly; (2) those of low acceptance are pupils having little interest in other persons, are quiet or shy or noisy, boastful, and rebellious.

As an outcome of the interview, both parents have at least some understanding that for their youngster to be socially acceptable, he must, in general, have certain qualities but not to excess; be interested in others, but not to the extent that he is too obvious in seeking of that attention; be active but not hyperactive; and he must be confident, yet not boastful.

TEACHER INTERVIEW CAUTION: In the normal course of events a pupil becomes more social as he grows older. He builds relationships with other people and acquires values that others share. The interviewer who seeks only to report these types of relationships may have forgotten to look at those streaks of individuality which makes the child increasingly aware of himself as a separate being. Thus, the interviewer must make a conscientious effort to search out what a child does that makes him socially unique and how he goes about winning friends and influencing moves on the part of others to respond to him as a socially active being.

Emotional Growth and Development

The teacher should observe most carefully the child's general pattern of emotional development and his individual variations within that pattern. Patterns of emotional involvement have many variations, fast and slow, steady and irregular. For example, a child of good mentality, whose over-all pattern of development is slow, may be ready for grade five at the age of ten, but in social and emotional ways he may be more of a seven or eight year old. Such a variation in emotional growth makes it necessary for the teacher to study the emotional level of maturity reached by each child so that he can report these conditions. As the teacher and parents talk about the child's emotional strengths and weaknesses, the more likely he can be helped to develop a more stable pattern of emotional control.

What Should One Report About a Child's Emotional Adjustment? Children are always exhibiting reactions to happenings and situations in their school life. The teacher should observe the stability with which the child faces successes and achievements as well as disappointments and failures.

In reporting information about the emotional growth and development of a child, it is desirable to include some items of behavior that illustrate adjustment patterns as well as those that depict undesirable behavior. One must not forget that the poorly adjusted child will have in his possession some desirable traits, and to report only undesirable trends tends to give a perverted evaluation of the pupil.

If a child's emotional conflicts are so difficult for him to accept that he represses his feelings altogether, it will not take long for him to be no longer consciously aware of them. He may begin to develop a headache or stomach-ache before test sessions, oral classroom reports, and similar things he doesn't want to do. This is an example of the unconscious mind's protest against something which causes tension, anxieties, and frustrations. When symptoms such as these arise, the teacher must help the parent recognize the importance of emotions in influencing bodily health. The child's mind and body work together with the body reacting upon the mind, and the mind upon the body. If the parent is made aware of the fact that illnesses must be considered and treated in relation to the whole person (*psyche*, mind + *soma*, body), the more likely they will seek expert help on psychosomatic illness if such therapy is needed and recommended for their child.

How Should Information about Emotional Growth and Development be Reported? Deviate behavior can be indicated by discussing whether or not the child is easily upset, readily hurt, or extremely restless in school. It may be necessary to indicate specific symptoms and indications of emotional difficulty. These often include: thumb-sucking, nail-biting, temper tantrums, lying, unacceptable language, tattling, and stealing. Such indications of emotional tensions are reported to parents in order to secure their assistance, if needed, for discovering and treating the underlying causes.

The teacher must exercise much tact in leading the parent to see that their child seemingly is experiencing deep-rooted emotional problems. Although crying-spells and outbursts of temper are usually punished, the parents commonly give no explicit attention to the education of emotional behavior. As a result, parents frequently take a negative attitude toward this knowledge and do something to inhibit effective learning.

Examples of the child's general pattern of adjustment should be cited to parents. This would allow most parents to formulate their own judgments (e.g.; "Billy was fighting after school two weeks ago; last week he pushed a girl down the steps; yesterday he was arguing about a bicycle parking space.") After citing specific examples the teacher should remark that he believes the problem to be one requiring *understanding* more than the administration of punishment. As discussions of this type terminate, there should be some move on the part of the parent to seek out the underlying causes of the misbehavior. If there is not, then the teacher must suggest the need of referring their child to the school counselor or psychologist if the case seems serious enough.

Extreme caution should be exercised when a parent seeks information which lends itself to comparing their child's emotional behavior with other children. Finally, the teacher has a responsibility to the welfare of the child by refraining from making statements of judgments without illustrating incidents (e.g.; "Billy is always in trouble."). Such statements are rarely helpful, and most likely very detrimental.

TEACHER INTERVIEW CAUTION: Information imparted to parents concerning their child's pattern of emotional development should be screened carefully. The following statements might serve as guidelines when dealing with reporting information about emotions: (1) avoid making comparisons and judgments with any degree of "certainty"; (2) indicate the problem and let the parents strive for its solution; (3) recognize that reporting information about the emotional growth shown by the child depends to some degree upon how well the parent accepts the judgment of the teacher, and whether the parent had previously been informed about the quality of control exhibited by the child; (4) discuss those emotional problems or conflicts which are directly effected by home environment, such as the child's outbursts of crying to obtain his way with the parent; and (5) report information only if it will enhance the emotional growth of the child.

Physical Growth and Development

The elementary program of physical education should be directed toward improving the development of the child's whole personality insofar as this activity can contribute to this end. A strong physical education program is centered upon personal relationships, mental learnings, the development of esthetic qualities, social relationships of group orders, and appropriate emotional responses developed in and coming from each individual child.

Safety education is also an integral part of the instructional program. Accidents are responsible for one out of three deaths of school-age children. Teachers should observe the extent to which pupils have developed a sense of responsibility for themselves as well as for others.

What Should One Report about Physical Growth and Development? At primary grade levels one should expect some change in weight and height at nearly every three month cycle. Hence, the teacher's charts and graphs which contain a series of heights and weight measurements of each child bear consideration for reporting purposes.

At the intermediate grade levels parents may need to know what to anticipate both in bodily changes and in new emotional reactions which will become observable during the coming adolescent years. They need to know what is important to pass along to their children. Therefore it is necessary that intermediate grade teachers prepare themselves well to give clear, simple, understanding help to parents about the physiological changes related to menarche and related adjustment problems of the young girl. The school nurse might be invited to sit in on those problems which seemingly merit close scrutiny and in which the problem is somewhat more technical than a teacher might desire to discuss. In general, however, each teacher must be prepared to discuss the characteristics of the sexual development of young girls and the way in which these factors could affect the emotional and mental development of females as observable through fatigue, inner-tensions, and irritability.

The teacher must also encourage parents to be more concerned about the physical development of their boys. Before the onset of puberty there is usually a resting period. Growth increments are relatively small. Then comes a period of rapid growth in height. Following the growth in height, there is an accompanying period of growth in weight. Simultaneously the rest of his body is changing and developing rapidly. It would not be unlikely for some pupils to become self-conscious because of overdeveloped portions of the body, or for them to be embarrassed because of the awkwardness accompanying this age. Thus the citing of examples of the activity of the child, and the use of terms which help to explain to parents the depth of the problem may lead some parents to a greater understanding of their child and cause some action to be taken on suggested solutions. For example, "As you know Mary is developing more rapidly than the other girls in her group. Therefore, she doesn't want to participate in P.E. because all girls are required to shower. Mary must be encouraged to use the private facilities and continue with her physical education class."

How Should Information about Physical Growth and Development of the Child be Reported? In the primary grades, few actual tests of performance need be shown in the conference. The teacher can judge, for example, as to whether a certain child is full of energy, recovers quickly from strenuous activity, enjoys several different activities, displays good coordination in movement, and is growing in motor control. These capacities can be recorded at regular intervals and the results of which can be reported at conference time.

Records of specific achievements should be kept on third and fourth graders. The objective evidence of achievement can be charted and shown to parents. Simple tests requiring the child to sit up when his feet are held, to touch finger tips to the floor without bending the knees, and similar movements designed to show body strength are examples of appropriate activities (see Table I).

For fifth and sixth grades the results of various tests that measure strength, endurance, speed, agility, flexibility, balance, coordination, and the like can be charted and shown during the conference (see Table II). An analysis of a pupil's individual score on the rating chart may reveal several significant facts about a child's progress. For example, the

TABLE 1

MINIMUM MUSCULAR FITNESS REPORT FOR PRIMARY GRADES

Pupil _____ Level _____ School _____ Date _____ Teacher _____

Your child made the following scores on his physical fitness tests of MINIMUM muscular fitness. The results of the tests are recorded below. Failure to obtain a FOUR rating on any one of the six test items indicates a lack of strength or flexibility of certain key muscle groups which may affect the functioning of the whole body as a healthy organism.

TASKS*	WHAT IT TESTS	UNDERSTANDING THE RESULTS	RATINGS**
A. Straight Leg Sit-up	Abdominal muscles plus psoas muscles	Child sits-up from lying position.	4 3 2 1
B. Bent Knee Sit-up	Abdominal muscles minus psoas muscles	Child sits-up from lying position.	4 3 2 1
C. Leg Lift	Psoas muscles plus lower abdominal muscles	Child lies on back and holds feet off floor 10 seconds.	4 3 2 1
D. Upper Back	Upper back muscles	Child lies on stomach and lifts legs off floor for 10 seconds; partner holds feet down.	4 3 2 1
E. Lower Back	Lower back muscles	Child lies on stomach and lifts straight legs off floor 10 seconds; partner holds chest down.	4 3 2 1
F. Toe Touch in standing position	Flexibility of back and hamstring muscles	Child touches toes with knees straight and holds for 3 seconds.	4 3 2 1

*Four trials are given on each task
**Key to Ratings:
  4—Excellent   2—Satisfactory
  3—Good   1—Poor

TABLE II
SAMPLE-PHYSICAL FITNESS TESTING SCORE
SHEET FOR 12 YEAR OLD GIRLS

Jane Doe (Pupil)	1st Test—red 2nd Test—blue 3rd Test—black		Laboratory School (School)	

EVENTS	Sit-ups	Modified Pull-ups	Broad Jump	50-Yard Dash	Softball Throw
Excellent	50	(45)	5'8"	7.2	94
Good	47 46 45 (44) 43 (42) 41 (40) 39 38 37 36 35 34	44 (43) 42 (41) 40	5'7" 5'6" 5'5" 5'4" 5'3" 5'2"	7.3 7.4 7.5 7.6 7.7 (7.8) 7.9 8.0	91 (90) 89 88 (87) 86 (85) 84 83 82 81 80 79 78
Satisfactory	33 32 31 30 29 28 27 26 25	39 38 37 36 35 34 33 32 31 30	(5'1") 5'0" 4'11" 4'10" 4'9"	8.1 8.2 8.3 8.4	77 76 75 74 73 72 71 70 69 68 67 66 65
Poor	24 23 22 21 20 19 18	29 28 27 26 25 24 23 22 21 20	4'8" 4'7" 4'6" 4'5"	8.5 8.6 8.7 8.8 8.9 9.0	64 63 62 61 60 59 58 57 56 55

Height 5' 4½"   5' 4½"   5' 4¾"

Weight   94   94¼   94½

Date   9/15/65   1/15/66   5/15/66

elements of the tennis serve can be shown when an area is marked off and the number of times the pupil is able to place the ball in those areas is recorded. Though this does not reveal exactly how a pupil may play an over-all game, it does indicate his progress on certain fundamentals. Much can be learned by observing the pupil in action when his form, force, speed, and effectiveness are noted. Style forms can be devised for all skills, analyzed with care, and the more significant facts revealed to parents in the initial conference.

For a more elaborate system of judging and reporting, "grids" are recommended. The use of grids, such as the *Wetzel Grid*[5] and then interpreting pupil progress in the light of uniformity and consistency, would be a desirable way of reporting information about a pupil's physical status and growth.

Parents often learn much at the conference from such statements as, "Bob's achievement is limited because of poor habits in practice and drill sessions." Comments of this type can be reinforced by showing them charts dealing with his practice sessions, attendance data, capacity and performance tests.

TEACHER INTERVIEW CAUTION. While the teacher may have some understanding of the child's general physical growth and rather clear-cut evidences of his mental health, it would not be assumed that he knows more about a child's physical patterns of development than parents or their physician. The teacher's responsibility is to make the parent aware of how the physical education program will be adjusted to meet their child's health needs and to give them insight into their role if special help is needed.

Attitudes and Values

Educators have concerned themselves for so long with "facts" that youth should possess that the values and attitudes that our pupils hold have been neglected. Most likely many of these *facts* have been forced upon the minds of pupils, and some would even strive to impose adult *values*

---

5. Norman C. Wetzel. Known as "Wetzel's Grid." Published National Education Association Service, Inc., 1200 West Third Street, Cleveland, Ohio.

upon children. But the approach advocated here is to try to extend a pupil's values in terms of the standards and background experiences he now holds irrespective of the standards held by the parents or teacher. This does not mean that a pupil lowers his standards nor does his teacher, but that instead of providing standards beyond the reach of children the adult seeks to extend pupil values by helping them to understand better the reason for which they hold certain views in the first place. In other words, if a child holds a certain attitude toward selected individuals in his peer group or toward a facet of learning that his subject matter promotes, it is better to increase his understanding of the value he holds so that he can take in newer or additional concepts for enlarging his point of view. To expect him to simply substitute new values for his old ones at a moment's notice not only is foolish but contrary to the known principles of child growth and development.

The teacher must be accepting of his pupils as they are, making use of the attitudes, values, and traits they already possess. This enables him to enjoy and profit from intellectual pursuits and may open doorways to learning when pupil intake on values is operating at a minimum level. If a pupil comes from a home where high values are upheld then the teacher may simply reinforce the goals already sought. But for the child who has lacked appropriate home stimulation, the school becomes his last chance to upgrade his values. If pupils are to adopt values, interests, and attitudes that are consistent with a free and orderly mind, then that mind must be stoked with common activities and examples so that he can react sensibly to his own strong emotional impulses.

A class will have as many attitudes as a group as they have as individuals; composite thinking and concerted opinions bring forth new attitudes. But there are some unique attitudes that are prevalent in today's society which mark the signs of our time. Among these attitudes which are evidenced in adults and in turn inculcated in our youth (they model after us) are the following which merit attention and concern in the parent conference:

1. If I'm not going to make the highest grade in class, why try?
2. If I'm not going to get to do something special then I won't participate.
3. If I do anything in class, then you'll have to make me.
4. What's the percentage in learning anyway? What's in it for me?

5. The things you want me to commit myself to as a pupil won't get me ahead in later life or on the job.
6. Get ahead at any cost; cheat or hurt your friends if you have to.

The statements above are exemplars of negative attitudes that seemingly are being perpetuated by adults in some youth. If such attitudes are allowed to go unhampered, spiritual problems and moral issues will become much harder to deal with in our society. Hence, the inculcation of desirable human values must accompany the development of intellect, academic progress, and fact-getting in all of our schools if any notable progress is to be made in living in an increasingly crowded world.

To offset the imbalance of attitudes and values relative to the child's growth toward more acceptable standards of behavior information should be reported to parents about the "rightness" or "wrongness" of the child's acts as they affected the well-being of others and himself. The teacher must be ready to deal with problems of abnormal behavior exhibited by certain children who exhibit habits of delinquency, school truancy, and dishonesty.

There are certain types of information about the child's growth and development of aesthetic values which should be reported in each parent teacher conference. These should include a discussion about the child's understanding and growth in aesthetic preferences and appreciations. For example, parents should be told about the child's reading of literature of high quality, listening to good music, and his school habits of studying those products and talents of persons who have made notable contributions in art.

The importance of reporting the child's development in selected aesthetic values and of citing his experiences is twofold. Information is imparted to the parent about the way in which the child has learned to detect and describe certain types of artistic talents. Subsequently, the parents may be led to develop an interest with their child in the appreciation of artistic work as obtained through extended reading, observation of finished products found in the local community, and for planned discussions in out-school situations of a descriptive nature. A child's special talents in the arts and the experiences which indicate his desire to be creative, such as his receptive regard of beauty, should not be neglected during the conference report.

Summary

The old saying has it that "an ounce of prevention is worth a pound of cure." Educators and parents would agree that it is far better not only to prevent the occurrence of some abnormal condition which may then lead to secondary complications for a child, but also to provide a healthy environment for maximal growth and development. In order to do this, teachers and parents must confer.

A healthy environment grows out of several pertinent factors: (1) a child's basic trust in himself; (2) the understanding that his parent's have about him; (3) the stimulation that he receives that is appropriate to his particular developmental level; and finally, (4) the understanding by the teacher, parent, and child that healthy growth is characterized by periods of progression, integration, and regression. Summarily then, basic trust of a child in his adult instructors is conducive to healthy growth; understanding by the parent leads to a child properly gratifying his needs; stimulation of a child to meet his needs relates to an important principle of pacing oneself to his growth increments; and understanding one's physical, social, mental, emotional, and psychological growth reduces the risk of child frustration and immature modes of his behavior.

Parent teacher interviews that promote thorough discussions of a child's growth and development patterns would not entirely prevent some difficulties in growth and adjustment. However, the precepts that parents hold may be guided by the teacher during the interview session thus preventing a child's mild upsets or minute disturbances from becoming major ones.

Selecting
and Reporting
Information
From Specific
Curricular Areas

The curriculum is as good as the learning it inspires.
—Hanne J. Hicks

Introduction

The matters which relate to a child's progress at school that might be discussed in parent interviews cover a vast territory. From the curriculum comes so much that could be reported that the interviewer often feels at a loss as to what ought to be imparted. Where he should commence his report becomes of even greater concern. The information contained in this chapter serves to identify what the teacher should report in an interview that is of a curricular nature. How one should report the selected information is also discussed.

Special Skills and Abilities

Educators deal with content, skills, and the reasoning powers of their pupils. The parent not only needs to know

6

how much his child is learning but how well he can use the skills necessary to the mastery of content materials. The interview report should include information about the child's progress in both general and specific skill areas. It is conceivable that some children will know skills in general, but will have difficulty in applying these specific knowledges to actual problem situations. Perhaps some will show greater difficulty in transferring what they have acquired as a given skill to its effective utilization in a new experience. Parents should be informed of their child's ability to use the information and skills which have been acquired through school experiences.

Reporting About Reading

Reading is more than word calling or word naming. There are two major acts to be performed as the child learns to read: (1) recognizing the printed word on the page; and (2) understanding and dealing with the meaning presented or inferred in the passage. After the word is recognized and understood, a third significant thing should happen to the child: as he comprehends what has been read silently, his behavior should be changed. Therefore, parents should leave the interview with the understanding that reading is a process of recognizing and comprehending words for the purpose of changing their child's behavior.

What Types of Special Reading Skills Should One Report? Teachers and parents should be less concerned about what a child gets through reading, and more with what gets *through to* the child. Silent reading is done *to get* something from the printed page quite likely for his own use. On the other hand oral reading allows one *to give* an author's interpretation to others. Therefore, oral and silent reading are done for different purposes. For the former, a child develops his ability to deal with an audience, while the latter is more individual and personal in nature. Parents should be informed of these basic purposes of the reading act.

The tables which follow illustrate the types of skills that should be reported to parents during the interview setting. Table I deals with the *skills* which are involved in the beginning reading act, while Table II contains those skills that a child must learn after having acquired initial word attack skills.

TABLE I

READING

General Skills	Specific Skills
Word Recognition	Can the child make the necessary mental associations regarding the form of the word, its meaning, and its sound?
Comprehension	Can the reader fuse into thoughts the words of the sentence or passage?
Reaction	Can he detect the mood, tone, and intent of the writer?
Integration	Can he blend the ideas obtained from reading into his actual life experiences?

TABLE II

SKILLS NECESSARY TO SUCCESSFUL READING IN THE CONTENT AREAS

General Skills	Specific Skills
Previewing	Can the pupil find the main ideas?
Skimming	Can "cues" to important ideas be found at a glance?
Scanning	Can he refrain from reading the entire page?
Graphic	Does he know how to get specific types of information from maps and diagrams?
Reporting	Can he write and read summaries efficiently?
Notetaking	Is he accurate and precise in note taking? Are his listening habits good?
Organizing	Can he outline? Can he identify the main sections of a good report?
Reference	Can he effectively use the dictionary, almanac, guides, and encyclopedia?
Speed	Does he know how to adjust his reading rate to his purpose and to the content?

How Should A Child's Reading Skills be Reported? That a given child has learned a certain skill is not as important as the fact of whether or not he can apply it effectively. For example, the teacher should report the success that a child is having (or lack of it) with respect to general skills of reading. General skills include: organizing paragraphs, arranging ideas in order, and summarizing information. Specific reading skills to be reported include such factors as the child's ability to perceive cause-effect relationships, graph reading, and drawing of inferences from passages.

Most commercial test companies provide "profile charts" upon which a pupil's reading progress is to be plotted. These pictorial graphs should be shown to parents so that they can tell at a glance the major attributes and handicaps of their child when it comes to his personal skills of reading. Workbooks in reading can also be shown to parents for these same purposes.

TEACHER INTERVIEW CAUTION: Parents should be brought up-to-date on the fact that their child is being encouraged to evaluate his own progress in reading. In a realistic way the pupil is taught to think about his work and given ways in which to determine if he is making progress, what phase of reading still gives him trouble, what he has mastered, and what experiences are to be forthcoming. For the teacher or parent to merely concur that a child's reading is of "good" or "poor" quality is inadequate and really not the point of conferring. The concern should be for a child's own conscientious effort (or lack of it) to strive for progress in his reading. An analysis of his work to that end should be sought.

Handwriting and Penmanship

An organized program for reporting the handwriting practices of children yields far-reaching returns to both parents and teachers. Most parents realize that handwriting is a neglected subject in many elementary school classrooms. They want their children to show proficiency in penmanship legibility, neatness, and correct letter alignment, as well as to develop speed and ease of writing. Good teachers want these same proficiencies stressed.

What Should One Report About the Child's Handwriting Technique? Handwriting skills involve a complex type of visual-muscular co-ordination. If the written product is to possess the desired level of legibility, speed of production, and general aesthetic qualities, then a very high standard of performance and coordination must be developed. Legibility and physical appearance are key elements affecting the quality of written expression. The teacher is thus confronted with a real need for instruments to appraise the results of instruction in handwriting. These same instruments can be used to diagnose individual difficulties in writing. Scales, graphs, and handwritten samples can serve well these needs.

From the practical point of view and the essentials of the program, parents need to know what constitutes efficient handwriting and how it can be recognized. Among the factors that should be reported about handwriting skills are: (1) *speed* as obtained from timed tests; (2) *quality* as observed in copies of daily papers and commercial scales; (3) *uniformity* as noted by slant and alignment of the letters; (4) *letter formation* as distinguished by its legibility, style, and beauty; (5) *spacing* with respect to distance between words, letters, and lines; and (6) *posture* which promotes self-control, sound health (breathing, heart development), and good writing.

How Should Information About Handwriting Skills be Reported? Parents should be shown the results of handwriting instruction through means of quality or merit scales. The scales should include the number of letters per minute at which the copy was written (see Table III).

TABLE III

QUALITY AND SPEED STANDARDS FOR HANDWRITING

Grade Level	2	3	4	5	6	7	8
Quality on Ayres Scale	44	47	50	55	59	64	70
Rate in Letters Per Minute	36	48	56	65	72	80	90

The table above indicates that pupils at the end of the second grade should write 36 letters per minute and that the typical quality of their samples should average approximately 44 on the Ayres Scale.[1] By the end of the third grade they should write 48 letters per minute and increase to a rate of 90 letters per minute at the end of the 8th grade. It should be remembered that quality "60" meets all of the legibility requirements of social usage.

The child's writing in the Language Arts should be compared with his writing assignments in other subjects. However, this would not give a parent a very clear picture of what his child should be doing. A good commercial scale

---

1. Leonard P. Ayres. *A Scale for Measuring the Quality of Handwriting of School Children.* Bulletin No. 113, New York: Division of Education, Russell Sage Foundation, 1912.

must be selected since it should not only convey the progress of an individual in class, but should also indicate something of the progress of the class as a total group after each four or six weeks' rating episode. To make the chart more meaningful, the teacher should draw in the norm with a colored pencil so that the parent can compare their child's earned rating with this previously established norm (see Figure No. 1).

A GRAPH SHOWING A PUPIL'S HANDWRITING SCORES AND PROGRESS IN HANDWRITING QUALITY

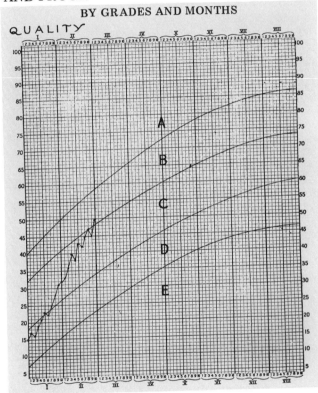

Figure No. 1

A very effective tool for scoring each pupil's handwriting *quality* and *speed* is the measuring scale developed by W. S. Benson[2] and Company, Austin, Texas. Their graphs give a

---

2. W. S. Benson and Company. *Graphs Showing a Pupil's Handwriting Scores and Progress in Handwriting Quality and Handwriting Speed.* Austin, Texas.

progressive curve in both quality (Figure No. 1) and speed (Figure No. 2) by months and grades. The parent can see how their child's grade was recorded and how many points he must raise his quality or speed to make the next higher grade on his profile card. Moreover, the parents can note the *grade median* above which their child should be expected to excel as he strives to exhibit steady progress in both speed and quality.

Figure No. 2
A GRAPH SHOWING A PUPIL'S HANDWRITING SCORES
AND PROGRESS IN HANDWRITING SPEED
BY GRADES AND MONTHS

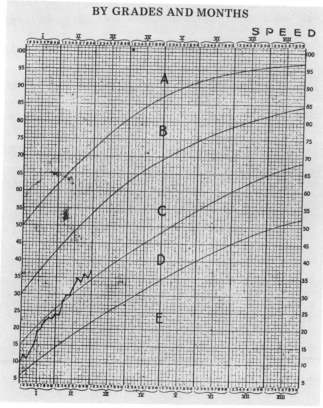

In interpreting these graphs to the parent, the teacher should indicate that a line is on each graph to represent each month of the school year. A dot is placed on the first vertical line in the proper grade which designates the pupil's earned score. The following month the same test should be given and the score recorded on the second vertical line and so on throughout the school year. If the validity of this procedure is questioned by any parents, it would be wise to indicate to them that twenty thousand children's papers were used as the basis for making the scales and progressive graphs against which their youngsters are now being compared.

As shown in Figure No. 2, the pupil will receive for his grade in speed or quality of handwriting, one of the letters A, B, C, D, E (unsatisfactory), or its equivalent in some other method of marking. The completed graph can then become a part of the child's cumulative record folder to be shown again the succeeding year. Last year scores are to be contrasted with the newer recordings plotted as the child advances.

For remedial cases, it would take only a few seconds of conference time to use a transparency in an Over-Head Projector to flash a scale or style of handwriting on the screen and concomitantly show the work of a child. This would allow the parent to see at the onset their child's handwriting before remedial work, his writing six weeks later, and the norm standard for that age group.

TEACHER INTERVIEW CAUTION: Handwriting was once thought to be a skill that was not affected by the content material which was being expressed through written measures. However, handwriting as it is generally viewed today, is affected greatly by both the purpose and the type of subject in which the skill is being used. Thus parents should be led to recognize there is justification for bringing materials from all subject matter areas into the practice sessions and that educators expect the child to attend to good handwriting habits in *all* subjects during the entire school day.

Oral Communication

When an individual speaks without drawing adverse attention to his manner of speaking, he is said to have *normal* speech. If a child's oral communication is unintelligible or inaudible, unpleasant to hear, or is characterized by repetitions or blocks, this may cause its user to become less efficient, anxious, or in some extreme cases, maladjusted.

The teacher has many opportunities to work with a child's oral communication since most pupils are actively engaged in conversing. . . .telephoning, interviewing, giving or seeking information, reading aloud, storytelling, dramatizing, and participating in oral class reports. With proper assistance from the professional speech therapist and by support of the child's parents, the classroom teacher can contribute a valuable service in making the pupil aware of his own speech patterns. To the extent that a pupil becomes aware of how others speak, to that extent he is more likely able to determine his own habits by introspection.

What Should One Report About the Child's Manner of Speaking? Since social success is shown by one's ability to handle himself well in ordinary speaking situations so as to mingle freely with other people in any walk of life, then conferences with parents designed to help their children develop positive habits and attitudes toward *good speech* are mandatory. The following questions are suggestive guides for the teacher to use in preparation for reporting information about a child's speaking habits. Does the child:

(1) express himself clearly, interestingly, and sequentially?
(2) have a good posture when speaking to the class?
(3) observe the social courtesies while speaking?
(4) seem free and natural in speaking situations?
(5) exhibit progress in eliminating his personal speech errors?
(6) show signs of originality when he expresses himself verbally?

In reporting information to parents concerning their child's skills in speaking, their attention should be directed also toward analyzing his ability to select and use a wider vocabulary, determining any noteworthy improvement of sentence structure, and assessing his preciseness in reporting relevant facts and ideas.

How Should Information About Oral Communication be Stated? In addition to answering the questions outlined in the preceding paragraph, during the course of the conference, it may be desirable that a tape recording be played which contains a two or three-minute recitation by their child, a portion of his oral reading assignment, a selection from his poetry reading, or a verse from his singing lesson. This would allow the parents an opportunity to hear for themselves significant instances to which the teacher refers. Moreover, it provides a very sound basis of referral when other points are made throughout the ensuing interview regarding the child's verbal growth and development.

TEACHER INTERVIEW CAUTION: The speech program should help the child establish correct attitudes toward the speaking situation, make him conscious of his own speech patterns, help him to detect speech handicaps that are serious and those that are merely functional, and to promote the use of good speech-making skills. However, most speech habits are learned by imitation. Hence, parents should be urged to tactfully encourage good speech from their child at home and to set appropriate standards that the child can reach without being continually corrected in the home situation.

Social Studies

Social studies content includes basic concepts from many of the social sciences. Its subject matter content is drawn from history, geography, sociology, political science, social psychology, anthropology, and economics. Since history is an integral part of the social education of youth at the elementary school level, and units of work are built around it, then some emphasis should be given to reporting information about this area during the conference.

History is man's orientation to time. Geography is his orientation in space. Therefore, to understand man and the record he has made, or is going to make, one must not divorce these two dimensions. For one to comprehend history well, it requires that he master a set of special skills. These include: making comparisons and contrasts, noting sequences of events, and responding on a higher intellectual level as a result of "critical reading." One's *critical* analysis serves as a means of separating fact from opinion, analyzing propaganda, and evaluating what has been read.

A major part of a child's experience in history should include: round table discussions, keeping scrapbooks, conducting mock radio and TV news programs, dramatizing events in history; drawing of cartoons, posters, and murals; making charts, graphs, and maps; viewing telecasts, and listening to resource persons who deal with the very nature of history-making experiences. This latter group might deal with talks delivered by the Mayor, local politicians, Directors of Foundations, and newspaper editors.

A study of history should include those significant facts and interpretations found within every culture. The following concepts are exemplary of people of all major cultures in that they are known to:

1. produce, exchange, and distribute "goods" for self-survival;
2. have a system of transportation;
3. have concern for human and natural resources;

4. construct and provide tools for services;
5. provide recreation within their groups;
6. have some form of organization and government;
7. express moral, ethical, and religious behaviors;
8. have a way of expressing and satisfying esthetic needs.

The above mentioned concepts lend structure to units of work centered upon the social studies premise, *the expanding environment.* An explanation of what underlies the purposes of social studies will help many parents to implement these constructs through field trips, museum tours, and extended readings during the evening hours.

What Should One Report About a Child's Skill Development Obtained Through the Study of History? Motives, attitudes, and feelings are essential elements of historical study. The writer of history deals with these elements and so must his readers. Parents should be familiarized with their child's ability to discern how a historian draws conclusions, formulates principles, and make generalizations regarding a significant episode of history.

A pupil must obtain an orderly procedure for studying history. Hence, he must deal with chronology. Chronology is a device—a tool of the reader of history. Through understanding facts in the light of the time in which they occurred, the more likely one can obtain *order* out of history.

History furnishes some guidelines to which man might look as he seeks to determine his future needs. The pupil who learns that the consequences, choices, and actions of people can be reviewed in historical writings, is one who sees possibilities and relationships between what *has* happened and what *might* happen.

Events in history must be studied in the light of the time in which they happened. In other words, it is unfair to judge all events of history in terms of present day standards and conditions. Therefore, the parent should learn the extent to which their child can draw inferences as to the causes of an event in history after having reviewed the standards, customs, values, and beliefs predominant at that time. In this way, the child learns to recognize that historical events have multiple causation. Rare is the case when an historical event can be explained in a one-to-one relationship.

How Should One Report Information Concerning a Child's Acquisition of Understandings and Skills Derived from Instruction in History? One unique way of showing parents information that a child has learned in history class is by recording selected social studies concepts on 4x5 cards.

By showing certain parts of these cards, a child's parents can see some of the *historical understandings* and *relationships* that their child is obtaining from his history lessons.

A strong teacher-made test or a commercial battery that measures both factual and interpretative skills learned by a child from the history unit should become a part of the conference report. Pre- and post-tests of the teacher-made types reflect some measure of growth since they reveal something of the extent of a pupil's accumulation of concepts, facts, skills and social experiences. It is more important for parents to see their child's actual test paper than it is to report to them only raw scores.

Current events of historical significance are also a major part of social studies lessons. The extent of a child's contribution to this aspect of work should be of interest to parents.

Many basic ideas of social studies are taught through the use of cartoons, scrapbooks, and murals. These materials should be saved and shown to parents during the interview.

TEACHER INTERVIEW CAUTION: There are so many facts to be learned in the social studies, particularly in the area of history, that one may find himself relating mainly a statistical report to parents (e.g.; "On the last major test Bob obtained twenty out of 30 responses correct."). But test results, as well as informal measures, must be interpreted in terms of pupil abilities, the curriculum, and the educational purposes set forth in the history lessons and units. Ideally, some measurements must be taken of a community-wide nature, since the ultimate test of one's learning of history is his exercising of competent citizenship. This latter point deals with the extent to which a child sees history being developed around him, whether or not he sees himself as a contributing citizen to patriotic pageantry in his locale, and the part he expresses that he wishes to play in preserving the American heritage.

Listening

When teachers observe how much of their personal time and that of their pupils is devoted to listening, most are astonished at the lack of any adequate consideration of this skill at the time a lesson or unit idea is being planned. Educators consciously teach children to read, write and speak, but seldom is equal time given to teaching them to listen intelligently. In modern day with so many media available to which one must learn to listen intelligently and discriminately, guidance in pupil listening is most important. The pupil must be directed not only in "how" and "why" to listen, but to "what" and to "whom" to listen.

What Should One Report About a Pupil's Skills and Abilities in Listening? Parents must be informed that listening is not something inherited; it is an acquired skill. They should be made conscious of the skills and abilities to be developed in the listening program as the child's homelife provides so many excellent opportunities for guidance in listening. The specific aims of an effective program in listening includes those activities that will help the child (1) to listen with a purpose, (2) to listen accurately, (3) to listen critically, and (4) to listen responsively.

How Should Information About the Child's Skills and Abilities in Listening be Released? The conversation exchanged between the teacher and parents about a child's listening activities should center upon answering such questions as:

(1) Can the pupil summarize accurately what a speaker said?
(2) Can he detect false reasoning exhibited as a result of biases of a speaker?
(3) Does he show evidence of being able to follow the speaker's presentation by asking relevant and intelligent questions?
(4) Is he a polite listener?
(5) Does he show evidence of understanding the significance of listening well?
(6) Does he demonstrate the ability to follow oral directions?

For some children who do well in the skills of listening a brief discussion of the aforementioned questions will be sufficient, but for those who have specific listening disabilities it is suggested that Table IV be used in the conference as the criterion sheet for showing in more explicit detail those areas of greater concern to the teacher and his pupil.

TABLE IV

SKILLS AND ABILITIES TO BE DEVELOPED IN AND THROUGH LISTENING

Kinds of Listening	Skills and Abilities to be Developed
CRITICAL	To detect biases of a speaker To detect emotionalized terms To seek evidence for statements made To sort out fact from opinion To hold judgment until facts are weighed
PRECISE	To take directions and follow them To repeat initially what was said To follow methodically a point of view To organize and summarize accurately
PURPOSEFUL	To seek an answer to a question or idea To find grounds for a strong argument To obtain new ideas To enable one to follow directions To encounter new ideas, words, and phrases To pursue one's own area of interest
RESPONSIVE	To be a courteous listener To respond to the beauty of words and sounds To consciously react to another's feelings To grasp the desired fact or thought To be socially appreciated

As the chart above is analyzed in the conference session, the parent soon finds out that as the teacher talks about *listening skills*, he is referring to more than the child's quietness or attentiveness in class. What appears to be a good listener may be in fact, a very poor listener. Good listeners participate by hearing and responding then to what has been heard. A quite child is not necessarily the "hearing" child; he may be tuning out his teacher. By reviewing this chart with certain parents, it is more likely that they will see their child's listening skills as a systematic teaching procedure; one to which they can contribute as their child increases his understanding and appreciation in listening situations at the home level.

TEACHER INTERVIEW CAUTION: Most children only "half listen." That is, they have poor listening habits. They listen without purpose. Most people listen expecting entertainment rather than listening for educational information. Therefore, parents should be urged to be generous with praise and recognition for the child's efforts and progress in listening to directions in the home, for interjecting information in home conversations which shows he has listened accurately, and for evaluating statements of others upon the basis of previously learned statements of worth. If parents show interest in how well their child is listening at home and school, more likely he will develop a keen sense of security, self-reliance, self-respect, and importance.

Spelling

Naming, writing, and printing of letters in proper order constitutes what is known as "correct spelling." In learning to spell the emphasis should be placed on visual presentation, *seeing the word.* It is also recognized that to increase the effectiveness of learning, the child should *say* and *write* the word as well. The end and purpose of a child's educational program in spelling is to fulfill his needs to communicate with others through the medium of written words. Therefore, he must learn to reproduce *speech sounds* accurately in his written work.

What Should One Report About the Child's Spelling Habits? Essentially, correcting pupil errors in spelling is a task requiring daily diagnosis. The factors which follow are in rank order and comprise the major types of errors which occur at all grade levels:

  (a) substitution of letters
  (b) omission of letters
  (c) addition or insertion of letters
  (d) transposition of letters
  (e) spelling the wrong word.

The parent should be made aware of any gross errors his child is making which corresponds to the aforementioned categories. If it seems feasible, he can then be asked to supplement the daily training program in spelling with additional activities provided by his child's teacher.

How Should Information About Spelling Skills be Reported? Most workbooks in spelling that are used to supplement the total spelling program contain charts in the back of the book for tabulating a child's weekly scores. These graphs can be shown to parents with the major emphasis given to citing the number of words spelled correctly rather than the number of misspellings. If one has kept a record of the types of words a child is misspelling, then it becomes an easy matter to find specific words that a child needs special help with and which might very well come under the guidance jurisdiction of the parents. When certain types of words are indicated as ones which need further study, it is more likely that parents will become involved in thinking positively about their child's problem, and less likely, that they will dwell on the number of words missed.

TEACHER INTERVIEW CAUTION: Evaluation of spelling growth must include evidences that the child is making progress in appraising his own spelling progress. To emphasize only the accuracy of one's spelling to the neglect of increasing his *meaningful vocabulary* would be a serious misrepresentation of the teaching task. Therefore, as a result of an effective interview, the parent should leave the conference with some understanding of how their child is currently: (1) proof-reading and correcting spelling errors, (2) assuming more responsibility for mastering words he needs as an individual, (3) showing improvement in his method of studying spelling, and (4) increasing the extent to which he seeks help in spelling new words rather than only using words presently in his spelling vocabulary.

Written Communication

In written communication one is concerned with the child's efforts to express his ideas in writing. Often it does not occur to parents how very useful the trips they take, the places they visit, or the things they say, are to aiding their child's written communication. Parents should be praised for this in the interview. The child's program for written language is based upon the stimulation of ideas as well as principles, techniques and skills coming from the structured language lesson.

What Should One Report Concerning a Child's Skills in Written Communication? Every written lesson in language comes from a motivation based on the child's experiences, in or out of the classroom. He must have ideas to express. Parents should be encouraged to talk with their children, to read to them, and to take them on educational excursions. With respect to written communication specifically, the teacher should report how well the child has accomplished handwriting mechanics, composition, manuscript form, capitalization, punctuation, correct usage habits in grammar, and creative ways of expressing himself.

How Should Aforementioned Written Communication Skills be Reported? A major asset of the child's learning experience is his ability to take notes. Efficient notetaking leads to self-improvement. Some of the daily notes of intermediate grade children should be collected for an analysis during the conference. In some classrooms this will mean that special lessons must be prepared and instructional techniques must be offered for two or three weeks in *how to take notes.* Notetaking is a sadly neglected art in most elementary schools. A few samples of a child's composition work should be collected prior to each conference and an analysis made as to the extent of the pupil's awareness of appropriate paragraph structure and its sequence in narration. A search can be made as to the consistency with which the pupil arranges sentences in order of sequence or events of the story.

A sample of a child's written work should be shown to his parents so that some evidence is given of the extent to which his self-improvement is being sought and stressed. This paper should contain evidences of the child's revision and proofreading practices. Mention should be made of the extent to which the child looks for specific errors in words, usage, and mechanics previously studied in his classwork. The teacher should comment also with respect to how much "teacher-help" is needed when the child is doing this type of proofing and editing.

Some of the papers shown to parents should contain evidences of their child's creative treatment of a topic. As the teacher discusses the creative paper, primary emphasis should be on the ideas expressed, not the mechanical features of the writing. The intent should be to show a child's attempt to create a mood, an unusual line of thought, or a provocative idea.

TEACHER INTERVIEW CAUTION: Many parents are more concerned with the *form* (margin, punctuation, grammar) of their child's paper than they are with the *creative* content. The teacher must point out that form is secondary to ideas and serves merely as a means of making the content correct, attractive, and presentable. Although correct form and neat handwriting do have a place in written communication, parents should leave the interview with the feeling that the quality of ideas and clarity of expression thereof, are the major issues with which they must learn to deal if they are to help their child extend and broaden his understanding of written and creative exposition.

Science

The concepts which incorporate knowledge of the broad fields of science have become tremendously numerous and expansive. Those chosen for elementary school programs must be carefully selected so that they not only are within the grasp of children but have permanent value. The parent should be informed about his child's participation in the various types of science activities. These would include scientific discussions, experiments, instructional excursions, and his extent of reading science materials in other than classroom texts.

The processes of science grow in importance in our increasingly complex society. Learning to discern, create, and delineate problems is a major function of the pupil in a science class. Accurate observation and/or measurement in the testing step is essential. Elementary pupils must learn to make refined observations so that they are less apt to draw unwarrantable inferences. For example, any conclusions drawn from an experiment should relate primarily to original hypotheses. From studying the data gleaned from the subject under investigation, the pupil learns to make appropriate generalizations. Such is the process of science and it is to these steps that information for parents must be directed.

What Should be Reported Regarding a Child's Progress in the Area of Scientific Study? By the time a child has completed the sixth year, it is expected that he will have developed some fundamental experiences dealing with concepts, attitudes, knowledges, and skills basic to the area of science. For example, the child who is to become well-grounded in scientific laws and principles must learn the relationship of cause and effect; distinguish between fact and fancy; suspend judgment until all facts are in; make accurate observations; know how to locate information on a problem; learn to think critically; be willing to change ideas; learn from demonstrations and experiments; be able to collect, organize, classify and identify data; and be efficient in the use of common scientific instruments.

The goals mentioned above, for the most part, are not measurable on teacher-made tests or commercially constructed instruments. Nevertheless these are desirable behavioral objectives in science teaching and parents are deserving of the type of knowledge which illustrates the extent of achievement of their youngster in this specialized area.

How Should Information About a Child's Progress in Science be Reported? If classroom science experiments are recorded in consecutive order, then the parent's attention can be directed to specific notations made in his child's science notebook. An analysis of the notebook should reveal whether or not the valid conclusions sought from an experiment were accurately "nailed down." Standardized tests of commercial varieties can be used to indicate how well children have mastered factual and procedural scientific knowledge. Teacher-prepared unit tests will augment impressions gained from commercial tests. The need for supplementary instruction is often revealed when a careful analysis is made of test results. For example, a quick perusal of specific test items will show whether the child is having difficulty with recalling his scientific facts, or if greater difficulty is experienced in "reasoning out" correct answers. In the former, one is dealing with his ability to memorize or recall; while in the latter, the attention is focused upon his ability to use his reasoning processes.

TEACHER INTERVIEW CAUTION: There are difficult but desirable behavioral objectives in science teaching for which the teacher cannot construct an adequate measuring instrument. Questions to which answers must be sought are:

Does this child *enjoy* science?
Is he enthusiastic about observation and experimentation?
Does he reflect accuracy and objectivity in observing scientific phenomena?
Can he apply his knowledge about scientific ideas to appropriate situations in life?

A child's scientific attitudes can be more accurately observed over a period of time than measured at the end of a unit by paper and pencil tests. The *application* of what he has learned in science to life situations can be sought through demonstrations, discussions, essays, and observations. It is important for parents to know if the elementary program in science is providing their child the foundational experiences and attitudes necessary for more advanced science work he will encounter at forthcoming high school levels.

Geography

Geography is a physical-social science. Its purpose is to describe, map out, and explain interrelationships. These interrelationships are composed of two major elements, the physical and cultural. Through a study of geography the child is provided with a way of looking at the earth; it is not simply a study of its contents. Geography also has historical dimensions. Judgments can be made with respect to the type of world that existed centuries ago.

What Should One Report About a Child's Geographical Skills? Children must be taught to realize that geography has its own terminology and devices for developing meaningful insights. The child should learn to detect, for example, that likenesses and differences of the earth's many surfaces can be developed into a *regional* concept (e.g.; sand-desert; icepacks-arctic). Geographical position is a determinant of the productivity, societal, and technological factors observable within given areas. Helping the child find his place with respect to the nature of the land and what can come from it, in large measure gives him a picture of the character of people with whom he will associate in reading or in real life as an active citizen.

Plotting where places and things are located on a map is an essential skill to be developed during geography study. Parents should learn of their child's "physical sense" of orientation. For example, the report might well include the depth of the child's understanding of man's relationship to his surroundings (land, water, climate).

A child can become an expert in his ability to make inferences from landscapes, maps, globes, statistics, graphs and pictures. If major geographic principles are going to be thoroughly developed, then it is mandatory that some instructional time be given during a child's school life to training him in *reading ideas out of* facts, content, pictures, contour lines, maps and globes, and the like appearing in printed materials. A child's ability to make such inferences can be evaluated and those observations can then be reported to parents.

Man's environment is constantly changing. Thus, geography is never static. Consequently, children should learn what influences these changes. Man has sought to alter his natural environment. Children should be taught how man has attempted to control, restore, change and shape the geographical features of the land and water about him. The extent to which the child can make such inferences should be of much concern to parents.

How Should One Report Information Concerning a Child's Skill Development in Geography? Teachers of geography are constantly dealing with images, concepts, and attitudes; therefore they must select and organize materials for the conference report to illustrate the extent of the child's growth to this end.

The teacher should discuss the extent to which a child is able to use simple map symbols, keys, colors, shading, and legends. Each child should have completed several outline maps, developed a system by which he studies a country, and have learned how to "orient" a map for direction finding and grid work purposes. All of these projects can be developed into concrete experiences. Projects of this nature yield much information when shown to parents at conference time.

A standardized test such as the *Iowa Test of Basic Skills* (Houghton) should be used for measuring the progress of the child in map reading skills and techniques. The results obtained from this type of commercial test can be charted and shown to parents. All children need some experience in making their own maps and legends. In the conference, the teacher should point out the extent of the child's ability to note familiar distances, whether or not his map is a good "ground" plan, and the extent of originality he exhibited in devising new symbols for the legend as well as the accuracy with which he plotted these symbols on his map surface.

Outline maps which contain the results of the pupil's efforts to demonstrate his ability to locate cities, states, nations, rivers, mountains, and the like, are types of teacher-made tests which should be previewed before parents. Plotting skills, however, are only a small segment of a child's modern geographical knowledge.

Many parents, until they are conferred with, will see the study of geography only as a separate subject. Their own school experiences will suggest it is only a study of technical terms and the location of states and capitols. The teacher must help them recognize that geography can be correlated with study in other subjects. For example, the study of a Haitian boy and his way of life makes an interesting fourth grade composition; a spelling list of meaningful geographical terms such as sextant, zenith, isobar, and the like can be an exciting spelling lesson; or a speech by a third grader on Spanish life in old Mexico as studied from *National Geographic Magazine* has much to offer to a child's experiences in geography. Though terminology is important and it must be thoroughly understood, the teaching of it should not replace opportunities for the child to put into practice its concepts and ideas.

TEACHER INTERVIEW CAUTION: Most parents will see their child's growth in geography much the same as it was taught to them in their school days—a memorization process (i.e. matching states and their capitols; associating cities and populations, etc.). Parents may seek to help their child by outmoded methods. This may create a conflict between school and home or between the child and his teacher. Therefore, the wise interviewer will inform parents about how the teaching of geography has changed in the last few decades.

Foreign Language

The initial emphasis of the foreign language program in the elementary school is upon the listening and speaking of a nation's language. Reading and writing of the language usually follows at the appropriate time and grade level. Since it is believed that a child can learn a foreign language the same as the mother tongue providing he has the innate ability and the setting in which to operate, then it is logical that this program should be in harmony with the laws governing child growth and development.

What Should One Report About a Child's Progress in the Learning of a Foreign Language? Some consideration should be given to discussing a child's ability to understand a native speaking at normal speed. For example, a student of Spanish listening to guest speakers, special radio programs, or television presentations with primary emphasis given to communication in Spanish, has an excellent opportunity to evaluate his own Spanish-speaking ability. The child also uses his foreign language skill in a creative way when he acts out plays, presents monologues, or reads poetry. Essentially, the parent should learn that as their child experiences a new language, new avenues are opened for him to more thoroughly understand another culture. If individual growth in the language studied is satisfactory, there is some assurance that opportunities were provided for critical reasoning about *why* certain cultures behave as they do. Critical thinking leads to the encouragement of attitude shifts. For example, it is one thing to learn about another country and judge it by one's own standards. On the other hand, however, new insights are opened up when one analyzes the habits, customs, and culture of a country through its own language.

How Should One Report Information to Parents About

Their Child's Progress in Foreign Language Study? The teacher should discuss individual "work samples" collected from regular classroom assignments. As the folders of work increase over a period of time, the parent can more likely comprehend a child's progress when they compare his recent work with earlier, less experienced attempts. A battery of tests of a commercial variety should be selected and used for gathering achievement information. The results of these tests, along with findings derived from teacher-made tests, can then be released to parents.

TEACHER INTERVIEW CAUTION: The purpose of the foreign language experience is to offer children both aesthetic and practical values they cannot obtain from other content areas of the curriculum. But parents often overlook this fact and seek greater attainments in communication skills (verbal accuracy) from their youngsters. Therefore, it is essential that teachers express to parents the point of view that children should not be forced into translation practices too early. If one is to translate, it would be better that the new language be translated into "action" experiences. Love of action seems universal with elementary school children.

Arithmetic

Arithmetic deals with the elementary areas of mathematics. The teacher of arithmetic acquaints his pupils with fundamental ideas of quantity, size, shape, and order. The ability with which a child is able to deal with the instruments, symbolisms, and processes which lead to his understanding of these elements is of major importance in the conference report.

What Should One Report About a Child's Progress in Arithmetic? The goals of arithmetical instruction are such that an effective report of a child's progress in this subject must be more than simply indicating the number of correct answers the child obtained during computation drills. The conference should deal less with *what* a child misses, and more with *why* he missed it. Since a sound arithmetic program should not consist of all children doing the same things in the same way, then individual parents will need to learn something of how their child is able to read, plan strategies, compose problems, estimate answers, and compute arithmetic on his own.

How Should One Report Arithmetical Information? Some of the very recently revised standardized tests are beginning to include items which measure much more than the computation and problem solving abilities of children. These tests and their results, supplemented by teacher-made tests which generally serve to emphasize computation abilities, should be reviewed in the conference. This procedure will give parents some understanding of how their child is responding to the present emphases being given by educators to meaningful understanding of processes and mathematical structures.

TEACHER INTERVIEW CAUTION: In the current manner used for checking arithmetic papers in elementary schools (red marks placed on problems missed), it would not be uncommon to find a large number of children displaying feelings of failure regarding their daily work. Feelings of failure are emphasized when only those problems found incorrect are identified. As such papers are shown to parents, they, too, tend to see only the glaring marks placed on problems that have been worked incorrectly by their child. Therefore, the helpful teacher will, as he has already done upon several occasions with the parents' child, always call parental attention to the large number of problems that a child has worked accurately in his daily arithmetic lessons. The conference emphasis is then upon the child's arithmetical successes, not his failures.

Summary

This chapter has dealt with selected kinds of information that should be reported during parent teacher interviews when curricular topics are the point of concern. Certainly one should not attempt to report all of the information contained in this chapter at any one conference. However, one should take definite steps to report something significant about a child's work in a few curricular areas at every interview.

A parent generally views the work of the schools from the perspective he acquired when he went to school. Thus, it behooves the teacher to re-train him to view his youngster's work in accordance with modern trends and methods of instructing a child in selected areas of curriculum content. It may be wise to dwell at some length on new areas of curriculum adopted for educative purposes. This would include discussions focussing upon sex education, drug abuse, and similar innovative programs.

Although it has been emphasized in this section that the parent should be shown through interview techniques that curriculum patterns are established primarily to help his child learn (1) how to think, (2) how to reshape ideas to fit his needs, and that (3) unless knowledge is doing something to change his behavior it is of little worth, one should still seek to bridge the "thought gap" between *facts* as viewed by parents and, *thinking processes* and *strategies* as viewed by educators. As the following stanza from a humorous poem illustrates, in the minds of some, a child's *thoughts* are secondary:

A Parent's Plea

They teach him physiology
And oh, it chills our hearts
To hear our prattling innocent
Mix up his inward parts.

He also learns astronomy
And names the stars by night,
Of course he's very up to date
But I wish that he could write.

It seems as if this poem is taken from a recent magazine criticizing what is learned from an interview situation. But it was actually published in 1907. Today, as if it were 1907, a typical parent's concept of the curriculum is much too narrow. There is no better place than the parent-teacher interview for such conceptions to be cleared up and the likelihood of children being hurt in the process is minimized.

Interview Guidesheets-- The Major Interview Tool of the Classroom Teacher

Even a modern sea wary Captain doesn't feel secure on a short voyage in friendly waters without his compass.

Introduction

7

Teachers, like most professionals, develop their own special techniques for dealing with educational problems. But when it comes to the area of reporting, it is essential that there be some consistency and continuity in what is reported to parents. One of the major criticisms offered by parents who have participated in interview programs is the concern they had for the lack of consistency in what was reported.

In other words, a parent gains little from his teacher interview if he goes to one teacher of his grade-two child and gains one type of information, and on the same day goes to the fourth grade teacher of his other child to be confronted with other types of information. He is frustrated by the lack of continuity between the two reports. Moreover, as parents and teachers talk among themselves they need to see some common threads of information running through every conference if interviews are to be meaningful and satisfying to all concerned, particularly the child.

The Interview Guide—Its Major Purposes

An interview guide not only provides the teacher with a plan of "attack" for his conferences, but also it can be used for several other significant purposes. Among the major purposes are these:

* An interview guide is a means of pulling ideas together about each child before the scheduled interview. One is never certain the direction an interview might need to take; therefore he needs all of the data beforehand so that certain judgments can be thought through much before he is confronted by the child's parents.

* Parents appreciate a well-organized teacher. They respect what he has to tell them. Interestingly, too, people often accept what comes from a sheet of paper if it is interpreted correctly by the interviewer. If there are strong disagreements, the issue is more often directed to what the paper states even though the teacher wrote them, than are comments made against the teacher. An interview guide removes some stigmas of fault-finding from the shoulders of the classroom teacher. The facts on the guidesheets are accumulative and parents can readily see "how the facts add up."

* Interview guides are growing in recognition because of the advantages associated with various patterns of cooperative teaching. As a result, it seems safe to predict that the reporting of each pupil's school progress will shortly be the joint responsibility of several teachers and its contents shared with the ones who are responsible for the initial interview with the child's parents.

* Teachers of kindergarten and the early primary years, particularly, should be prepared to spend more time in the functions of reporting than is usually expected of upper grade groups. Hence, the interview guide can be used to report information over two or three conference sessions. The information that has been reported can be checked off with a red pencil, thereby reducing the probability of duplication over the series of conferences.

* An interview guide is helpful with the talkative parent. For instance, the teacher can interject by stating: "Your point

here is important, I note the next item that we should take up is . . ." As the teacher points at the interview guide, the parent must look, ceases talking, and the conference has a new direction.

* There is inevitably a period of time during which the child and his teachers are unfamiliar with each other and when it will be especially helpful for his teachers and parents to talk together about the child's apparent strengths, weaknesses, preferences, and so forth. Obviously, then, the interview guide can serve as a formal plan for seeking information from parents and for making recordings on it which can be of great value at the onset of each new period of the child's school life.

* The interview guide prepared on each child reduces the possibility of reporting the wrong types of information. After a teacher has completed 15 to 20 conferences, it is entirely possible that the remainder of the conferences could sound alike if he did not have specific data before him to guide his thoughts. Guidesheets keep the teacher alert to the fact that the right data is being released on the right child.

* Many of our elementary schools are becoming highly specialized. In addition to the varying needs of *the school principal*, the school counselor, school nurse, school physician, school social worker, speech therapist, remedial reading teacher, coach, and other special service personnel find it necessary to confer at length with the teacher. A guidesheet which can be pulled from the classroom teacher's file gives a historical record of a child's progress and makes the task of reporting to special service people not only easier, but much more helpful and revealing.

Recording Information on the Interview Guide

Before each interview session the classroom teacher makes a judgment of each child in terms of the type of schoolwork that he has been able to achieve. If a child has performed in an outstanding fashion in relation to his ability and has surpassed the class arithmetic averages in large measure he receives an "A." If a child shows normal progress in his school subjects and skills in relation to his own ability, he receives an "N." If a child's progress is not in accordance with his measured ability, than a "U" is given since this would represent unsatisfactory progress.

The significance of this type of marking procedure lies in

the fact that the class average is only a check-point against which all children are compared. The teacher and parent will want to know where each child is regarding what the total class has been able to accomplish. However, the major point of concern is whether or not a given child is working up to his own ability. In other words it would be possible to have a child who is scoring below the general class average to have earned an "A." For instance, a case in point would be the child who has an I.Q. of 90 and who cannot possibly under traditional grading practices score above the class average. He has always heretofore, scored and "M" or average (perhaps even "I") grade. Though he worked up to his ability, his ability has always been low. Under this modern schema, however, he is able to earn an "A" because he has worked to full capacity (potential) although he has not measured up to the "class averages." Thus, he is rewarded for his efforts; he has a feeling of success.

On the other hand, bright children have always received high scores simply because they were of high intelligence. Educators will find academically talented "top" all of the tests and generally are "well-rounded" pupils. All too often they receive the "A's" with very little or no effort. Shouldn't our grading system be somewhat reversed to care for these differences?

For example, a typical case in the elementary classroom is somewhat as follows:

> Joe, of average ability, works steadily, strives hard, doesn't give up and manages to obtain a grade of "A".

> Jim, of above average ability, works little, hurries along and makes an easy "A".

Joe is using nearly all of his ability; Jim is using little of his. Situations like the example proposed above are replicated in every elementary school classroom in this nation thousands and thousands of times a day. Therefore, it seems that elementary educators should seek out answers to these types of questions: (1) Aren't children really rewarded for their efforts by the measurement coming from the results of some end product (same questions, identical objectives, etc.)? (2) Isn't it possible to judge some children not so much for obtaining the same answers, but by judging the way, technique or means by which they arrived at them? (3) Shouldn't a different value be placed upon Jim's work, since he got there first, with minimum effort? (4) Isn't one similarity becoming more evident about a pupil's work today—more pupils will soon find out that true education is taking place when they can do a task with minimum effort, rather than to be judged by how long they stay at a task?

If the teacher but agrees that the questions above are significant ones to be considered, then there is a need of defining accurately these same scores to parents—not just in terms of what is expected of the group, but in terms of what an individual has been able to accomplish. Thus, under the system of grading advocated by this author, it would be entirely possible for the brightest child in class, who under traditional systems would get his automatic "A", would likely receive a "U" because the expectations for him were too low and his intellectual power has remained unchallenged.

The philosophical idea of the interview guide is based on the fact that children are not developing an "even front"; they have serious peaks and falls; not likely to be at the same level in all areas developmentally or academically. In addition, it must also be recognized that nature does not compensate for weaknesses in some characteristics by providing strengths in others. Therefore, the idea of pupil differences must be considered in this light when scores are being sought for a comprehensive report to parents. What strength of a child is it that we want to foster? What evident weakness is the one that needs to be resolved? What weaknesses must he learn to live with? These three questions are more aptly answered through the use of the interview guide in a conference situation conducted with a child's parents.

In marking on this interview guide, it is recommended that two colors of pencil be used (red and blue). If one uses red checkmarks (✓) under the appropriate columns to check observations which are to be reported during the first Fall conference, while on the other hand one uses blue marks for the Spring conference, it becomes an easy task to make comparisons of gains or losses between the two interview settings.

There is no system of reporting that meets all of the varying needs of the pupils for whom it is to serve. However, the *interview system* comes closer to meeting a larger number of those needs than any other system or groups of systems combined. A major factor which makes the interview system an outstanding report procedure is the opportunity presented for *recommendations*. Each interview guide has a designated space for recording a teacher's recommendations. It may be necessary to record additional information and recommendations in the initial interview which may very well come from the insights of parents. In any event it is important to make a written record of the recommendations so that what is tried and is found to be satisfactory and helpful, might be continued. By the same token, recommendations which did not work can be checked off and next year's teacher will not need to suffer the same types of mistakes.

Succinctly, then, a separate interview guide is to be completed by the teacher for each child. It is to be taken into the initial conference with his parents. From it the interviewer is to select the most pertinent data and information that he believes the parent should have in this conference. The interviewer will make marginal notes and add personalized data to this guide in the light of individual characteristics of the given case for whom the conference is conducted. After the completion of the interview, the guide is to be filed for future conferences and for use with special service personnel when the need arises.

Interpreting Information to Parents

An interview guide is a tool of the classroom teacher and will only be as effective as is the one who interprets its information to the parent. It seems likely that improvement in reporting to parents by the interview procedure will be made when more *substance* is put into the teacher's remarks during the interview. Therefore, in interpreting information from the interview guide, the following cautions should be observed by all interviewers:

CAUTION ONE: AVOID THE USE OF EDUCATIONAL VERNACULAR WHICH MAY LEAVE A FALSE, OR UNDESIRABLE IMPRESSION.

Words to Avoid in Interview	More Positive Words to Substitute
Profane	Uses unfavorable language
Shy	Reserved
Prevaricates	Stretches the truth
Below average	Works at his own level
Steal	Takes without permission
Cheats	Depends too much on others
Trouble maker	Disturbs the group
Lazy	Can do more

Must	Should
Uncooperative	Should develop better group skills
Mean	Has difficulty getting along
Rude	Intentionally inconsiderate
Selfish	Lacks sharing skills
Show-off	Strives for attention
Is going to fail	A chance to pass, if he. . .
Impertinent	Lacks courtesy
Is never right	Should learn the right thing

Simply knowing the right words to use is not enough. The interviewer must always be alert to how he presents these words in context during the interview. Some illustrative categories follow below:

Interviewer's comments	A more refined presentation
1. Your boy seems lazy.	1. I find it difficult to challenge him. He can do more. Do you think these things I'm trying are right?
2. She irritates us all.	2. Our class is learning to live in a democracy with every one waiting his turn to contribute. Mary needs to learn better group skills. For example, these sharing skills need . . .
3. Sue received an "A" on this interview guide.	3. Here are the criteria I used to score Sue. Here is the evidence upon which I based her grades.
4. Bob barely passed with an "S".	4. Bob should not be expected to make top grades in class; however, his potential suggests he might have done better. Here is what I propose to do.
5. I've judged Jim this way. Tell me if you think I'm wrong.	5. Let me summarize my descriptions of Jim's behavior. If you consider it as behavior we should try to change, feel free to indicate it.

Thus it can be seen through the rewritten statements above that some emphasis must be placed upon more specific constructive suggestions in direct talk to parents. The interviewer will also note that it is essential to substitute "censorial language" for those types of comments that are more diagnostic in nature. In pointing up critical areas of a child's school life to parents, there is always need of pointing out the next steps that should follow in furthering the child's development.

One should also glean from the afore-mentioned presentation that parent-teacher interviews do dwell on specifics. The information that is recorded on the interview guide comes from a study of the pupil's daily work, tests, and teacher observation conducted over a period of time. Therefore, parents must be shown some of the data and information while comments are simultaneously being made about their child. When the teacher presents the criteria against which the work of a child is being compared or described, they are more likely to be followed by action on the part of his parents.[1]

CAUTION TWO: CHECK THE PARENT'S SEN-
SITIVITY TO YOUR INTERPRETATIONS.

The purpose of the parent-teacher interview is to share information. After presenting a portion of the initial remarks one has prepared to share with a child's parents, the teacher should ask questions intermittently during the conference to establish whether or not points of view are clearly understood. For instance, such questions as: (1) How do you feel about this? (2) What suggestions do you have to offer here? (3) Does this seem to be the correct inference to make? (4) Have you noticed this reaction at home? (5) What would you like for me to do as the next step? (6) Could you tell me more about this?

CAUTION THREE: REPORT, BUT SEEK INFOR-
MATION FROM PARENTS THAT CAN BE USED
LATER ON IN THE SCHOOL YEAR.

Each teacher will want to know certain kinds of information about every child whom he teaches. This confidential information must be sought from the parents and should come from the interview situation. The questions which follow should serve as a guide in obtaining that information:

1. John J. Jessel and J. W. M. Rothney. "Evaluation of Parent-Counselor Conferences." *Personnel and Guidance Journal.* October 1965. 43:142-46.

1. What is your child's general reaction to school?
   a. Is there something he especially likes?
   b. Is there something he especially dislikes?
   c. Does he feel able to do the work assigned?
2. How is your child's mental health?
   a. Has he had any recent illness?
   b. Does he have any emotional problems?
   c. Does he sleep well at night. (e.g.; bad dreams; awakening early).
   d. Are there any unusual or "little things" troubling him?
3. How does he spend his leisure?
   a. Does he have a job after school or of the early morning hours?
   b. How much does he TV?
4. How do you discipline him at home if he breaks your regulations? What discipline works best for you?
5. What are his special interests and hobbies at home?
6. Does he have special home responsibilities?
7. Do you provide him with home study guidance?
8. What would you like for us to do better for your child?

Certainly each interviewer will have his questions to add to this list. But if one wants his interview to be successful, he must *seek* information from parents as well as *report* it.

THE INTERVIEW GUIDES

After having read and studied all   preceding chapters including this special section directly related to the effective use of the interview technique, the *guides* which follow need no further introduction. Conferring, like many things, improves with practice. But practice becomes valuable only when the interviewer corrects his mistakes as he goes along. Each interviewer who uses these guides should try them out in four or five interview situations before he goes into a lengthy interview session with 25 to 30 parents. This pilot run will enable him to make essential additions, deletions, or changes to the guide to further standardize it for his local school system and the clientele to whom it is directed.

A PRACTICAL GUIDE FOR TEACHERS WHO CONFERENCE WITH PARENTS OF CHILDREN IN KINDERGARTEN

A—Indicates outstanding achievement in relation to child's ability.

N—Indicates normal progress in relation to child's ability.

U—Indicates unsatisfactory progress in relation to child's ability.

I. SKILLS

A | N | U

Expresses ideas well orally.
Takes part in group discussions.
Shows ability in creative activities.
Can match tones and sing independently.
Controls bodily movements in directed games and dances.
Shows interest in books.
Exhibits evidences of readiness to read (left to right).
Pronounces selected words and letters clearly.
Recognizes and names colors.
Counts ten objects.
Can plan and judge attack upon some activities and small projects.

II. PERSONAL AND SOCIAL DEVELOPMENT

A | N | U

Listens to and follows directions.
Relaxes during rest period easily.
Practices safety habits.
Is happy, cheerful and friendly.
Claims only his share of attention.
Is dependable in carrying out responsibilities.
Arrives at his class on time.
Puts on and takes off his wraps with a minimum of help.
Replaces work and play materials.
Finishes his work.
Makes good use of his school time.
Cares for his own and others' possessions.
Exhibits some understanding of his environment.
Is physically active in individual and group play.
Practices desirable health habits.
Enjoys listening to stories, poems, and plays.
Likes singing and listening to music.
Practices good manners in the lunchroom.
Shows some degree of self-control.
Has some concern for personal appearance.
Helpful and considerate of others to some measure.

III. RECOMMENDATIONS:

A PRACTICAL GUIDE FOR TEACHERS WHO CONFERENCE WITH PARENTS OF CHILDREN IN THE PRIMARY GRADES (1,2,3)

A—Indicates outstanding achievement in relation to child's ability.

N—Indicates normal progress in relation to child's ability.

U—Indicates unsatisfactory progress in relation to child's ability.

I. SKILLS

A | N | U

Reading Level of child:
_____ Pre-Primer
_____ Primer
_____ 1_2 _____ 3_2
_____ 2_1 _____ 4_1
_____ 2_2 _____ 4_2
_____ 3_1 _____

Has an adequate interest in reading.
Can use phonics for word attack.
Can use word-form clues in unlocking words.
Can use structural analysis in attacking words.
Can use contextual clues in figuring out words.
Is using the dictionary properly. (Or pictionary)
Has interest in recreational reading.
Expresses himself well orally.
Can relate important facts in sequence.
Respects the opinions and expressions of others.
Is presently developing proper usage of
    grammar in written expression.
Spells words correctly in written work.
Uses correct writing position.
Forms letters correctly.
Is developing an understanding of our number system.
Works arithmetic accurately and carefully.
Responds to rhythm in music.
Participates in singing activities.
Exercises standards for living in a Democracy.
Is creative in art.
Shows evidences of acquiring taste for good art.
Is learning principles characteristic of art projects.
Is learning to solve some problems
    methodically and scientifically.
Is learning historical and geographical facts.
Is developing an awareness of the world about him.

II. PERSONAL AND SOCIAL DEVELOPMENT

A | N | U

Shows some degree of self-control.
Uses time to good advantage.
Takes care of materials.
Works well with others.
Works well independently.
Obeys safety rules.
Shows good sportsmanship.
Has good lunch room manners.
Selects food wisely.
Practices good posture.
Is courteous to those in authority.
Is thoughtful of rights of others.
Takes pride in his school work.
Accepts responsibility for own acts.
Begins and completes tasks on time.

Makes wise use of leisure time.
Is learning to evaluate his own work.
Willing to take turns.
Listens closely and follows directions.
Takes part in class activities.
Shows good muscular control (larger and finer muscles).
Exhibits good classroom behavior.
Is building some standard of measurement
    of his own values.
Reasons well in thinking through problems.

III. RECOMMENDATIONS:

A PRACTICAL GUIDE FOR TEACHERS WHO CONFERENCE
WITH PARENTS OF CHILDREN IN THE
INTERMEDIATE GRADES

A—Indicates outstanding achievement in relation to child's ability.
N—Indicates normal progress in relation to child's ability.
U—Indicates unsatisfactory progress in relation to child's ability.

I. REPORTING THE CHILD'S QUANTITATIVE AND QUALITATIVE GROWTH AND DEVELOPMENT IN: . . .

A. Reading

A | N | U

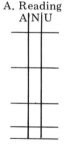

Applies correct reading skills (i.e. word recognition skills—phonics, contextual clues, structural analysis).
Shows evidence of good comprehension (finds answers to questions, understands sequence of events).
Enjoys reading rich literature (i.e. prose, poetry).
Does recreational reading.
Shows evidence of integrating and reacting well to what has been read (i.e. reading the examples in arithmetic and working story problems without additional help; reading a poem and then describing the possible feeling or mood of the author).

RECOMMENDATIONS:

B. Spelling

A | N | U

Spells with accuracy.
Shows evidence of growth in skills. (i.e. prefixes, etc.)
Spells accurately in all subject matter areas.

RECOMMENDATIONS:

C. English

A N U

_____ Uses correct grammar.
_____ Knows rules of grammar.
_____ Applies knowledge of rules in other subjects (i. e. correct grammar used in social studies work).

RECOMMENDATIONS:

Composition

A N U

_____ Writes well-organized ideas.
_____ Employs a good vocabulary.
_____ Shows originality.
_____ Is brief, concise, thorough.

Oral Communication

A N U

_____ Expresses ideas well (Use of voice, content and quality of speech considered here).
_____ Enters freely into class discussions.

RECOMMENDATIONS:

D. Writing

A N U

_____ Forms letters legibly in written work.
_____ Writes with sufficient speed.
_____ Writes neatly and with good form (i. e. spacing).
_____ Takes pride in writing well.

RECOMMENDATIONS:

E. Academic Progress in Creative Expression

Art

A N U

_____ Shows skill in working with several media (i. e. crayon, chalk, paper cutting, and the like).
_____ Gives attention to detail and selection of pleasing color schemes.
_____ Shows originality and good form in creative work.
_____ Participates enthusiastically in group projects.
_____ Enjoys "art appreciation" activities (i. e. likes studying works of the "masters").
_____ Shows some degree of skill in judging "great works" of art and music.
_____ Resourceful in use of materials (not wasteful, extravagant).

RECOMMENDATIONS:

F. Music

A | N | U

____ Understands the language of music (i. e. notes, technical vocabulary).
____ Uses singing voice well.
____ Listens attentively to good music.
____ Enjoys participating in musical activities.
____ Is giving attention in special classes.

RECOMMENDATIONS:

G. Dramatics

A | N | U

____ Shows a talent in writing or producing skits.
____ Enjoys acting.
____ Participates in class contests in speaking (i. e. debates, poetry reading, etc.).
____ Enjoys professional entertainment and the purposes of visiting speakers (i. e. assemblies, guest speakers).
____ Uses good body movements.

RECOMMENDATIONS:

H. Arithmetic

A | N | U

____ Has facility in fundamental processes (i. e. understands addition, subtraction, multiplication, & division).
____ Shows facility in problem solving (i. e. two or three step problems emphasizing reasoning).
____ Shows facility in use of interpretive skills (i. e. maps, charts, graphs).
____ Sees number relationships.
____ Understands common fractions.
____ Can work with denominate numbers (i. e. knows table of measurements).
____ Applies some principles to everyday living (i. e. shows some understanding of savings and cash accounts; buying at reduced rates, etc.).
____ Understands theory of "sets."

RECOMMENDATIONS:

I. Science

A | N | U

____ Has abundance of factual information.
____ Applies scientific method satisfactorily.
____ Participates in science activities (i. e. experiments—contributes materials, ideas, etc.).
____ Understands technical vocabulary (i. e. principles, hypothesis, and the like).

RECOMMENDATIONS:

J. History

A│N│U

____|__|__Shows interest in the study of history (i. e. study of famous men).

____|__|__Understands technical vocabulary (i. e. chronology, political, militia, and the like).

____|__|__Understands sequence of historical events.

____|__|__Knows how to live and work in the classroom democratically.

____|__|__Relates the study of history to everyday life (i. e. comparing early Roman laws to current rules and regulations; follows parliamentary procedure).

RECOMMENDATIONS:

II. EMOTIONAL GROWTH AND DEVELOPMENT

A│N│U

____|__|__Emotional pattern of behavior (i. e. exhibits self-control, calm, stable).

____|__|__Emotional tensions (i. e. evidences of daydreaming, nail biting, and the like).

RECOMMENDATIONS:

III. PHYSICAL GROWTH AND DEVELOPMENT

A. Health

A│N│U

____|__|__Knows health facts (i. e. functions of the body).

____|__|__Reflects good health habits (i. e. cleanliness, posture, diet, rest).

____|__|__Observes safety rules (i. e. pedestrian, bike riding).

____|__|__Has a good disposition (i. e. pleasant, cheerful).

Special Health Problems

At this point discuss physiological changes if there seems to be a problem (beginning of menarchy; age of puberty; period of rapid growth).

Discuss physical manifestations if any (headaches, and other illnesses that may be symptoms of emotional tensions).

RECOMMENDATIONS:

B. Physical Education

Has scored satisfactorily in Physical Fitness Test work with respect to:

A│N│U

____|__|__Pull-ups

____|__|__Push-ups

____|__|__Sit-ups

____|__|__Knee-bends

____|__|__Soft ball throw

____|__|__Standing hop, step, and jump

____|__|__30 second run

Has made satisfactory progress in:

A N U

___ Volley ball activities
___ Soccer activities
___ Fundamental rhythms
___ Basketball activities
___ Stunts and tumbling
___ Track and field events
___ Softball
___ Football
___ Sportsmanship and teamwork

RECOMMENDATIONS:

IV. SOCIAL GROWTH AND DEVELOPMENT

A N U

___ Has respect for property of others.
___ Associates well with others.
___ Is helpful and courteous (i. e. contributor to a common purpose).
___ Has respect for rightful authority.
___ Is truthful.
___ Practices self-control (i. e. deals well with situations and people).
___ Recognizes how others "see" him as a member of the group.
___ How he "sees" himself as being worthy of acceptance by the group.
___ Has friends within whom he can confide.

RECOMMENDATIONS:

V. COURTESY

A N U

___ Pays attention when others are talking and does not interrupt.
___ Talks and laughs quietly.
___ Claims only his share of attention.
___ Takes correction nicely and tries to profit from it.
___ How he responds to me. (teacher).

RECOMMENDATIONS:

VI. CHARACTER TRAITS

A N U

___ Shows growth toward more acceptable standards of behavior.
___ Shows loyalty to the group.
___ Evidence of having strong character.

RECOMMENDATIONS:

VII. WORK HABITS

A N U

___ Assumes responsibilities and carries them out.
___ Uses leisure time well.
___ Completes assignments within given time allotment.

_____ Follows directions with little additional guidance needed.

_____ Amount of effort expended in performing school tasks (i. e. ease with which he grasps abstract meanings and relationships).

_____ Discuss quality of work produced (i. e. depth of understanding; thoroughness; penetrating analysis of the subject).

RECOMMENDATIONS:

VIII. MISCELLANEOUS

School Rules and Regulations

A|N|U

_____ Follows rules and regulations willingly.

_____ Lunch program (i. e. behavior in cafeteria).

_____ Class schedule (i. e. punctuality in changing classes).

_____ Absenteeism (i. e. remembers to bring excuse note from parent).

_____ Phone calls (i. e. remembers that most calls are restricted to emergency situations).

_____ Transportation (i. e. bike parked properly; school bus behavior).

_____ Playground behavior.

_____ Library (i. e. assumes responsibility for books used).

_____ Health service (i. e. keeps appointments; follows advice).

RECOMMENDATIONS:

IX. TESTING

A|N|U

_____ Report converted scores (not I.Q.) obtained from standardized tests.

_____ Compare converted scores such as his percentile scores with past information (i. e. compare results from Fall and Spring tests relative to norms for class, school, and nation).

_____ Report scores from teacher prepared tests (i. e. 17 right out of 20 words on the spelling test).

RECOMMENDATIONS:

X. ATTENDANCE

a) Discuss attendance only if a problem exists.
b) Report "times tardy" if habitual.

XI. FOCUS SOME ATTENTION UPON:

a) How the parent can help the child in his school work.
b) How you, the teacher, intend to help the child in his areas of strengths as well as in areas of limitations.
c) How the child can help himself.

Summary

Effective parent-teacher interviews are not easy. They take plenty of planning, patience, and practice by their participants. If carried off poorly, interviews can mutilate whatever understanding does exist between the parents and the teacher. Interview guides eliminate much of the "uncertainty" of conferring with parents. Specifically, by the use of an interview guide the teacher: (1) has all essential materials summarized before him; (2) establishes from it a "plan of attack"; and, (3) gains confidence in himself since he is ready for the conference.

Some things that one cannot afford to overlook if the conference is to be effective are: (1) the terminology to be used during the interview exchange of ideas; (2) the tactfulness with which data and information are imparted; (3) the kinds of information to be sought from parents; and (4) the necessity of adherence to reporting similar information about every child while at the same time allowing ample time to talk with parents about their child's special talents, abilities, and aptitudes.

In conclusion, the oral conference is justified when each teacher, child, and parent benefits from the time and effort which must go into it. The impersonal nature of an increasing complex society brings into sharp focus the need for far more *personalized conferences* with parents. Children need to be brought closer to what the school is trying to do for them. Interviews are a means to the realization of this end.

Helping Parents Counsel Their Own Children

Let us aid the schools with missionary zeal not because they're so good for Little Jimmy, but because they're so necessary for America.
　　　　　　　　　　—Jean Worth (Escanaba Daily Press)

Introduction

8

Many parents do an excellent job of counseling their own children because human understanding became a part of their general education as they grew up. Nevertheless, at one time or another, the teacher will find that some parents seek his advice on how to deal with certain matters involving a child. It is paramount that the teacher help these parents find more ways of dealing effectively with their offsprings so that the lives in the household can contribute healthfully and with greater sensitivity to human needs. The parent is in a strategic position to give the greatest emotional help to his child.

The qualities which really count in life are learned best when they are given to a child by his parents. The child who learns about love, kindness, understanding, and other human attributes from his parents is a step ahead of those pupils who must learn of such attributes from his teachers. A child cannot give these values, attributes, and qualities to others in later life if he has not received them.

Parent Education Through Interviews

Some teachers may find it most beneficial to confer with parents outside of the regularly scheduled interview sessions. These private consultations should focus upon helping parents to develop high level interpersonal relationship between parent and child. The type of relationship should be one that seeks to provide understanding, exploration of problems, clarification of feelings, and an array of patterns of adjustment which might be beneficial to the training of their children. By no means is conversing with parents about how to help the child express and clarify feelings and emotions a "sacred" subject to be left only to trained counselors. There are certain principles that lay people can learn about and ascribe to in managing their own children.

Principles to Adhere To. The teacher who would confer with parents for child guidance purposes would help the interviewee to:

(1) understand that his child is a worthy human being who is capable of a wide span of human feelings; that is, he will be both good and bad at times.

(2) accept his child as a person of worth even though his behavior does deviate from what is acceptable at given moments.

(3) recognize that as a parent he may be the center or focus of hostility, yet he must learn to analyze his youngster's feelings and work with negative feelings in constructive ways.

(4) help the child emote in acceptable ways with the end result being the development of a child who achieves emotional control.

(5) help his child assess conduct respectable to selected circumstances and to set standards of conduct that are within the child's ability to understand, accept, and achieve.

(6) provide opportunities for his child to verbalize his feelings, to air points of view, and to express negative expressions in some acceptable word form and manner.

If a teacher can help a parent to achieve the emotional

hurdles enumerated above, the parent will be able to decipher the coded messages often communicated by his children.

The teacher should help the parent recognize that communication with children is based on respect and on skill. The code requires that messages preserve the child's as well as the parent's self-respect; that statements of understanding precede statements of advice or counsel; and that the language used for communication be something other than everyday language.

Help Parents Mirror a Child's Feelings. A child learns about his feelings when adults mirror his emotions. If a person looks in a mirror he sees his physical image; likewise when an adult communicates to a child what actually his emotions are doing to him, he hears about his feelings. Therefore, he learns about his emotional likeness by hearing his feelings reflected by his parents.

The teacher should encourage parents to reflect emotional images without adding flattery or faults. The parent should give an image not a sermon. When a child hears about his emotional image from his parents, the feelings reflected should be as they really are, without distortion. "It sounds like you had a bad day at school." "You seem disgusted with yourself." "You really don't like him, do you?"

If a parent helps a child to obtain "clarity of emotional image," he shows his child what his feelings really are. This provides his child with an opportunity to do some self-initiated grooming. Parents who learn how to provide a child with an emotional mirror will cause their offspring to:

(1) come to see himself differently.
(2) accept himself and his feelings more fully.
(3) become more self-confident and directing.
(4) become more the person he would like to be.
(5) become more flexible, less rigid in his perceptions.
(6) adopt more realistic goals for himself.
(7) behave in a more mature fashion for his age.
(8) change his maladjustive behavior.
(9) become more acceptant of others.
(10) change in his basic personal characteristics, in constructive ways.*

Good mental health consists in striving for a balance between

---

*Adapted, Carl R. Rogers. *Client-Centered Therapy.* Boston: Houghton-Mifflin Company, 1951.

these various objectives. Teachers will do well by their pupils' parents if they give some moments of conference time to helping parents relate to their children.

Guidelines to give Parents. The parent will want to know specifically what he must do to become an effective manager of his child. First, he must explore the answers to the following questions:

(1) What are my own emotional needs as a parent?
(2) Do I expect this child to make up for my own deficiencies?
(3) Are my own deficiencies real or imagined?
(4) Am I afraid of my own children?
(5) If I find out how he really feels, can I take it?
(6) What can I do to make my children feel secure and happy?
(7) What do I believe is a fair request in helping my children meet certain selected standards I have set for them?

Direct presentation of the questions above to a parent, like direct sunlight, would be uncomfortable and blinding. It is embarrassing at times for a parent to be told exactly what to do. No doubt greater gains will be achieved when the teacher puts it thusly, "I would like to suggest some things from which you might select the more appealing to try. Perhaps these questions will trigger off newer and more important types of questions as relates to your own situation."

The Parent as Counselor

Process Requirements. As one deals with his own children he must first deal with his own emotions. The part that an adult's feelings are playing in the relationship have much to do with the ultimate conclusions reached. The teacher must share with the parent such process requirements as these:

1. As parent-counselor you must seek to understand how your child really feels. (What is his real problem?).

2. As parent-counselor you must accept your child's feelings. The child who is allowed to "talk out" his feelings is generally one who has not been told that he doesn't or shouldn't feel that way.

3. The parent-counselor must mirror the child's feelings. Statements used by the parent must be of the nature that the child knows and understands that his feelings have been recognized. The parent truly knows how he feels.

4. The parent-counselor helps his youngster to express even

his most vehement feelings. Guilt springs from deep feelings often suppressed by unknowing parents.

5. The parent-counselor resists the use of dialogue. The tragedy of dialogue lies in the fact that the parent criticizes and instructs while the child denies and pleads. The wise parent eludes to a reflection of what the child is actually saying irrespective of the words that a child might be uttering to convince his parents about a certain issue.

6. The parent-counselor must help his own child to plan future actions. Appropriate planning will help the child clarify, cognitively speaking, future problems.

The teacher who observes a conversation between a parent and a child will note with surprise how little each listens to the other on strong points of view. In the conference session, the teacher should point out the fact that a child, much like the adult, when in the midst of strong emotions, cannot listen to anyone. It is a wise parent who seeks to understand what is going on inside of a child and particularly at moments of intense frustration.

Supply Parents with Illustrations. The teacher should discuss several ways of dealing with statements that a child may make about himself in the home environment. When a child says, "I am not good in Spelling," the parent adds little by agreeing or disagreeing. Disputing his opinion ("Why you're good at Spelling!") is as bad as offering him cheap advice ("If you would do your homework, you'd get better grades.").

The interviewer should suggest to the parent that he must give the child enough details about the comment that the child can anchor meaning to the conversation which tells him his parents really understand. Any one of these comments would suffice in most instances:

"When your test on Wednesday is over, I'll bet you feel safer."

"You must feel we are disappointed in you."

"I'm sure you will do your best."

"Some words must be real hard to memorize."

"The teacher doesn't help when he needles you about it."

"You do other things well. I have faith you will overcome some of the learning problems you now face."

A third grade boy related that when his mother put her arm

around him and said, "I'm *not* disappointed in you. You just do all you can," his inner reaction was: "Gosh! She believes in me. I can make it!"

An Exemplar of Family Dynamics. Mr. Bradley, Mrs. Bradley, R. C., Junior, and Danny Ray are having their evening meal. Throughout the dinner Mr. Bradley has been explaining the problems of getting one of his student teachers at the college to assume responsibility. Mr. Bradley, being in a position of authority, feels most secure if he knows that when student teachers know his wishes, they follow his judgment and do not question his requests.

Midway through the meal, Mr. Bradley remarks to his wife: "I guess I'm going to have to move Susan. She seemingly can't accept the responsibility of handling first graders."

R. C., Jr., (a first grader) has been toying throughout the dinner with his food, eating very little. Mother has praised Danny Ray (kindergarten) for eating well and has remarked on occasion, "R. C., eat your supper." Mr. Bradley has not noticed R. C. and the whipped look on his countenance. R. C. has brought home a note from the P.E. Instructor which says, "Unless R. C. pays attention in physical education class, he is to be taken out of flag football."

After a few more negative comments by Mr. Bradley and nods of affirmation from Mrs. Bradley, Mr. Bradley pounds the table and states, "I know what I'll do, I'll take Susan out of student teaching for a week!" At that moment, R. C., turns over his tea glass, pushes himself away from the table, and runs to his room. As he passes Mr. Bradley grabs him by the arm, shakes him, and says, "See what you did to the new tablecloth!" "Apologize to your mother!" R. C. retorts, "I won't! I won't!"

How can a teacher help a parent like this who finds himself in this situation? Is it possible for a teacher to help through interviews only? Is it only a job for a counselor? The wise teacher will develop several illustrations and specific hints to share with groups of parents in school settings and with selected parents in private interviews who seemingly seek out such help. Certainly, in the case of the example above, Mr. Bradley can be helped.

As a parent Mr. Bradley might be brought to realize that his concept of authority was shaken when the student teacher refused to do the tasks which were outlined for her. In seeking the apology, it should be remembered that Mr. Bradley asked R. C., Jr., to respond to his mother. Thus it seems, Mr. Bradley was willing to have it appear that Mrs. Bradley's authority was flaunted rather than his own. Consequently, Mr. Bradley must reflect on the questions presented earlier in this section:

1. What is Mr. Bradley afraid to find out? That his son must make up for his own deficiencies? Or, that his son must meet certain emotional needs by force?

2. What is Mr. Bradley going to do to find out his son's true feelings? What should he say? What should he ask? What should he accept?

For one thing, he must reflect on the dinner conversation and recognize that his discussion centering upon his own problems has caused his son to feel that his father must prefer the troubles of Susan over his own because he spent the entire meal discussing them. His father did not get after Danny Ray (his brother) at all during the meal and his mother praised him for eating. Therefore, it is little wonder that R. C. feels neglected, forgotten, and perhaps somewhat jealous of Susan and Danny. This feeling is compounded for after all, he has a problem with his coach and no family member has let him talk about it or even ask about it. What should Mr. Bradley have done?

First, Mr. Bradley should observe R. C. once in awhile throughout dinner for facial expressions which reflect "troubles." Second, he should help R. C. express his most negative feelings. At the moment, Mr. Bradley must recognize that R. C. has feelings of hate, resentment, jealousy, and pent-up emotions which are directed toward him, his father.

The teacher, who is sharing this example in an interview, might cite the type of conversation which should ensue. "R. C.," Mr. Bradley says, "you're upset about this matter and mad at me." Only a moment's reflection upon the dinner episode will show these feelings were present—the upset tea, the apology sought, the shaking, the rush for his room. Mr. Bradley repeats, "Why don't you tell me about it?" Statements of this nature will let R. C. know that his dad is trying to discover and accept how he feels. Mr. Bradley further states: "I know you are angry with me but I can't let you spill food over the table because of it. Tell me in your own words what you feel like saying. It's all right!"

Perhaps R. C., Jr., is still reticent but states finally, "I'm so mad I could pour tea all over this table!" At last, he is no longer concentrating upon the evening's incidents—he is now challenging and threatening his father. Threats of pouring tea all over the table is R. C.'s way of releasing anger. His father can now mirror (reflect) this feeling back to him. An attack can now be made on R. C.'s problem.

"Does it make you feel better to threaten me?" asks Dad.

"Yes!" R. C. mumbles and his voice has already lost some of its edge. "You care more about Susan than me getting to play flag football all year long." "You don't care what the coach says to me." At this point it can be seen that Mr. Bradley has disarmed R. C. through asking the right types of questions. R. C. is letting his feelings flow openly now. The crisis is past. R. C. is able to express feelings to the person with whom he wanted to share them, his own father.

It would be prudent for Mr. Bradley to follow up with a summary-type statement so that his son really sees that his father truly understands his position and his feelings. For example, Mr. Bradley might say:

> "I'm sorry son. I can see where I spent all of the dinner conversation time on Susan. I was so worried about her I didn't think of you and your problems."

> "Yes, I can see how you feel and why you would feel that way. I can also see that Susan might be as concerned about me and her problem as you are concerned about yours and your Physical Education instructor."

Mr. Bradley, additionally, is planning for the future by letting his son know that he can always come back to talk over his problems: "Next time if I do this son, come over and ask me to listen to your problems, too." R. C. is beginning to recognize by this time that although his father might simultaneously be upset about another problem, he will still take time from hereon to listen.

Time alone would not permit the teacher to cover all household situations, nor would he be able to serve as counselor to all parents. Nevertheless, the episode described above is so very typical that it might be shared in some form with several types of parents. Obviously, however, an experienced interviewer will inform his parents that at the evening meal it is wiser to engage children in conversation, letting the children talk the most, rather than keeping children quiet while Mother and Father mull over only adult experiences encountered during the day. If children become the center of attention during the evening meal, generally there is an atmosphere set which characterizes the type of homelife that improves the mental health of those within it.

Study Family Relationships

Family Patterns Differ. When the teacher interviews he should seek to determine who is head of the household. In many subtle ways the daily behavior of parents conveys to their children traits of masculinity and femininity.

Girls who come from homes where the woman is the boss may develop feelings that the mother is the last court of appeal in all matters of importance. Boys in these same types of homes receive the message that the female is boss. In homes where the father is the boss, boys will behave differently, and unknowingly so, toward female teachers. Consequently, in some homes children will obtain a different message. As one husband humorously puts it: "I decide the big things, whether or not President Nixon should stop the war in Vietnam, or whether Braniff should build bigger airplanes. My wife decides the smaller things: what house to live in, what car to buy, what college to send the children to." It is reasonable to assume that when men of this type are asked for decisions, the youngsters are referred to mother.

Weak fathers and dominant mothers affect both sons and daughters. Boys at intermediate grade levels particularly try to overcompensate and to prove their masculinity by fighting, swearing, and shoving the girls around. Girls may become tomboyish and seek to rule the playground in baseball, football and other masculine types of games. It may be impossible for the teacher to discuss openly in conference the competition and rivalry that is observable in selected homelife, but life is made easier for most children coming from such environments when their behavioral patterns which deviate from their sex roles are identified and the reasons for such deviations can be applied to the home patterns established by parents. The probable reasons for such behaviors should be conveyed tactfully to these unfortunate parents.

Seek to Improve Home Ties. Parents sometimes have to learn from the teacher that school years are a good period for intensifying a son's relationship with father and a girl's with mother. But it still remains the home's concern to choose willingly the roles deemed more acceptable to the given sexes. Imitations of language and manner will likely lead to the emulation of interests and values. A major role of the teacher in conferring with parents is to show the extent (and sometimes the lack of it) to which a child is mirroring the values held sacred by his parents. Parents derive much pride in learning about what the teacher sees as exemplifications of "like father, like son" and "like mother, like daughter."

Summary

Many conscientious parents need school guidance in bringing up children. The interview is an excellent setting in which to discuss what it means to be loving and devoted parents and teachers. Preoccupation with school achievement may become detrimental if the homelife of a child is overlooked. The child's life at home in large measure influences how he views his life at school. Likewise there is little reason to continue to administer social penicillin at school if the infested area is not corrected in the home.

The classroom teacher is the best counselor some parents will ever get to know. This role should not be taken lightly. Some parents linger on every word of the teacher in the interview. Much is still true to many parents merely because, "John's teacher said it." The parent can be educated to serve as a better counselor to his child. Preparation for this counseling might well come from qualified classroom teachers who have a keen sensitivity to parents and their children, problems and their solutions, and techniques and methods for implementation of selected therapy. The parent-teacher interview is an excellent means of making richer a parent's responsiveness to needs of his child.

How to Drop Report Cards in a Hurry

Introduction

9

    It should not take twenty years for a school district to adopt an interview method as its system of reporting. Changing to a conference system can be accomplished in a matter of months. All too often, however, new programs to be adopted in schools are referred to a committee for study. Although the logic may be questionable a poignant observation is that if Moses would have been a committee the Israelites might still be in the wilderness. The picture is, nevertheless, not entirely bleak. Most leaders and teachers in elementary schools hail the recent development concerning the demise of the abominable report card. Surely some member of each school system in this country will step forward and lead the way to a more adequate system of reporting to parents.

    Consequently, for purposes of expediting the change to an *interview system*, the work presented subsequently in this chapter deals with information and ideas that committees should consider with great haste if the report card method is ever to be eliminated. The home-school communications system must be improved and the time is right to organize for realistic home-school cooperation. In this light, then, it will be readily recognized why the provocative work selected for this chapter deals with reasons for dropping report card methods, how to encourage parents to visit their schools for informational and guidance purposes plus the need of their determining which way the "wind is blowing" (see, "The Weather is B Minus"), and how to organize for home-school cooperation.

IF YOU'RE THINKING ABOUT DROPPING
REPORT CARDS . . .

In Bellevue, Wash., report cards are out, parent-teacher conferences are in. Why? Read on, and discover a school-home communications system that *you* can adapt right now.

There's nothing wrong with the good old ABC method of grade reporting . . . except if a student is doing well or badly in a subject, that's the only story the report card tells. It never tells why.

As the chief means of communication between school and home, the report card simply doesn't do the job. It is superficial. It is often misleading. It doesn't tell parents what they can do at home to help their children in school; it doesn't give teachers any insight into the family background and personal problems of students.

Communication is a two-way street; the report card, too often, is a dead end.

This problem has been recognized for years. The key question: What to do about it?

In Bellevue, Wash., the answer is: *Eliminate* the report card.

Instead of sending report cards home, Bellevue elementary schools are sending invitations. That's right —*invitations* . . . to parents to periodically visit school for an information-exchange with teachers. And that—the parent-teacher discussion—is the Bellevue "report card."

The result: Today, when Bellevue elementary students are doing poorly in school, their parents know why and get a pretty good idea of what they can do to help.

Finding a better way

The quest for a better system began some years ago and

was reviewed last year, when the Bellevue school board appointed a citizen's committee to study the feasibility of a new elementary school reporting system. Many parents had expressed dissatisfaction with the standard report card.

"It just wasn't doing a good communications job," recalls one board member.

The committee quickly discovered that parent-teacher meetings—not report cards—were considered by most parents to be the most effective way to exchange information between home and school.

The committee relayed this information to the board with the strong recommendation that parent-teacher discussions serve as the foundation of a new reporting system—a system *without* misleading letter grades. A second citizen's committee was promptly assigned the task of putting a new system together. The system was implemented this fall.

It's inordinately simple and sensible. It works like this: Six days are set aside in November and February for conferences. Students are dismissed at noon on conference days and the conferences—one half-hour each, *at least*—are held in the afternoon.

Parents are notified of their appointment well beforehand, via an appointment slip sent home with the children. The slip indicates the time and date of appointments. Parents who can't keep their appointment merely indicate another time when they can make it at the bottom of the slip and send it back to school with their child. The teacher then reschedules the appointment.

Also listed on the appointment slip *(see page 141)* are possible topics for discussion: student work habits, growth as an individual, growth as a group member, comparative grades, reading, writing, speaking and so on. Before sending the slip back to the teacher, the parent checks the areas she is particularly interested in discussing. This primes both teacher and parent for the conference; time-consuming groping during the conference is eliminated.

Along with the appointment slip, the parent receives a four-page "conference guide for parents and teachers." This, too, is designed to prepare parents and teachers, in considerable detail, to get a lot out of the upcoming conferences.

The first page simply invites parents to review the guide to see how *they* can profitably *contribute* to the conference.

On the second page, the guide lists three key subject areas: work habits, growth as an individual and growth as a group member. Under work *habits,* several questions are posed: Is the student attentive? Does he follow directions? Is his work accurate? Does he begin work promptly?

Under *growth as an individual,* similar questions: Does the student assume responsibility? Does he respect rules? Does he show a questioning mind? Is he learning to apply the processes of rational analysis and critical thinking?

The same kind of questions are posed under the heading, *growth as a group member.*

All of the issues thus raised cue the parent—and the teacher—to the kind of information they will be discussing.

The third page of the guide provides space for parents to make notes before, during and after conferences on such important questions as: What is your child's attitude toward school? What are his out-of-school activities? What are his special interests? Does he assume responsibility appropriate for his age? This is, in effect, a record of the information the parent and teacher give each other. These notes are especially useful when, as so often happens, one of the parents is not able to attend the discussion.

The fourth page of the guide focuses attention on the student's academic progress: communication skills, social studies, science and mathematics, art and music, and all the rest. Here, too, space is provided for comments on the conference . . . but *not* for grades.

Bringing the student in

Obviously, the parents' guide sets the stage for the conference rather well.

One final step, as part of the preparation: bringing the *child* into it. Just prior to the conferences, the teacher takes each student aside to discuss his problems and progress in some detail. This makes for a cooperative effort on the part of teacher and child—i.e., the conference does not become just a report "about" the child by the teacher to the parent.

In both conferences during the year, the teacher uses a form called the "cumulative record of conferences." During the conference, the teacher capsules the most significant parts of her talks with the parent on the record sheet. The form is in triplicate and, at the end of each conference, the parent gets a copy. The original goes into the student's file.

At the end of the school year, the parent receives a "year-end pupil progress report." This is a one-page, written report that describes the student's personal and social growth, academic progress, attendance for the school year and assignment for the next school year *(see page 141)*.

This report is prepared in duplicate. One copy is sent to parents and the original is placed in the student's permanent record file.

This report is mainly a conference follow-up and answers the basic parental queries: Is he doing as well as he can? On what can I build in the next year and the years to come? How well is he doing in terms of the goals and plans discussed in previous conferences? And have there been any significant changes in attitude or achievement in the final weeks of school?

In this report, areas of weakness still remaining are brought into focus and significant or new data about the child is emphasized. If a third parent-teacher conference is needed, this report serves as the vehicle for planning that conference.

HOW BELLEVUE TALKS WITH PARENTS

Here are three forms that keep Bellevue's conference program rolling. Below, the cumulative record of conferences that gives the parent and the school a permanent record of the comments and recommendations made during the conference. Opposite above, the appointment slip that sets the stage for the conference and, below, the year-end pupil progress report that summarizes the student's progress over the past year—without letter grades—and points out problems that still exist.

That's all there is to it.

Cumulative record of conferences

This is Bellevue's report card. No A's and B's. Just a short but sensible report on progress and problems.

Student___Steven Smith___   Teacher_Mrs. Mary Jones_   School _Viewridge_

CUMULATIVE RECORD OF CONFERENCES

What are this child's strengths and weaknesses? What activities were recommended for the continuing growth and development of this child?

First Conference:
Date _November 7, 1966_

Has difficulty being attentive and concentrating on any activity for more than a few minutes. This hampers progress in all areas.

Oral reading and comprehension skills are developing satisfactorily. Word recognition and phonetic skills will require major emphasis. We will begin new approaches to developing spelling and writing skills which should improve performance.

Enjoys and is most successful in mathematics. Understands meaning of numbers and recognizes quantitative differences.

Does very well in art and handcraft activities. Able to visualize objects in two and three dimensions.

It is vital that teacher and parent build confidence through an acceptant attitude.

Second Conference:
Date February 27, 1967

Work habits have improved. Begins work promptly but is still easily distracted. Is able to participate more effectively in group projects.

Word attack skills have improved. Should be encouraged to read for enjoyment and of books on my recommended list. Has improved significantly with individualized spelling program. Will be working to improve form and spacing in cursive writing.

Continues to perform well in mathematics. Work with drill cards will help in mastery of multiplication facts through sixes.

Your parent-teacher conference is scheduled for

Date_____ Time_____

Please indicate below any area(s) that you are particularly interested in discussing.

____Work habits	____Social studies
____Growth as an individual	____Science
____Growth as a group member	____Mathematics
____Comparative grades	____Art
____Reading	____Music
____Writing	____Physical education
____Speaking	____Health
____Listening	
____Spelling	____Other: ____

Please detach and return prior to the conference. If you are unable to attend at the time above, please indicate other convenient dates and times.

Parent's Signature

Appointment slip

Appointment slip provides teachers and parents with an outline for the upcoming discussions.

Year-end pupil progress report

The parent receives this report at school's end. It's a tally of the year's parent-teacher conferences.

YEAR-END PUPIL PROGRESS REPORT (8-year-old)

Student _____Steven Smith_____ Teacher ___Mrs. Mary Jones___

School _____Viewridge_____ School Year 1966—1967

This report is based on our previous parent-teacher conferences and incorporates a summary of your child's progress to date. Items considered in evaluating your child's growth and progress are listed on the reverse side of this form.

Personal and Social Growth:

Steve is now able to complete most of his lessons in the specified period. He has more confidence and his work is self-motivated. It is important that the school and home provide activities that Steve can complete successfully.

Steve should enjoy some of the activities on my "Summer Fun" list. I recommend he participate in the community swimming program.

Academic Progress:

Steve is now able to read in a third-grade basic reader. His weakest area is word meaning. We need to provide various experiences to increase speaking and reading vocabulary. I suggest he enroll in the library's reading program.

A summer trip to the Seattle Science Center will help maintain the strong interest Steve has developed in science.

Steve has continued to meet our expectations in other areas of the program.

Your child has been absent___ days during the current school year. The assignment for next September is to___Room 500.__

Report cards not holy

"Once we discovered there was nothing holy about the old quarterly report card system," says Alden Clarke, director of curriculum development, "it was easy enough to devise the new system."

To familiarize teachers with the rationale and technique of the new system, a "teacher's guide to reporting practices" was developed.

The guide includes information such as:

1. What each parent-teacher conference should cover— i.e., comparisons with other children, expectations for the child and action to improve the child's learning process.

2. The use of the cumulative record form.

3. Directions for using the year-end-report.

4. A few rules of thumb for conducting the conference.

A similar guide was issued for parents.

But, from the very outset, some parents have insisted on having *letter*-grade reports. They feel lost without them. So the teachers, as a matter of course, do prepare grades for all students, prior to the conference. However, these comparative grades are discussed only briefly and are not reported on the cards.

It's too soon to tell whether Bellevue's system is *the* answer to the long-time reporting problem. But several conservative conclusions can safely be made.

It makes sense, educationally. It eliminates misleading "grades" and helps parents see education as *individual* development.

It's simple enough to be effectively used by teachers and easily understood by parents.

It's ripe for adaptation by other school districts. As a starter, simply consider using the materials reproduced on pages 141 and 142 as "report cards" in *your* schools.

FOR YOUR TEACHERS:

The success of Bellevue's new reporting system depends on how well teachers conduct conferences.

To help its teachers organize and pilot effective discussions with parents, Bellevue administrators have prepared the following tips.

Be professional
Observe professional ethics at all times. Don't comment

about other children even if the subject is introduced by the parent.

If a former teacher or school is brought into the conversation, let your attitude reflect only good.

Treat these conferences as highly confidential. Never repeat any matters of a personal nature about a child or family to other parents, even teachers, except when professionally necessary.

Parts of a conference
The parent contributes information about the child to aid the teacher in understanding him.

The teacher tells the parent about his child's progress in school, his work and study habits, and social and personal growth.

Recommendations for the continued growth and progress of the child are discussed by parent and teacher.

Preparing for the conference
Be informed about school purposes, methods and program.

File representative samples of the pupil's work over a period of time. Children can participate in choosing samples of their work.

Review your record of significant observations of the child's attitudes and actions.

Review data in the pupil's cumulative folder.
Evaluate recent test data in light of the pupil's performance. (Compare with daily work.)

Write brief descriptive phrases which are personally meaningful under headings of the Conference Guides. These notes are for the teacher's personal use. Leave space for additional notes during the conference.

Try to have a conference with the pupil before the parent conference.

Conducting the conference
Let the parent know what you would like to accomplish during the conference.

Establish a friendly atmosphere. Remember you are a host or hostess just as though you were in your own home. The parent may be uneasy and fearful about the conference.

Have an informal setting. *Sit on the same side of a table* with the parents, rather than at your desk. The desk between you is a barrier to free and fruitful exchange of ideas.

Remember that you are dealing primarily with one individual child, not comparing him with other members of his or of her class.

Be positive. Begin and end by enumerating favorable points. Stress the child's strengths.

Help parents to achieve a better understanding of their child as an individual. Don't attempt to interpret the curriculum in a short conference. This is more appropriate for a group conference.

Be sure to have at hand samples of the child's work—the whole range, not just those you consider adequate or inadequate.

Base your judgments on all available facts and on actual situations. Preparations should be made to discuss any standardized group tests that are available.

Keep vocabulary simple.

Accept the parent's reason for a child's behavior without showing signs of disapproval or surprise. If necessary, lead the discussion into additional possible causes of action or attitude.

Be truthful, yet tactful. The parent should be aware of the child's weaknesses, but nothing is gained by an unkind remark or by putting parents on the defensive.

Remember that parents are subjective and emotional about

their children. Put yourself in the place of the parent and try to see what effect a given remark would have on you.

Don't use expressions that imply placing of blame for unacceptable performance.

Remain poised. Avoid defensive arguments. Talk calmly.

Select for emphasis from among the child's weaknesses only those the child and parent are ready to deal with constructively.

Be constructive in suggestions. Don't "load" parents with suggestions. A few are more effective than many.

If excessive note-taking during the conference seems to be impeding the easy flow of communication, you might suggest that there will be time at the end of the conference for notes. Help parents to find their own solutions to problems. Agree upon action needed. Go only as far as the parent is ready to accept. We are all afraid of ideas we do not understand.

At the close of the conference summarize points covered and suggestions agreed upon. This is the time to record notes of these points and suggestions on the "Cumulative Record of Conferences."

Set a time limit. If another parent is waiting, tactfully conclude the conference; suggest further conference at another time.

The parent should receive a copy of the notes on the "Cumulative Record of Conferences." Copies are to be reserved for the second conference and the permanent record folder.

End on a note of continuing cooperation. Cordially invite parents to visit school. (You will probably wish to ask for prearrangement.)

The parent's contribution

Encourage the parent to talk. Be a good listener. You are interested in the information the parent brings to you about this child.

"The Conference Guide for Parents and Teachers" includes many questions that the parent will have had an opportunity to review. These may be used as a basis for discussion. Be sure to give the parent the opportunity to discuss those questions raised on the "Conference Guide." It isn't necessary to cover each question. Focus upon those in which you or the parent are most interested for the particular child. For example: If the child seems worried you might ask: How is his health? Any recent illness, accident, etc.? Any problems concerning sleep, bad dreams, etc.? Any early illness?

But don't diagnose health conditions or suggest treatment. Keep discussions to such aspects as fatigue, restlessness, irritability.

Don't tell a parent that a psychologist or psychiatrist should be consulted. Problems too severe for the school to give sufficient help should be referred to the principal.

Respect information as confidential. Don't pry.

WHAT'S ALL THE FUSS ABOUT
REPORT CARDS?

If you haven't seen a public-school report card since the last time you straggled or strutted home with one, you may be due for a shock when your youngster comes in with his first report. Every year chances get better that it won't resemble any report card you have ever seen.

It may be a letter from the teacher. It may be a folder full of check lists. It may contain unfamiliar terms—"acceptable growth," "learning activities." Unfamiliar symbols may replace the A-B-Cs or E-G-Fs or percentages of your youth—Ns or Ls, plus and minus signs, check marks. You may find much space devoted to marks or comments on such items as "contributes to group discussion" and "assumes responsibility," with relatively little—if, indeed, any at all—devoted to the list of academic subjects you were used to.

Your reaction may be frustration, bewilderment, anger, curiosity or admiration. And if you follow through on your reaction, whatever it may be, you are going to find yourself embroiled in a hot and perplexing debate.

Reporting methods have been a field in which educators have been most insistent on the need for re-examination and revision. And the field is one where innovations have often collided violently with established ideas and standards. The result: a lot of changes, a lot of experiment and a lot of controversy.

Here's what the fuss is all about—a guide to what is involved, what lies behind, what lies ahead. It may help you get more out of your child's report card and help you do an intelligent job of appraising and shaping practice and policy in your own school system.

What's a report card for?

Think back to your school days. How did you feel about your report card? Too often kids think of it as an end in itself—the goal toward which they work, a definitive judgment, a periodic reward or punishment. That attitude often sticks with them as adults.

Actually, though, the function of a report is quite different. First of all, it is not a goal, but a measurement of progress made toward a goal. You send your youngsters to school to learn certain things and grow in certain ways. Their marks are merely information on their advance toward those objectives.

Second, the report is not *the* definitive judgment, but only one part of a broad and continuous process called evaluation. Most school systems maintain cumulative records on students throughout their entire school careers. Report cards represent one of many measurements, records, test results, health data, family information, teacher recommendations, etc., all of which are collected and analyzed to evaluate a youngster's development.

The moral is, Don't overemphasize report cards. Keep them in perspective.

But what, then, are the functions of reports? Here are some of the jobs that they do. Which do you consider most important? Which does your school system stress?

1. Help the pupil do better work by showing him what progress he has made, where he has made it, where he has failed to make it, and what he needs to do in the future.

2. Inform parents on their children's progress, on the kind of guidance they need, on the nature and aims of the schooling.

3. Help teachers reach conclusions about their pupils, make plans, judge the effectiveness of their own work.

4. Provide an incentive for the pupil to do his best by recognizing top effort and achievement or pointing out the lack of them.

Much argument revolves around that. Some educators are dead against trying to motivate children this way and some parents deny there is any other effective way. The middle ground is described in an information sheet on marks put out by the National Education Association: "People should do their best for the satisfaction good work brings, but . . . children do not always see and accept the goals of schoolwork, which may be too distant or too intangible to appeal to them. Marks may furnish a substitute for more desirable motives."

5. Help school officials appraise the workings of their school system, assign and counsel pupils, plan for the future.

6. Help pupils, parents and guidance officials decide on courses and vocational preparation.

7. Provide information to other schools, colleges, prospective employers.

What makes a good reporting system?

Most of the discussion about report cards focuses on forms, marking techniques and similar details. But you will be putting the cart before the horse if you try to judge a system by starting there. Instead, start by looking for standards that can be used to measure the effectiveness of report cards in general, whatever form they happen to take.

Are there such criteria? Yes. Not all are universally agreed upon, but all are widely enough accepted to provide a reasonable basis for investigation and discussion. Here are some suggested hallmarks of a good system:

It is easily understood by all parents. They represent all sorts of backgrounds, viewpoints and interests. Systems that are too complex, that are easily misinterpreted, or that contain a heavy dose of unfamiliar professional terms rate poorly on this point.

It has been worked out cooperatively. Teachers, parents and administrators all shared in developing the system. It reflects the requirements of them all.

It agrees with the objectives, policies and practices of the school. Sometimes the educational theories represented by the card do not square with the theories upon which the school is run. They obviously should match.

It reports on the child as an individual. It describes his progress and achievements and problems in terms of his own ability and personality. It does not rate him *only* in comparison with a norm or his group.

It reports on the child as one member of a group. It describes his progress and achievements and problems in terms of what is expected of his age and grade. It does not rate him *only* in comparison with himself.

It concentrates on fields of behavior and learning that are of primary importance to the child, now and later, and to the community. In other words, it puts first things first.

It is accurate. Judgments are fair, thoughtful, correct and clear. Parents and children have confidence in them.

It tells how and why as well as what. It tells the causes of difficulties, pins down specific types of progress, probes under the surface of classroom behavior and performance.

It is efficient. It does not put an out-of-proportion clerical load on teachers or school. It does not demand more skill or training than the average teacher has at her command.

It is flexible. Everthing that may need to be said can't be put across with symbols and pre-selected phrases. The card should provide for the special situation as well as the routine.

It fits with other records kept. Useful information from the latter can be adapted to the report, and vice versa. There is no unnecessary duplication, no inconsistency.

Parents, teachers and children are helped to understand and use the reports. The school system provides such aid and encourages everyone to take advantage of it.

Methods of reporting

Schools use many different methods to try to turn out report cards that will do the required job and meet the agreed-upon standards. The following are the usual ones, with brief statements of arguments commonly made for and against each. Percentage grades, the oldest form of marks, are getting rare nowadays, so they are not discussed separately. What is said about letter grades applies generally to percentages.

Letter grades. This is the A-B-C (or E-G-F) system you probably remember. The pupil's performance is compared with a norm—either a minimum standard for the grade or a class average. If his achievement matches it, a C. Better or worse, a B or D. Way above or far below, an A or E. Effort, conduct and other nonacademic traits may be similarly rated.

Pro: It measures the child's performance with a specific, objective standard. It reports the degree of achievement in skills and knowledge considered necessary for competence in adult life. It gives recognition and reward for extra achievement, and reproof and an incentive to improve for inadequate achievement. It does so in terms the child can understand. It gives concrete information needed in choosing courses and careers or applying for employment.

Con: Grades are not objective because teachers differ in applying standards. (C work in Miss Grim's class would rate a B in Miss Cherry's room.) It makes kids work for grades, and grades are not effective incentives for learning. It does not explore whys and hows. It tries to isolate academic progress from general social and emotional growth, which is wrong. It is unfair to below-average children and discourages them. It encourages bright children to be satisfied with good marks they don't have to work hard for.

Progress reports. Instead of marking by an achievement standard, these evaluate progress made in terms of the child's own individual ability. Doing one's best becomes a basic criterion. Check marks, symbols or letters may be used. Some systems use only two marks—S for "satisfactory progress for this child" and N for "needs improvement," for example. Others add an equivalent of O for "outstanding progress" and U for "unsatisfactory progress." Personality, social adjustment and work habits may be marked. Academic subjects may be listed in regular form or broken down into subdivisions, as when separate progress ratings are given on ability to read with expression, understanding of what is read, etc.

Pro. The system rates the child only in terms of what he as an indvidual is capable of; demanding that he do more is unfair and pointless. It encourages both the bright and the not-so-bright to put forth their best efforts. Poorer students are not discouraged or upset by repeated failures. Undesirable competition for marks is eliminated. Emphasis is properly placed on the growth and development of the whole child instead of on certain arbitrary academic fields.

Con: Students are conditioned to think of "satisfactory" as good enough. There are no incentives to do better. Progress reports are not diagnostic, that is, they offer no whys and hows. Good students get no reward or recognition for top-quality work; slow ones are falsely encouraged and led to think that poor achievement is acceptable. Schoolwork is devalued by becoming the one area in which the child gets no special recognition for excellence, with open rewards going only to those who excel at play, socially, in sports, in the arts. No achievement data is available for use in choosing courses, appraising aptitudes, measuring vocational skills. The system is based on subjective opinions, and there is just as much room for variation among teachers as there is in letter-grade systems. (Miss Grim suspects Johnny is only half trying, while Miss Cherry always gives her students the benefit of the doubt.)

Narrative reports. The teacher writes a letter, goes over it with the child, sends it home. She comments as she feels needful on any or all phases of the child's development, performance and problems. She may stress either progress or achievement.

Pro: A letter is flexible and diagnostic, providing a maximum of truly useful information. It is always constructive. The stigma of low marks, the competition for marks and easy self-satisfaction on the part of bright students are all eliminated. No arbitrary standards impede the child from progressing at his own best rate.

Con: Letters take too much time and effort to prepare and often report on the child as he was a month or six weeks back. Too much teacher skill is required; all are not able to turn out good narratives, and letters in practice fall short of what they are in theory. Teachers tend to pull their punches, say only "nice" things. Letters can be hard to understand, easy to misinterpret. Many arguments made against progress reports apply even more forcefully to narratives.

Conferences. Instead of writing a report, the teacher delivers an oral one at an appointed conference with one or both parents. Parents are free to request, and teachers free to offer, any type of information they they feel is important.

Pro: There is full freedom to explore every phase of the child's development. Competitive aspects are completely eliminated. Misunderstandings can be straightened out at once. Teachers get helpful information from parents.

Con: Fathers are usually left out. Demands on the mother's time are a nuisance or, if she works, a hardship. Conferences use up the teacher's time or classroom time. Written records must be supplied as an extra. There is no adequate report to the child. Criticisms of progress reports and narratives apply again.

Combinations. Some schools use several types. Conferences may alternate with written cards. Narratives may be used only in the first few grades, and letter grades only in junior and senior high. Other schools have developed cards that combine the features of several marking methods. Some give dual ratings, one set on achievement and one on progress. Space for teacher comment may supplement marks. Subjects and subdivisions of them may both be rated. Physical, emotional and social development may be reported through one system and academic learning through another.

Pro and con arguments are hard to generalize. But combination cards have one big advantage: They offer a way of compromising divergent viewpoints. They have one big disadvantage: They tend to be complicated.

How to find your way around

If the pros and cons on different reporting methods confuse you, if you have difficulty making headway in discussions of reporting methods, it may help to note that all of the debate tends to reflect one of three viewpoints.

One viewpoint emphasizes standards of achievement. It says schools are not intended to raise children for parents but to equip them with certain desirable skills and knowledge. It stresses the need to measure actual achievement against community-set minimums or standards. Making this kind of measurement has important incentive value.

The second viewpoint emphasizes progress according to individual ability. It says that education is supposed to develop the fullest capacity of the individual. It stresses the uselessness and danger of measuring by standards that all are not able to meet and the incentive value of rating effort over rigid performance levels. It stands on the proposition that kids learn best if allowed to progress at their own rate.

The third emphasizes the diagnostic type of information. It says that schools are supposed to lead children into socially desirable skills and behavior. It stresses that a child must be considered as an individual and as a whole; that academic growth is inseparable from other kinds of growth; that *wanting* to learn is the only workable incentive. It holds that children must be analyzed and described, not rated.

And, of course, there are many who can't ally themselves with one camp but find valid arguments in two or even all three. That is what produces combination reporting systems, which may turn out to be the real current trend in reporting methods. Up to now, though, the two most noticeable trends have been a movement away from the use of academic letter grades alone and a movement toward the full or part-time use of conferences.

The final puzzler about reports is this: What are your responsibilities as a parent with respect to them? Here are three:

Use the report and use it wisely. Read it carefully. Digest all the information that it offers. Ask questions if you need to. Discuss it constructively with your child. Do not overemphasize it; keep it in perspective as an along-the-way measurement and as just one of many types of information available.

Understand it. Talk with the teacher about the reporting method the school uses. Learn the mechanics of it and the philosophy behind it. Find out about all the records kept. Study any printed material put out about reports.

Help develop it. When studies are undertaken, changes proposed, and complaints aired, get into the act. Don't sit on your hands, and don't go off halfcocked either. Investigate, debate, help decide. Be wary of aligning yourself too closely with noisy pressure groups on either side of a report-card argument, for such groups frequently devote themselves to broadcasting preconceptions instead of examining facts. There's no need for you to be stubbornly critical or docilely uncritical.

It is sad but true. You didn't finish with report cards after all when you got out of school. They are just as important, just as perplexing and maybe just as worrisome now as in the days when you were the one who brought them home instead of the one waiting to read them.

DANGER HANDLE WITH CARE!   3

The report card can be a dangerous weapon.

Have you ever thought as you distribute report cards to your class that you may be passing out a hand grenade which will explode in the living room of a well-ordered home, or a bankruptcy notice which will insure an early school dropout, or a badge of honor to be worn in street-corner society?

Even though report cards are a favorite topic for cartoons—witness the ones scattered throughout this feature—reporting is nevertheless a serious matter and carries great emotional impact.

Nothing will break the calm of a middle-class household

like a "bad" report card. Achieving, going to college, and improving the mind represent dominant concerns of the family. The terrible story of school failure spelled out in the report card when aired at supper time will contaminate the evening meal. The dining-room table becomes a verbal battleground.

Most parents take their child's failures personally. When the report card indicates that their youngster may not be able to get into any college, let alone the college of their choice, they are faced with a terrible loss of status.

"Why," feels the father, "when you were born, the first thing I did was to buy you a bib with HARVARD printed on it. Now you won't even be able to get into West Podunk College. You . . . you saboteur!"

The apprehensive, crestfallen, and defeated parent will counsel, beg, admonish, or cajole the youngster: "Please, please bring up your marks." He paints the future as bleak and foreboding. He threatens, "Until you get better marks, you get no allowance, you can't use the car (or bike, according the pupil's age and grade), and you can't watch TV!"

One of the few "safe" ways that the middle-class student can strike out at his parents is through failure in school. With this youngster three failing marks can mean three stiletto wounds in the parent's back. The report card thus becomes a lethal but concealed weapon, and the parent had better watch out.

On the other hand, the middle-class parent whose youngster brings home "all A's and B's" basks in the reflected glory of his offspring's achievement. He may even show off the youngster's school report to his fellow employees at the office or to his neighbors at the bridge table.

And usually, rewards—in accordance with the family's socioeconomic level—are forthcoming. An A can be worth a dollar or a dime, depending on the current state of the family exchequer. In this way the school report may become a vehicle for barter or blackmail.

By way of sharp contrast, the teacher's report to the lower-class home carries radically different symbolic overtones for Harry, a member in good standing of the street-corner gang.

On their way home from school, members of the gang—all thorns in the side of the school staff—compare their marks. Gleefully they check to see who has the most failures and absences.

Harry, with five failures and a sharply written comment from his homeroom teacher complaining of his inattention and low achievement which "is far below his ability level," earns prestige and the approval of his confreres. In fact, Harry tops the gang's "honor roll."

But woe to any member of the street-corner group who finds himself on the *teachers'* honor roll. His "rep" and his status with his peers are immediately jeopardized. The fact that his report card also shows a perfect attendance record for the last quarter sets him up as a target for the jeers and jibes of the gang.

The "professor" will have to be tough indeed to endure the climate of the gang and the rigors of their criticism. There is no honor for him in his street-corner society—only dishonor. He will quickly discover that he has betrayed them and will soon be betrayed himself. His report card, like the deciding Greek ostrakon has banished him from his group.

The report forms are not without their symbolic overtones for the school staff. The special marking system employed by the teachers often will reveal the school to be suffering acutely from institutional schizophrenia.

Most reporting devices today, especially at the elementary-school level, optimistically attempt to appraise growth and development of "the whole child." This is consonant with the broadened objectives of the modern school. The result is a six-page report form listing personal and social traits and habits in addition to the traditional skills and substantive headings.

The switch to a more complicated system is regarded as proof of an alert administration eager to change or to implement lessons learned at the Institute on Appraisal during the past summer session at State U. But changes do not always mean improvement.

At the same time the new school reports reveal a personality-splitting ambivalence in marking or rating. The appraisers waver between marking the pupil's performance in terms of his own capacity and appraising his achievements in terms of the modal performance of his grade or age group.

A glance at the report forms now in use would indicate that the mental hygienists have won out and most youngsters, particularly in the elementary grades, are being evaluated against the criterion of their own potential or individual capacity for learning. The result is a school report that informs the parents that the pupil is doing what is considered to be a "satisfactory job *for him.*"

Ultimately this kind of appraisal will only confuse the youngster and his parents since he must still face the comparative appraisal against the performance of others in the competitive market of the outside world. The student should not be protected from comparison with his peers, for the world outside the classroom represents a highly competitive culture which, at its worst, approaches a "dog-eat-dog" rivalry.

The only way the evaluators in school can solve this personality-splitting dilemma is to provide two marks: one indicating the level of the pupil's performance measured against his potential; the other reporting his achievements against the performance of other pupils of his own age or grade.

A few schools have already moved in this direction. But a study of the appraisal and reporting methods in any one school system will usually reveal that the elementary schools are using the criterion of individual capacity whereas the secondary school tends to rate in terms of the average or modal performance of all the pupils in a grade.

In a cartoon by a well-known artist who is given to commenting in two panels on "the good old days"—a pupil is depicted quaking with fear as he carries his report card home. In "today's" panel the parent is shown fearful and trembling as his youngster brings the report in to him for signature.

It is true that the report cards sent home by the modern school have become more complicated and much more elaborate. Many schools have felt the need for supplementing the written report with a "parent conference" to make sure the complicated message is not misunderstood. In one school system, the teacher carries the report card home to the parents and confers with them regarding the meaning of the written message. In other communities, written reports are being replaced entirely by teacher-parent conferences. In some cases, doing away with the report card eliminates the only pipeline between schools and home—particularly when both parents of many pupils are wage earners.

Progress reports, home-school communications, achievement reports, or just old-fashioned report cards, call them what you will—they provide a real-life experience of being judged and evaluated. Not the worst thing between teacher, student, and parent is the communication device reporting growth and progress that has or has not taken place.

Unfortunately, because of the periodic nature of such reporting, it has some Day of Judgment overtones. Every day should be report card day—at least for the student. And every teacher should remember that in his appraisal of his students he appraises himself.

"Of course, that's only one person's opinion."

ARE YOU KEEPING PARENTS OUT OF YOUR SCHOOLS?

4

"Stop by and see us—any time!"

If you're like most superintendents, you make this carte blanche invitation to parents at least a dozen times a week. And, like most superintendents, you'd be appalled if they took you up on the offer.

This kind of insincere heartiness doesn't fool anyone. Parents know they are *not* welcome to "stop by any time." It's been made clear to them that they would disrupt classes and interrupt the busy days of administrators.

When we tell parents to stop by for a visit, *we mean it.* We don't just say "any time"—we set a date and make sure they keep it. This is a carefully planned visitation program that has resulted in markedly increased community interest in the Galesburg schools. Through it, parents learn firsthand about their child's school and its activities, and a true home-school rapport is established.

How it works

Each week, every elementary classroom invites one set of parents to visit their room as their "Parents of the Week." The invitations are written by the students in the intermediate and upper grades, and by the teacher in the primary grades.

Included with the invitation is the room's study schedule so that parents can tell what subjects they'll be observing. Also included is a letter from the superintendent's office that explains the reasoning behind the district's visitation program.

This letter of explanation tells the parents that, by attending, they will be able to:

1. Know their child's teacher personally.

2. Observe their child when he functions as a student in the classroom.

3. Support the child's interest in school by showing that they themselves are interested.

4. Know what their tax money is purchasing and, perhaps, discover what further support is needed.

R.S.V.P.

Parents are asked to reply to the invitations, stating on what day they would care to come. Mondays and Fridays, because they're heavy teaching days, are discouraged; but if parents notify the school that they choose to come on a Monday, they receive no argument. They are *always* welcome. It is suggested to the parents in the invitation that they will feel less encumbered if they leave infants at home. This suggestion, if heeded, makes the day more comfortable for teachers as well. If parents are unable to find a sitter for small children, they are advised to plan a future visit, at a time when a sitter will be available to them. The schools make no provision for baby care services.

If parents do not reply to their first invitation of the school year, their name comes up in rotation for a second. Since the rotation permits only about two invitations per year for each family, those who decline the last invitation are not hounded. If, however, they cannot accept because their job does not permit attendance, they are encouraged to come during their lunch hour, to make special arrangements that will give them at least a half hour free from work. About 90% of those invited do participate.

Although both parents are invited, it is usually the mother who attends. In one of the smaller schools in the district, average daily visitations numbered about two or three per day—a number the student ushers handled with dispatch.

These ushers, members of the class that has invited the parents, greet the visitors at the school's general office and award them "Parents of the Week" badges, paid for by a local firm. The children escort them to the classroom, showing them the school's layout on the way. Parents are seated in the back of the classroom and are provided with copies of the textbooks that will be used while they are present. And then they observe. There is no written rule on how to handle a parent who calls out a question in the middle of a lesson; teachers have responded to such (infrequent) interruptions by politely telling the parents that questions should be asked at a more convenient time.

No novelty

Teachers and children quickly become accustomed to having visitors, and they cease to be a novelty. Classes go on as usual when parents are present. At noon, or during recess, parents and teachers have some time to visit with one another. But no appointments are made specifically for parent-teacher or parent-principal conferences. If they do drop in to visit, they're received cordially. But the visitation days are really intended to let parents see classroom activities. Conferences can always be arranged later.

During lunch hour, incidentally, parents may eat hot lunch in the cafeteria as paying guests. This direct experience goes far toward building support for the hot lunch program.

Most of the teachers have grown to appreciate the program, and the support that it builds for the school. And not a few of them appreciate the opportunity to exhibit their teaching skills. Some of them, without doubt, are still not wholly at ease when the parents are in the classroom. But the consensus, as expressed by one teacher, seems to be: "I was a little nervous at first. I don't like the idea of putting on an exhibition for the parents' sake. But after awhile, I could see that they really appreciated what I was doing up there. And they were beginning to understand what it means to teach 30 different children for a whole day."

How they react

To find out more precisely what parents think of the program, we recently initiated a reaction sheet. It's given to each visiting parent, who is urged to return it to the school. The top half of the sheet says, "What did you enjoy most about your visit?"

Reactions range from simple compliments ("Everyone did such a fine job") to, "This morning made me wish I were back in school."

The bottom half of the sheet is headed: "Is there further information we could provide to help you understand what the school is trying to do for your child?" About one parent in 15 makes a comment that leads us to make a follow-up contact. This procedure helps us to adjust potential problems and dissatisfactions before they become troublesome situations.

One parent, for example, wrote, "Why is my child's classroom so crowded?" The parent was contacted immediately; he was told that the district was concerned about classroom overcrowding, and was preparing to act. He was congratulated for his observation and interest. And he was told that the conditions he saw could be dispelled more quickly through public support of financing referendums. He was also told that the district was in the process of contracting with a university to do a pupil-facility survey that would lead, hopefully, to alleviation of the crowding.

Outlook is promising

The parents' response bolsters our belief that parents deserve to know as much about their schools as they are willing to learn. And the response supports our conviction that good school public relations is not incompatible with full-time devotion to academic concerns. The parents get to know about the schools, they support the schools at home; their children thus receive educational encouragement on a total scale. And "class" extends from the schoolroom to the living room.

That's why we don't tell parents to "Drop in—any time."

We do tell them to drop in. But we tell them when to drop in and we make it easy for them to do so. We're glad that they come, and so are they.

Badges worn by visiting parents are sought by children as souvenirs.

THE WEATHER IS B-MINUS: 5

Is an "Average" Mark Enough?

The United States Weather Bureau does an excellent job of gathering data on the weather and reporting it to the public. Conditions all over the country are systematically recorded and transmitted to a central office, where they are analyzed and the findings are released to the many interested persons and agencies throughout the nation. Local stations must report such records as temperature, barometric pressure, cloud conditions, wind direction and velocity, relative humidity, precipitation, and many other factors which contribute to the total weather picture.

It seems likely that the Weather Bureau could operate more efficiently and at a reduced budget if the report of each local station could be reduced to a single symbol and all these symbols in turn could be averaged to give the total weather condition throughout any given area. Under a simple method of arithmetical averages the entire weather condition could be expressed by a single number. A system could be worked out whereby the average of temperature, pressure, wind velocity, direction of wind (a numerical value given to each point of the compass), precipitation, and other conditions could be shown on a scale. On this scale any number below 70 could be expressed as "F." Averages between 70 and 78 could be expressed as "D," and between 78 to 85 as "C." The top averages, of course, would fall into the brackets designated as "A" and "B."

Not only would such a simplified system reduce telegraph bills for the Weather Bureau; it would also save many industries much time and money. Valuable radio and television time could be saved by the announcer merely saying, "The weather today is B-minus. The forecast for tomorrow is B-plus." The newspapers could save space and still tell the complete story with a single letter in the upper right-hand corner of the front page. An airline pilot could receive the simple message that the condition at the airport is "Baker-Minus," and thus know the cloud ceiling, wind velocity, precipitation, and other weather facts which are important for him to determine before he brings his plane to its landing.

Because of tradition it may be difficult to educate the public on a revolutionary plan of this sort. Some persons would insist on knowing how much rain fell or the exact temperature until they became accustomed to reading the single symbol to represent all of it. Of course some newspapers would probably aggravate this condition by printing the specific conditions which go into making the "average" weather. As a result we would probably have a few individuals more interested in the prediction of "rain" than in a prediction of "B-minus."

The American people have accepted such a system from their schools for generations without too many objections. They are convinced that they know the meaning of "B-minus" on a report card, yet that symbol represents the report on an individual child who is much more complex that the weather conditions. Many pages of printed materials would be inadequate to report fully on the child—yet the simple symbol of "B-minus" is accepted as being the total picture of his progress in school. Of course, on the back of the report card there is usually a superficial attempt to tell something about the child. Such terms as "citizenship," and "industry," "cooperation." and others are listed and usually evaluated. Most parents look at these terms, but as long as the total picture is "B-minus" they are not particularly interested in the other items because they "don't count."

Many elementary schools feel that the elements which go into an "average" mark are important within themselves and as a result have devised different ways of reporting to parents. Sometimes letters are sent out to describe the activities of the children along with specific information on the individual child's progress in these activities. Some schools hold parent-teacher conferences in which teacher and parent discuss specific strengths and weaknesses of the child. Because of the time involved in such reports it is very difficult to make them every month but two or three such reports each year are much more meaningful than monthly reports of "B-minus."

Reporting progress in high-school classes presents a different problem. A high-school teacher with four, five or six classes would have to write from a hundred to one hundred fifty detailed letters and hold conferences with as many parents. Each parent would have to go to four or five different teachers for conferences. Such arrangements would be difficult to schedule.

High schools have not found an answer to the problem of making meaningful reports to parents but a few schools are attempting to improve the existing practices. In place of a "B-minus," the pupil may be evaluated on several items which are important to school success. Such a list of items represents the working philosophy of the school. There is no longer a single mark for a given subject but an evaluation of the child in many areas which the school feels are important. It is not a terminal mark based largely on the results of a final examination, but a series of evaluations which will help the child to improve the quality of his work. A report to the parent in these terms will explain the strengths and weaknesses of the child—which a "B-minus" cannot explain.

Radical departures from traditional patterns in education are not always acceptable to school patrons, so it may be necessary to accompany a change with an information campaign. A progress report which evaluates a pupil in several areas of achievement will undoubtedly be described by some parents as a "personality rating scale" which does not reflect academic achievement. It must be pointed out to these parents that such items as "Works and studies effectively alone," "Expresses himself effectively in writing," and "Shows initiative" indicate some very important aspects of academic success. It isn't necessary for a teacher to hide these ratings in a "B-minus" when they can be shown separately.

If the weather is "B-minus" we would like to know what specific conditions make it that way. If Tom brings home a report of "B-minus" in algebra it would be nice to know what specific elements in his work made it "B-minus" and not "B-plus."

EDITOR'S NOTE

Drawing a parallel between weather reports and reports to the home, Mr. Brimm, principal of Teachers College High School, Cedar Falls, Ia., demonstrates why his school issues report cards that are complete enough to let parents know whether their child's progress is likely to be fair or stormy, whether his efforts are dry or humid—and, in short, which way the wind is blowing.

TEACHER AND PARENT
TALK IT OVER

6

In recent years more and more teachers and parents have come to realize how important it is for them to share their knowledge of each child's life at home and at school. For without such shared understanding a child's educational success hangs in perilous balance. More and more school systems have made a practice of scheduling regular teacher-parent conferences all the way from kindergarten through high school. School administrators are beginning to see the need for giving teachers released time to talk over mutual problems with parents in the natural setting of the school-room, where a child spends the greater part of his day.

These conferences should begin as early as possible in a child's school life. Some school systems give parents and teachers a chance to get acquainted even before a youngster enters kindergarten. One system, for example, schedules individual conferences for the parents of entering kinder-gartners. Sometime during the summer each parent receives a card telling the time and place of the conference, together with a booklet describing the educational goals of the kindergarten and suggesting how to help children get ready for their first school experience.

The child usually comes too. He has a chance to inspect the kindergarten while his mother and his teacher-to-be talk together. The conferences last, on the average, for about thirty minutes.

Last September the school officials of this system began to wonder whether parents were really interested in these early conferences, so they gathered some statistics. They found out that more than a thousand mothers—approximately 100 per cent—had answered the invitations, and in all but four interviews children had accompanied their mothers. As for the teachers, they generally agreed that the opportunity to meet mothers on the eve of a young child's great adventure and to gain insight into that child's world overbalanced any possible objections to the plan.

In the course of the talks, the teachers reported, they have a chance to explain the importance of kindergarten, to emphasize the need for safety precautions, and to urge that the youngster have a physical examination if his parents have not yet made an appointment for one. Most teachers also feel that a child's enrollment card can be filled in far more satisfactorily at a conference than when it is sent home with the child or filled in hurriedly on the opening day of school.

Do parents grow less and less interested in meeting their child's teacher as he moves up into the grades? If there is any doubt on this score, data reported last spring by one school system offer encouraging, convincing evidence. There were 5,970 children in the elementary schools, and 5,119 parents had appeared for individual conferences with the teachers—85.7 per cent! The percentage would have been even higher if some parents had not had transportation difficulties, baby-sitter problems, or illness in the family. And in some homes both mother and father were employed.

Only a few parents believed that the conferences were unnecessary and therefore did not keep the appointments made for them. Teachers and administrators tried various ways of reaching these fathers and mothers: telephone calls, personal notes making new appointments, even special delivery letters. If a parent could not come for a conference at the scheduled hour, the teacher's program was rearranged to suit that parent's convenience. Sometimes a teacher would offer to make a home visit. Or she might invite a parent to her own home for a chat over a cup of tea. Occasionally other parents were enlisted to talk to the reluctant fathers and mothers.

Preparatory Steps

Naturally, just setting up a conference schedule and getting the cooperation of parents will not assure the success of a teacher-parent conference. At any school level, careful preparation is necessary. The teacher must plan for the parent's comfort, knowing that a guest greeted warmly by name in a pleasant atmosphere will probably speak freely and listen appreciatively.

Sometimes teachers feel that parents will be more at ease if they have some questions to guide them in preparing for the conference. A certain elementary school teacher, who does an excellent job of counseling with parents, has a list of questions that they may want to ask. These are sent home prior to the conference. Some questions have to do with the child's social relationships: "Does my child have many friends or just a few?" Does he accept most children?" "Do children accept him?" "Is he a good leader? A good follower?" "Does he understand and accept authority?"

Other questions have to do with the child and the three R's: "Will you explain how reading is taught to young children?" "How does my child fit into the school program?" "What kind of reading material should I have at home?" "What can I do to help my child in arithmetic;" "Does he need extra practice?" "Is my child able to organize his thoughts into a story?" "Can he carry on an interesting and meaningful conversation?"

On the other hand, there is always the possibility of losing freshness and spontaneity when prepared questions are used to guide a conference. Therefore the teacher who wants to give parents advance preparation may find it helpful to have the room mother sponsor a preliminary meeting. Perhaps the meeting could feature an appropriate film. *Skippy and the Three R's*, for example, would give parents an excellent introduction to the reading program in the primary grades. Or there might be a discussion of a topic such as "Things I'd Like To Talk About at a Teacher-Parent Conference," including suggestions from both teachers and parents.

Parents having little or no experience with conferences may approach the meeting hour with some trepidation, possibly recalling their own school days when every teacher-parent conference had a bad-boy label. Here is an opportunity for the P.T.A. to step in and help pave the way for a pleasurable experience. Some P.T.A.'s ask parents to come to the school a few minutes early for a cup of coffee and homemade cake. In this way parents can chat with one another before the conferences start.

A P.T.A. might also plan a role-playing meeting that

would show different kinds of people at different kinds of conferences. Through brief dramatic presentations parents and teachers might see themselves as others see them—and learn a bit about themselves in the process. The not-too-cordial teacher and the blustering parent might be led to change their attitudes. The overly critical parent and the gushing, all-is-well teacher might decide that a down-to-earth conference based on the actual needs of the child would be most gratifying to both.

Once a friendly atmosphere has been established at the opening of the conference, the teacher may begin by explaining briefly some of the tasks of the child's group and his part in the work of the school day. The parent may then ask the question that is probably uppermost in his mind— "What kind of person is my child in school?" This type of question gives the teacher an opportunity to discuss the child's relationships with others, his attitude toward authority, his values, his strong and weak points.

Comparing Notes

Throughout the conference parent and teacher alike should bear in mind their chief aim: to share their knowledge of the child and plan together to guide his development. Sharing information and working together are essential for positive results. The parent should realize that Johnny's teacher can be of more help to Johnny if she knows something about his out-of-school activities, his home interests, his recreation, his friends. And the teacher should realize that the parent needs not only information about his own child but an understanding of the school's basic beliefs. Today, for example, the school recognizes that every child grows at his own rate. A parent, on the other hand, may judge a child's growth by comparing him with other children his own age. This difference in beliefs, unless it is interpreted to the parent, may well lead to an unhappy interlude for the child.

As the conference is brought to a close, the parent should have specific information about his child's strengths and needs and about plans for further cooperation of home and school. The teacher, likewise, should have information to aid her in guiding this child. And when parent and teacher talk together again they will both have an opportunity to list their recommendations in terms of Johnny and Susie as individuals.

Now, having considered the values and techniques of the teacher-parent conference, let us make ourselves an invisible third party to an interesting and revealing session between the mother and the teacher of Jo Ann, a second-grader.

Teacher *(going to the door to greet Jo Ann's mother):* Good afternoon, Mrs. Goodwin. Won't you come right in?

Mother: Yes, thank you. *(She stops to look at the bulletin board near the door.)* Oh, now I see what Jo Ann has been talking about the last two weeks.

Teacher: Jo Ann has told you about our flowers and our plans for a trip to the flower show?

Mother: Yes, and is she excited!

Teacher *(pointing to board):* This original poem and the picture of the daffodil are Jo Ann's.

[The conference is off to a good start. The mother has been put at ease by the teacher's friendliness and by the bulletin board display that she has heard so much about. The teacher has also pointed out some of Jo Ann's work. The conference continues.]

Teacher: Jo Ann and I have made a folder of her work. Won't you come over and see it? *(She directs the mother to a table, where both sit down.)* I think you'll find that Jo Ann has made a real effort to improve. She's completing her work—and neatly too.

Mother *(looking through the folder):* Her father will be so happy to see this. He was quite concerned, because Jo Ann's untidiness is a big problem at home, too, as I told you at our last conference. Her father and I tried some of the things we talked about then, and she really seems to be improving. Her room is a lot neater now.

[Jo Ann's indifference to neatness was the big problem discussed at the last conference. The teacher has begun with this point because it was of such concern to the parents. This device has also helped to give Jo Ann's mother a feeling of "on-goingness" from the previous conference.]

Mother: My husband would like to come too, but he can't get away from the office during the day.

Teacher: Perhaps next time we can make an evening appointment so you can both come.

[Parent and teacher continue sharing information.]

Teacher: I wonder if you might help me with another problem. Last week Jo Ann came to me several times in tears. She complained about not feeling well or about some child's bothering her. This isn't at all like Jo Ann. She is usually happy and friendly. Do you know of any reason why she should be crying?

Mother: She has been upset at home too, but I didn't realize it was carrying over into school. Her uncle died two weeks ago, and she. . .

Teacher: Poor thing. No wonder she's upset. I do appreciate your telling me this, Mrs. Goodwin. I think now I can understand Jo Ann's moods.

[Parent and teacher have felt free to discuss a personal problem, which seems to have been the cause of Jo Ann's unusual behavior. This part of the discussion reveals how home problems and behavior often show up in school.]

Teacher: Thank you so much for coming in this afternoon. I'll be looking forward to our next conference. I'm sure we can arrange a time when Jo Ann's father can come too.

Mother: Thank you, I appreciate your interest in Jo Ann. Her father will be pleased with this folder.

Afterward—Understanding

How does Mrs. Goodwin feel after the conference? Let's do a bit of mind reading.

"I hadn't realized Jo Ann was so upset over her uncle's death. I never would have known that it was affecting her work in school.

"I know now why Jo Ann likes school. The room looks so interesting, and her teacher is so friendly.

"The teacher really gives Jo Ann a lot of attention. She went right to that poem and picture of Jo Ann's and she helped her make that nice folder for Ralph and me. Maybe Ralph would like to go to a conference. I never thought about asking him before."

This conference indicates excellent preparation on the part of the teacher. Along with a friendly greeting, the parent finds her child's work displayed on the bulletin board. She also sees a folder that shows the child's progress in solving a problem discussed at the last conference. That helps to give her a feeling of continuity from one conference to the next. Taking the discussion into an area of unusual behavior helped the parent to understand how school and home need to work together.

. . . .

Considerable background and preparation are needed not

only for each individual session but for the entire program of teacher-parent conferences. Launching a program without sufficient knowledge and skill will very likely be unprofitable. Both parents and teachers need a solid understanding of the true meaning of education in a modern school. And here is a good reason why administrators and P.T.A.'s should continue to seek ways of communicating educational principles to the public.

One way of doing this is through public forums at which specialists explain modern educational methods and goals, leading up to an active, vigorous audience discussion at the close of the talks. P.T.A. workshop programs, in which parents and teachers are equally responsible for the success of the enterprise, are another popular means of interpreting the principles of modern education.

Then, too, perhaps the time for some reflective thinking is at hand. Change is all around us. Communities and neighborhoods, as well as life in general, are changing. Possibly we need to look at education in a new light. Do old rules, regulations, and procedures fit into a world where multitudinous forces are shaping a new civilization? For day by day that civilization is becoming an integral part of each child's life.

EDITOR'S NOTE

Parent-school decision-making emerged from this experiment and, along the way, many petty grievances were dismissed.

ORGANIZING FOR HOME-SCHOOL COOPERATION   7

IN A RECENT statement of the American Bishops on Catholic Schools,[1] a major point of emphasis focused on the place of the community in organized Catholic education. The Bishops not only emphasized the necessity for parents to respond positively to the school, but they commended the practice and necessity of the school inviting the community to participate in the decision-making councils of the educational institution.

---

1 Statement on Catholic Schools, National Conference of Catholic Bishops, Washington, D.C., November 16, 1967.

It is apparent that the Bishops have focused upon the immediacy of a serious problem. The inference is clear. The future existence and effectiveness of Catholic schools will depend in good measure, upon the school and community being tied together as never before in the total educative process.

The implementation of the Bishops' charge is by no means a simple task. It demands, however, that each school leader along with his staff begin organizing for effective home-school cooperation which is basic to overcoming, as the Bishops said, many of the trials and troubles of the present moment. Such a concern is a necessary first step toward a new era for Catholic education.

What Is Home-School Cooperation?

The term *home-school cooperation* frequently falls into the category of easily verbalized phrases which meet with everybody's immediate approval. Too little effort is spent analyzing what is meant by such a concept as *home-school cooperation*, and consequently definitive courses of action are seldom realized which might contribute toward the amelioration of problems indigenous to breakdowns and conflicts between home and school. A status quo type situation tends to exist which exemplifies home-school cooperation as:

1. Teachers criticize students and parents as not being cooperative when there are discipline problems or when assigned tasks are left undone.

2. Parental conflicts with the school or school conflicts with the home are frequently assessed as a lack of cooperation.

3. The cooperative parent is often identified as one who stays home, is sometimes seen, but never heard.

4. The cooperative principal and teacher make everybody happy.

In contrast to the above, the meaning of *cooperation* is the association of persons for their common benefit. It is a dynamic social process to achieve common goals. The common benefit and the common goal, in the school business, is the child who, without serious home-school cooperation, is often caught in the middle with parents and school clashing head-on. If home-school cooperation means *doing* whatever we are doing *together* for the benefit of the child, then the assumption is: give and take, mutual understanding, sharing information, an attitude of inclusion in decision-making, and thoughtful reflection, not reflexive emotional behaviors which say, "I'm right, you're wrong."

It is not for the personal satisfaction of the parents or teachers that the Bishops plead for wholesome home-school relationships, but for the personal satisfaction and benefit of the child—quick learner or slow, handsome or plain . . . this child. Every child.

The Experiment

Motivated by the statement of the American Bishops and having to face up to the problems stemming from the usual breakdowns of school-community relationships, a Wisconsin Catholic elementary school principal chose to risk other sets of problems which one has to face when organizing for effective home-school cooperation.

The first task of the principal was to obtain the services of an outside consultant to initiate the planning of a project to strengthen home-school cooperation. After lengthy conferences between the principal and the consultant at which problem areas are identified relative to the teaching staff, the parents, the curriculum, and the clergy, an exploratory meeting was held with approximately three hundred parents to inquire about the implications of the home-school aspects of the Bishops' statement.

Of the many dimensions discussed, emphasis was put upon the theory that home-school cooperation begins in the school, from the principal's office, through the teachers in the classrooms, through the pupil, to the home. When the home knows it is wanted, in the broadest sense, then the cycle is complete and home-school cooperation has a chance of becoming a reality for the benefit of the child. It was also emphasized that the school has the responsibility to provide:

1. adequate opportunity for the community to gain knowledge of what is going on in the school

2. opportunity for the community to question, doubt, and search for better answers in partnership with school personnel

3. opportunity for the community to suggest, evaluate, and decide with school personnel.

At the end of this meeting, the parents and the faculty made a series of significant decisions toward organizing for better home-school cooperation:

1. Procedures should be organized to involve both mothers, fathers, and school faculty in an intensive evaluation of the school, the curriculum, areas of strengths, and areas of weakness.

2. The consultant with the school principal should analyze and synthesize the dimensions in point one.

3. A program of observations, faculty conferences, community curriculum conferences, and evaluations should be decided upon and implemented by the principal and the consultant.

PRELIMINARY PLANNING:

The principal and the consultant met several times in an effort to identify significant problem areas related to the faculty, the clergy, the students, the home, and the curriculum. Because of the need for faculty involvement, an opinion inventory was constructed. The contents of the inventory were drawn from the principal-consultant discussions. From the faculty response to the opinion inventory, priorities were established for staff meetings and parent curriculum conferences. The following is a sample of the content of the inventory:

> *Directions:* In order to enhance the program of home-school cooperation we are asking each faculty member to help us establish priorities relative to various problem areas at_____ School. Please indicate (from high to low priority) your reaction to each of the following areas:

4. The need to examine student responsibility as related to the home and school.

High   Low
1   2   3   4   5

5. The frequent turn-over of administration at_____School.

High   Low
1   2   3   4   5

6. Parents supportive of the faculty vs. causes of non-supportive parents.

High   Low
1   2   3   4   5

7. How to make optimum use of new report card.

High   Low
1   2   3   4   5

8. Homework for learning—what is homework—climate for homework.

High			Low	
1	2	3	4	5

9. What is the real attitude of the faculty toward students and parents?

High			Low	
1	2	3	4	5

11. Fear that school decisions will not be supported by the clergy.

High			Low	
1	2	3	4	5

15. Providing for individual differences when giving tests and grading report cards.

High			Low	
1	2	3	4	5

Program Implementation:

Several days were spent by the consultant in total school and class-room observation. At the end of each day of observation, faculty meetings were held to discuss the visitations in view of the priority areas previously identified by the faculty. The major outcomes of these meetings, faculty suggestions, and decisions were issued in a series of written reports to the staff.

Immediately following the observations and the general faculty meetings, grade-level curriculum conferences, under the leadership of the consultant, were organized for the parents of the school community. Ten separate meetings were held. Three hours were given in both the morning and afternoon for the mothers' grade-level meetings. (Fathers who could attend were invited.) Two evening sessions were reserved for fathers' curriculum meetings, grades one through four, and grades five through eight. Following each set of daytime curriculum conferences, the respective grade-level teachers met with the principal and the consultant to discuss in depth the questions, comments, problems, and suggestions of the parents. A final follow-up faculty meeting provided opportunity to evaluate the total program.

Content of the Program:

The areas covered in the parent meetings included: the reasons for freeing the principal from teaching duties, current thinking underlying the need for lay boards of education, extending opportunity for educational excursions and physical education, the related values of cutting teacher-pupil ratio through the use of teacher aides in primary grades, sex education as a part of the curriculum, homework, yearly grade-level curriculum conferences, report cards based upon ability-achievement, and specific curriculum content areas. In addition to the areas listed above, the parents themselves brought up topics for group discussion. The parents were aware that all of their ideas, suggestions, and even their complaints would be and were discussed with the faculty. As the parent curriculum conferences progressed, it became apparent that criticisms of the school and teachers stemmed from two major sources:

1. Many criticisms and "gripes" were actually several years old, but this was the first opportunity parents had to voice them.

2. A major part of parent criticisms of teachers tended to be sparked by poor teacher judgment about "little things" as:

   a) refusing to accept a paper because of a wrinkle.
   b) students having to copy fifty pages from the encyclopedia by the next day.
   c) telling a child he is dumb.
   d) making children remove heel marks from the floor made through *normal* use.

Upon the completion of the program a final report on the project was mailed to all of the families in the school community. The faculty also received the report and in addition one focusing on an analysis of some clues as to why groups of parents become defensive.

Some Useful Conclusions

A major task of elementary school faculties is to develop problem solving methodologies which help to cope with school-community problems rather than keep the school and community apart as a devisive way of defending against such realities. Practice with the necessary processes related to inter-group relations is a necessary step toward the amelioration of such problems and is but a prelude to the tranquility of order and effective home-school relationships.

The fact that over 350 families were represented at the various curriculum conferences indicated a strong willingness on the part of the parents to strengthen home-school bonds for the benefit of the children. These parents became fully aware of the emerging role of the home in the decision-making process of Catholic elementary education by being active participants rather than passive recipients of "how things shall be done."

The faculty and the principal began to see new roles for themselves once they got beyond the nerve shattering risk of opening the school not only to the intensive observation of an outside consultant but also the invited scrutiny and forthright criticism of the parent.

This experimental program in home-school cooperation by no means solved nor attempted to solve all of the problems as seen by parents and faculty. However, a beginning was made which enabled the school and the community to embark upon a dynamic social process to achieve common goals for the benefit of the children. Plans have been completed to free the principal from a major portion of classroom teaching; materials have been purchased to improve the primary reading curriculum; planning is in progress to involve the use of teacher aides in the primary grades; and techniques for reporting to parents have been implemented to make evaluations meaningful to the home, the pupil, and the school. These were *parent-school* decisions.

Should the school continue in its initial experimental effort, it will come upon new and better ways to sustain and expand the meager gains derived from this first program. The chances of long-term solutions related to home-school co-operation will cease being status quo because the faculty and community will stop talking to themselves—they will be talking and working with each other for the personal satisfaction and benefit of the child. Every child.

REFERENCES

1. From James E. Doherty (Editor). "If You're Thinking About Dropping Report Cards . . . " *School Management.* April 1967. Reprinted by permission of *School Management.*

2. Reprinted by permission from *Changing Times,* the Kiplinger Magazine, (November 1955 issue). Copyright 1955 by The Kiplinger Washington Editors, Inc., 1729 H. Street, N. W., Washington, D.C. 20006.

3. From William C. Kvaraceus. "DANGER Handle With Care! The Report Card Can be a Dangerous Weapon." *NEA Journal* (now *Today's Education*). December 1959. 48:27-28. Reprinted by permission of *Today's Education.*

4. From Orval A. Trail. "Are You Keeping Parents Out of Your Schools?" *School Management.* September 1965. 9:82-3. Reprinted by permission of *School Management.*

5. From R. P. Brimm, "The Weather is B-Minus: Is an 'Average' Mark Enough?" *The Clearing House.* May 1954. 28:534-535. Reprinted by permission of *The Clearing House.*

6. From Mary Harden. "Teacher and Parent Talk it Over." *The PTA Magazine.* (was *National Parent-Teacher*). September 1956. 51:15-32. Reprinted by permission of *The PTA Magazine.*

7. From A. Gray Thompson. "Organizing for Home-School Cooperation." *Catholic School Journal.* September 1968. 68:68-70. Reprinted by permission of *Catholic School Journal.*

How to Get the Most From the Parent- Teacher Interview System

Introduction

The beginner in education sometimes looks for a short cut in schooling. The experienced person is likely to look for a secret weapon. But there is no substitute in developing or improving parent-teacher interviews for work by the student, or for an experienced teacher who is so impressed with the need for upgrading the school report to parents through personalized and individualized conferences that he is willing to pay the price of further study on the subject.

How does one become a good listener? What is meant by "the teacher as a counselor?" How should one report without presenting himself as an authority figure? Does one only report the things a child does well in the initial conference? Are there special approaches to conferring with parents on matters of pupil intelligence? What steps, if any, should one follow in preparing for a teacher-parent interview? All of these questions, and many other significant queries dealing with techniques of interviewing and reporting are presented and answered in the scholarly writings presented in this chapter.

10

LET'S LOOK AT PARENT-TEACHER CONFERENCES   *1*

OUT OF MANY EXPERIMENTS in group dynamics have come techniques for effecting changes in behavior which can be applied to various problems in the field of education. One technique which as been successfully used in the group process is the sociodrama. Through the dramatization of a problem situation the attention of the group is focused upon strengths and weaknesses in the performance. Out of the subsequent analysis comes practical help for all those who are participating in the group process.

Studying Parent-Teacher
Conferences Through Sociodrama

There is general agreement in educational circles that parent-teacher conferences are a very desirable means of furthering effective work with children in school. It has also been recognized that the area of parent relations is probably the most difficult one in which teachers have to deal and may very well be the area in which their performance is most inadequate.

While various reasons have been pointed out for teacher difficulty in this field, one of the most important may be that this is an area in which teachers have not been trained to work. Teachers, for the most part, have been taught to deal with children, not with adults. Although they have been told that conducting parent-teacher conferences is one of the activities in which they ought to engage, too often they are not helped to do a good job with these conferences. Even when some training in conferencing with parents has been given, one might question the effectiveness of a training which pretty largely relies upon the method of exposition. How the sociodrama became a means for clearer insights into problems of dealing with parents is illustrated in this account of one activity in a graduate course in education.

After a preliminary discussion of some of the psychological factors underlying parent-teacher conferences, the class agreed to try some role playing. A brief description of a boy who was to be the subject of the conference was presented to the group:

> Henry is a fifteen-year-old high school student with an
> IQ of 130. He is a tall, extremely thin, flat-chested, and
> sunken-cheeked boy with protruding teeth and receding

jaw. He has had many illnesses and must wear glasses.

This boy is always sloppy in appearance, seldom looks clean, and hardly ever has his hair combed. He often loiters listlessly in the school halls and he always looks fatigued and lacking in energy. In the classroom his attitude is one of languid indifference. He sits on the end of his spine, slouched down in his seat with his legs up or stretched out in front of him. His meager contributions to class discussion are made in a drawling monotone, except on the infrequent occasions when he becomes argumentative. When he does feel contentious his voice has a distinctly whining quality. In his attitude to school regulations he sometimes plays the role of indifferent or high-handed objector. Sometimes he is sullen, uncooperative, and intent upon "getting away" with as much as possible. He does not go out with girls, and in school appears indifferent to them.

One summer he thought he'd like a job and he asked his father to get him employment. When the father explained that he could not use his own position to help his son procure a job but urged the boy to find one on his own initiative, Henry refused on the ground that he knew he couldn't.

As for his classroom accomplishment, teachers note unevenness in quality and quantity of work, poor study habits, failure to meet requirements for written work, short span of interest, disinclination to accept responsibility to carry on work independently, an attitude of rebellion, inattentiveness and passivity, interspersed with occasional energy and co-operativeness. Only in athletics does he seem consistently interested; in spite of the handicap of a far from robust physique, he has attained proficiency in several sports. But although his skill is recognized by his peers, he is in no sense a leader in athletic activities.[1]

Following the description of Henry, one member of the class was selected to play the part of the teacher and another to play the part of Henry's mother. A wire recorder was set up to record the conference, and the scene opened with the parent at the door ready to come into the classroom. Following the conference the class attempted to clarify the role of the teacher in a parent-teacher conference. Several possible roles were described:

The teacher as sympathetic listener.

Some teachers use the conference to find out more about a particular child. When this is the teacher's purpose she asks

1 Adapted from Zachry, Caroline B., and Lighty, Margaret, *Emotion and Conduct in Adolescence*. New York: D. Appleton-Century Co., 1940.

a few leading questions about the child to encourage the parent to talk and makes sympathetic comments from time to time. She may end the conference with a few words of advice.

The teacher as imparter of information.

In some school systems the conference is replacing the report card as a means of communicating to parents a child's progress in school. The teacher will use records and samples of a pupil's work in reporting progress in school subjects as well as general adjustment.

The teacher as the omniscient one.

The purpose of this conference is to give advice to the parent. It is assumed that the teacher knows the pupil, knows the total situation, and knows what is best for both parent and child.

The teacher as counselor.

Here the conference is designed to help the parent, through discussion, develop insight into the causes of her child's behavior. As a result of such insight parent and teacher will work out a cooperative plan for bringing about a change in behavior.

Analyzing the Conference

With these roles in mind the students turned to an analysis of the conference with a view toward identifying teacher roles. Students recognized that the particular role the teacher played helped to evoke a particular response from the parent. A very important part of the analysis was to watch for such cause and effect relationships. A play-back on the wire recorder facilitated such an analysis. A verbatim account of the conference with comments from the class discussion is presented below.

Teacher: Good afternoon, Mrs. Smith. Do come in.
Parent: Good afternoon, How are you?
Teacher: Have a chair, Mrs. Smith. Wouldn't you like to take off your coat and make yourself more comfortable?
Parent: Thank you. I guess you sent for me because we've got quite a problem in Henry. Isn't that right?
Teacher: I'm afraid you are right, Mrs. Smith. Henry isn't doing well in any of his school subjects. In fact, the only thing he is doing well in at all is sports—the coach reports he is pretty good in some of those. I've been wondering how many clubs he belongs to. Does he belong to many outside organizations?

(Teacher begins with a negative report on Henry and immediately assumes the initiative for the direction of the conference by a question. The question is misleading because it might imply that if Henry does belong to many clubs he may be spending time on them which he should be devoting to school work.)

> Parent: Well, as a matter of fact he doesn't belong to any outside organizations. His academic work hasn't been good and we've sort of discouraged him; and he hasn't really been interested in joining up with any organizations or doing anything outside of school other than sports.

(Parent speaks confidently. She assumes she has a reason for keeping Henry out of clubs which will be accepted by the teacher.)

> Teacher: I think I can speak freely with you, Mrs. Smith, and tell you Henry's IQ is a good deal above average. Now it may be that because he is bright some of his classes aren't tough enough for him. It may be that if he were with a faster group of students he would be more challenged. Perhaps he is bored with some of his work.

(The teacher's role is now made very apparent. He is the omniscient one who will tell the parent possible reasons for Henry's behavior. Because of his own lack of knowledge, he is ready to jump to superficial explanations of behavior.)

> Teacher: I think there is something else, too, and that is if Henry becomes good enough in basketball so that he makes the team and then finds that he can't play because of his academic record, that may work as an incentive to get him to study more.

(Encourage students to make the team in order to give teacher a club which he can wield to get them to study. This is peculiar motivation to be advocating.)

> Parent: Yes, it may work out that way.

(Parent is not too enthusiastic about the teacher's plan. In fact, she has already been put on the receiving end in this conference.)

> Teacher: I think he should be encouraged to enter into some outside activities. He needs to become more social minded and I think if he were encouraged to join some organizations that that might help him. If I remember correctly from reading Henry's record he was sick a good deal as a child and it may be for that reason that you didn't

encourage him to mix with other children as much as he might have, and it may be that you favored him for fear of what might happen if you didn't.

(Teacher continues in his role of the omniscient one. He has gone into the conference with a preconceived idea of what is best for Henry and now reveals his plan. Again he advances a theory to explain Henry's behavior, for which there is little evidence. His explanation implies a criticism of the mother.)

Parent: There is another side problem and that is that Henry's father is a bit of a problem. He has never been a very encouraging kind of person and he has tended to put a damper on some of the things Henry has tried to do. Our ideas about the bringing up of Henry differ a good deal.

(Mother responds to the criticism by making the father a scapegoat. She can now effectively refute the teacher's suggestions without exposing herself to criticism.)

Teacher: It looks as if some of the missionary work will have to start at home with Henry's father, doesn't it?
Parent: That's a hard thing to do, you know.

(Mother is safe now. She can make father out to be a pretty tough customer.)

Teacher: Have you ever thought about a boy's camp? You're financially able to afford it and I should think it would be a good thing for Henry.

(Teacher is unable to get around the obstacle of the father so offers another plan.)

Parent: Well, there again I run into difficulty. Now I approve of camps for boys as the kind of thing I'd like to see Henry do, but his father has different ideas on the subject and every time it has come up he has put his foot down and said he didn't think that was the kind of thing we should spend money on. He thinks Henry needs more work, not more play.

(Mother has found an excellent alibi and continues to use father for all he's worth.)
(Teacher is puzzled. He can't figure out how to get rid of father. Meanwhile he asks a question.)

Teacher: What kind of work?
Parent: Well, there's quite a bit of asparagus grown around these parts and Henry's father thinks that he might get a job picking asparagus in the Spring, or he might get odd jobs of other kinds as they happen to turn up. But that

kind of thing doesn't seem to appeal to Henry and he hasn't wanted to do it. Now when there's a party or any entertaining going on he seems ready for that and that bothers his father a good deal.

(Parent lets the teacher know Henry is social under certain conditions and that his parents have a plan for Henry. Parent now has the upper hand in the conference.)

Teacher: Now, on the contrary, in school he is not social minded. He doesn't enter into any of the activities or social affairs and it was for that reason that I suggested the camp as one way of getting him into some of these things. After all, a boy can't pick asparagus forever.

(Now the teacher is on the defensive. He lets the parent know she's wrong about Henry's social adjustment. He ridicules the parent's plan for Henry.)

Parent: Well, of course we have higher ideals for him, too, but one of the difficulties is trying to realize them. Now I think what Henry needs right now is a chance to talk over his problems with someone, preferably a man, because it's hard for a boy as he gets older to confide in his mother. Of course, his father would be the logical one, but it seems as if there's a gap between Henry and his father. That's a real problem and it's one that I don't know how to handle. The other day I did ask Henry just casually which men that he knew he particularly liked and which ones he felt he was close enough to to talk things over with, and he did mention a few.

(Parent is reluctant to relinquish the reins. She continues in a dominant role in the conference by making another suggestion for Henry.)

Teacher: Who were these men? What kind of things do they do?

(Teacher is curious. Will he be one of the men Henry can confide in?)

Parent: Well, one of them runs a grocery near us. He's one whom Henry admires a great deal.
Teacher: Well, why don't you satisfy both Henry and his father by seeing that Henry gets a job in the store? Wouldn't that be a good thing to do? Wouldn't that be a happy solution for this whole thing? Henry's father would fall in line with that, wouldn't he? Henry could work there after school evenings and on Saturday.

(Teacher falls in line with the mother's ideas and makes a proposal in keeping with them.)

Parent: Well, yes, I suppose that would work. What would be your suggestion, that I contact this grocer to see about getting Henry a job?

(Parent is ready to act on the teacher's suggestion when it is in line with her own thinking.)

Teacher: Well, yes, I should think that that would be the thing to do. I'd talk it over with the boy's father first and then I'd contact this grocer to see what could be worked out. But then I think, too, we ought to see if we can't get Henry into some of the school clubs. What are his hobbies? What are some of the things he's interested in?

(Teacher comes back to original theme. But will Henry's difficulties be solved by mere joining of clubs?)

Parent: He seems to like machinery and he likes to tinker with things.
Teacher: He's interested in machinery, is he? Yet he isn't taking any of the machine shop courses—probably because his IQ is high and so he has been steered into the academic courses, which he dislikes. I don't know why he dislikes them but he seems to. It may be that they aren't tough enough for him. It may be that we could work him in with a faster group to provide more competition for him, but meanwhile let's see if we can't get him into some of these clubs and interested in some of the social activities.

(Is Henry's IQ really high enough to justify this theory?)

Parent: I guess the next step for me is to go ahead and contact the grocer and see if I can get Henry a job there.
Teacher: Yes, I think that's the best thing to do. Meanwhile we'll watch his progress and see what happens.
Parent: Yes, I feel that something has just got to happen so we can get Henry steered in the right direction. Well, thank you for all your help, and it's been so nice to have this chance to talk with you.
Teacher: Thank you for coming, Mrs. Smith, and I'm sure this will get Henry started in the right direction.

(Will it? Will Henry's apparent sense of inadequacy really be helped by getting a job? What if he falls down on the job? Parent has not been helped to think through the problems so that she has any real appreciation of Henry's needs. Emphasis has been placed on doing things to Henry—getting him into clubs and jobs—and Henry may fail in both because there has been no basic change in his feeling about himself.)

Pointing Up the Generalizations

A summary of the points brought out in the analysis of

the conference was attempted, and the following generalizations agreed upon:

The role the teacher plays in the conference bears a direct relationship to the personality pattern of the teacher. A dominant personality may overpower the parent with suggestions and advice to the point where the parent may temporarily acquiesce. An aggressive personality may be openly critical and attack the parent for her methods of child rearing. The sociodrama may enable the teacher to gain insight into the typical role he plays in a conference, to see what effect such a role has on the parent, and to bring about a change of role.

The role the teacher adopts helps to determine the response of the parent. The role of critic may bring about a defensive attitude on the part of the parent. If the criticism continues long enough, the parent may seek a scapegoat in the form of the other parent or a grandmother to whom the blame for the child's behavior can be shifted. The role of adviser may find the parent searching about for excuses as to why the advice won't work. "I tried that but it didn't work out for this reason . . . "typically prefaces such excuses. Then the teacher is put on the defensive, points out to the parent she really hasn't tried the teacher's solution because she got off the track at a particular point. Eventually the parent may end up by accepting a piece of advice which may or may not be followed and which may or may not be effective.

Attempting to shift roles in the course of the conference may be difficult to do. If the teacher starts out as the omniscient one, telling the parent the answers, she may establish such a relationship that when she later tries to establish an attitude of working together to solve a problem she will be unsuccessful.

Teachers need to know more about child behavior and development before they can counsel effectively. All too frequently the advice given to parents has been grounded in faulty notions of child psychology, and teachers have been ineffective in helping parents achieve insight because they are lacking in insight themselves.

PARENT-TEACHER CONFERENCES   *2*

Many teachers and school administrators have been laboring under the absurd assumption that the sole purpose of the regularly scheduled parent-teacher conferences is to report. If the parent-teacher interview is to have any meaning whatsoever, the primary purpose of such a meeting must become the obtaining of information. This stress is particularly important when the teacher is dealing with parents of children who are experiencing difficulty is school.

Many teachers as well as administrators are somewhat confused themselves as to the proper organization of a meeting with parents, and possess little skill in using proven interview techniques that effectively produce both information and a positive attitude on the part of parents.

First and most important, teachers engaged in conferences with parents must stop talking so much and learn how to listen. Many parents have questions concerning new teaching techniques, their child's relationships with other children, the reason for his poor grade in arithmetic, or his lack of or overabundance of homework. Listening can be a painful process and may take a terrific amount of self control. However, the teacher or the principal who grits his teeth halfway through a parent's comments and spends the remainder of the time formulating answers has already lost the battle.

It must be kept in mind that when one listens to parental complaints, the listener not only learns of parental attitudes toward the school but also gains respect for being a sympathetic and understanding human being. As basic as this first rule is, it is surprising that so few people are able to follow it.

Listening is not the only key to a successful interview. Reflection is an integral part. Reflection means to put into different words what the parents have said. Not every word, but key phrases, unspoken feelings, and half-understood statements. Reflection will indicate to the parents that you are paying attention and are trying to understand what they have to say. It may often function to head off a misunderstanding and may make it unnecessary to ask for clarification after parents have had their say.

Observation is also an important interview technique. Communication involves much more than conversation. The teacher should be able to determine whether the parents see their child's failure as a blow to their social standing, whether they consider it something they are directly responsible for, or whether they do not appear to be the least bit concerned. Dress and manner of speech will give an estimate of the probable socio-economic level of parents and will help the teacher or principal to determine what suggestions and level of conversation should be used. Certainly it would be a mistake for the faculty member to suggest referral to a private tutor when it is apparent from observation that parents may be in difficult financial straits. It may also be determined whether parents are likely to benefit from written materials such as pamphlets or bulletins. Too often, such materials are distributed indiscriminately to persons who border on illiteracy.

When parents have had their chance to speak, the teacher must direct his or her questions and conversation toward obtaining additional information. Standard questions which will draw yes and no answers should be avoided. For instance, if the teacher feels a particular child is not studying enough at home and asks the question, "Does Johnnie have a set time to study?" the typical answer will almost always be an emphatic "yes." The parent knows this is the correct answer and will try to report what he believes the teacher wants to hear.

One technique which is useful in circumventing this pitfall is to ask parents to relate a typical evening in their home from the time he goes to bed. A great deal of information concerning family dynamics as well as study habits can be learned in this way. It is also useful to listen to the adjectives each parent uses to describe the child. An overprotective mother or an exceptionally strict father can often be picked out in this manner. Such information is invaluable in working with a child and his problems in school.

Information obtained through listening, observation, and questioning should then be used to counsel parents on their child's problems.

Try to indicate areas of strength first. It helps to start with a positive picture. Gradually move into the problem areas, actively seeking parental cooperation. Observation is still important at this time. If negative reactions are detected, it is the teacher's responsibility to question them. By avoiding the unpleasant, satisfactory solutions are never reached.

Finally, the interview should be closed by having the

parents summarize what has occurred during the session. Such action places responsibility on the parents and promotes future communications. If the faculty member has demonstrated a genuine interest in the course of the interview, the parents should be most willing to engage in future discussions.

THE PRESCHOOL AND KINDERGARTEN LEVELS   3

Under the surface of parent-teacher relationships

Preschool teachers have opportunities to get to know the parents of the children in their classes in many different contexts. They may meet at parent-teacher meetings, in conferences (scheduled and impromptu), perhaps at home visits; in cooperative schools they may meet when the parents work at the school. In addition, preschool teachers see some parents at the beginning and end of each school day, simply because preschoolers are too young to take themselves to and from the school.

The frequency of these contacts requires that preschool teachers have much more skill in working with parents than is demanded of teachers in elementary school.

Some preschool teachers welcome all opportunities to see parents. Others find them a burden. Regardless of your preference the nature of your job demands that you meet parents rather regularly.

Most teachers would like to learn how to improve the quality of these relationships. Perhaps some of the ideas discussed here will help you find ways to make your contacts with the parents more fruitful for you, for the parents, and for the children for whom you both care.

Opening pathways to the future

The preschool teacher's work with parents may mean a lot to the families concerned. She is the child's first teacher, and she has a special nursery-school point of view.

Family-school relationships established in preschool may set the pattern for the kind and quality of such relationships in the future. Parents who feel welcome in preschool are likely to expect a warm welcome when they go to school in later years. If they get used to talking informally with the teacher about the child and his growth they are likely to try to continue this kind of easy exchange as the child matures.

A far wider range of attributes in children is valued by

the preschool teacher than by the elementary school teacher, who must focus more closely on academic skills. Each child is considered in depth—motor skills with large and small muscles; social skills as leader, follower, good mixer, and team member; artistic and other creative and performing abilities; intelligence, judgment.

By pointing out strengths of many kinds, preschool teachers can help families to appreciate a wide spectrum of values in their children—values which parents may never see on the elementary school's report-card evaluation.

Frustrations in working with parents

Some preschool teachers find work with parents easy and satisfying. They have been taught to work closely with mothers and they enjoy doing it. Many others find, however, that parent work is a discouraging part of the job and much harder for them than working with the children. Some reasons for this chronic dissatisfaction are worth exploring.

Preschool teachers would like to understand why mothers ask teachers to solve in two minutes some problem the family has been worrying about for two years. Why do parents demand for their own concerns time during the school day that teachers want and need for teaching children? More important, what currents of feeling beneath the surface of the relationship between parent and teacher act to disturb the rapport between them?

One answer to the last question is that the qualities which made us elect to work with small children are the very ones that make us feel ill at ease with adults. We may not care to admit it, but the special strength of many nursery-school teachers lies in their enjoyment of preschoolers. They should not expect that work with adults will be as satisfying.

Some of the negative undercurrents in parent-teacher relationships come from feelings most of us have about authority. We normally respond to those in authority in various ways, mixing hostility and submissiveness, the anxiety to please, awe, respect, and perhaps fear.

Parents and teachers tend to see each other as authority figures. Mothers bring with them from childhood the feeling that teachers are authorities. Teachers bring with them from childhood the feeling that mothers are authorities. These feelings distort the way each sees the other, so that they do not respond to each other in a truly personal way. They simply put the other person into the package where they keep their feelings about all people in authority.

The complexities of the parent-teacher relationships are intensified by the fact that many parents and teachers feel ambivalent about being cast in an authority role. They may enjoy the prestige it entails, but do not want to cope with the negative feelings that generally are directed toward those in authority.

Some of these distortions disappear as parents and teachers get to know each other personally, but the undertones may continue for a long time in their not quite conscious feelings. Recognizing them may lessen their force.

Teachers at every grade level are in a position to evaluate the children under their care, to form opinions about their abilities, to note areas where changes might be helpful, to judge each child as a whole. Parents are likely to feel that they themselves are being evaluated when a teacher evaluates their child. Most have mixed feelings about this evaluation. They really want to know "how they are doing" as parents, how their child stacks up against other children. But, knowing their child's shortcomings, they may also fear that the teacher will think their boy or girl does not measure up.

The nursery-school teacher is quite likely to be the *first* person (except perhaps the doctor) who does this kind of evaluating of a child. Parents, therefore, are likely to approach you with a mixture of hopes and fears that you sense carries a great deal of feeling.

If parents are ambivalent about being evaluated, teachers are ambivalent about doing this evaluating, perhaps because they sense how much weight will be attached to what they say.

The parent-teacher relationship in nursery school has many facets. Some are easy to see and comfortable to accept. Others can be puzzling and disturbing. You may be reassured to know many people in the profession of nursery education share ambivalent and negative feelings toward parents with whom they work.

As you think about the ideas suggested here perhaps you will be moved to explore some of the undercurrents of your own feeling in these areas. Your insights may help you to become more comfortable and more effective in your relations with parents.

GETTING THE MOST FROM   *4*
PARENT-TEACHER CONFERENCES

Traditional Reports—The Triple Threat

Through the years countless stories, jokes, and cartoons have circulated about what Father did when he saw Johnny's report card and what Johnny did to soften the blow—both to and from Father.

Many of these stories are amusing but underlying their humor is another, and a very disturbing, note. It is the tensions, the fears, the undesirable attitudes which were generated by report cards. These tensions were shared by children, parents and teachers.

The teacher had the problem of deciding what she meant by a grade or score. For example, did an A (Excellent) denote the amount known at a given time of the school year, or the amount learned during a given period of time? Did it refer to the quantity or quality of learning or to both? Did it take into account the child's ability to learn? Was his learning evaluated by comparison to what others in his group did or against a rigid standard? Did it indicate the extent to which the child could utilize his knowledge contructively or creatively? Next, she had to decide what grade to assign to each child in each area of the curriculum. This entailed the ability to justify or substantiate her decision. This may sound relatively easy until one thinks about assigning such a letter grade to the work of a first grade child in an area such as art or music or social studies!

Once she had resolved all these problems and sent the card home in Johnny's care, the parent was faced with the impossible task of accepting and interpreting her evaluation of his child without knowledge of how or why it was derived. His proper concern for his child frequently led to harmful reactions. Children were unduly praised or undeservedly punished. The bright child who received top marks for little effort in terms of what he was capable of doing often became dangerously over-confident because he was praised for "all A's". This competitive marking gave no indication of what the slow child could reasonably achieve and little or no credit for what he had accomplished. It gave no indication of what the lazy, bright child could do nor did it serve to disclose the nature or source of his lack of achievement. Such reports gave no certain guide for the parents in helping their child improve.

In the meantime, Johnny was caught in the middle, facing with anxiety the fateful Report Card Day. He would go home filled with pride, or disappointment, or shame. The teacher had become a judge instead of a guide, and the acquistion of marks had become the primary goal. Learning was no longer an exciting adventure.

Growth of the Parent Conference

In an effort to prevent this recurrent crisis and to provide a basis for more effective teaching and learning, many schools are turning to Parent-Teacher Conferences instead of relying solely upon the traditional written reports. The conference provides for two way communication between the parents and the school. It permits individualized reporting without threat to the individuals involved, particularly the child.

What Parents Can Contribute

The purpose of any report to parents should be to furnish the information which is necessary to their proper guidance of their child. The schools cannot truly fulfill this obligation without the help and cooperation of the parents.

Real learning involves more than the acquisition of marks, or even, the acquistion of facts. It involves growth that results in a change in the behavior of the individual. If this growth is to result in desirable changes of behavior the teacher must be able to provide the opportunity for him to discover and explore new and better meanings, to experiment, accept or reject new and better modes of behavior. Parents may be of inestimable help to the teacher in her striving to develop this sensitivity to their child's needs.

By the time the child is half way through the third grade, the school will have had contact with him as a member of a group for approximately four thousand hours. The third grade teacher will have had the opportunity to know him some seven hundred hours. The parents will have had the closest association with him for over sixty thousand hours. While these figures do not indicate the parent's ability to observe accurately and to interpret their observations free of emotional involvement, they do emphasize the importance of the home on the child's behavior and attitudes and the parent's responsibility in helping the teacher understand the child.

The parents may contribute much valuable information

about a child's interests, his attitudes towards himself and others, his health, his friendships, and associations in the home and neighborhood, his daily life. If the teacher knows that eight year old Jimmy shares a room with twin brothers four years younger, it will help her understand why he guards his possessions so closely and refuses to lend them to his neighbor because "They will be broken." She will be able to deal more sympathetically with Susan's untidyness if she knows that she comes from a home which lacks running water and where cleanliness is not a matter of much concern. Or, six year old Jack's loud voice may assume a different significance when the teacher learns that a grandparent who shares the home is quite deaf. The more the teacher knows about the home, the parents, and their attitude toward the child, the better she will understand how the child thinks and feels and reacts, and the better teacher she will be to him.

What the Teacher Can Contribute

Such conferences provide an opportunity for the teacher to explain in some detail the child's achievement in all academic areas. She is not restricted to deciding that he has earned a C in reading. She can describe his progress in terms of specific skills and understandings which he has acquired or failed to acquire. She can discuss possible reasons for success or failure. She can outline, for the parents, the goals which the school has for their child and she can evaluate his progress in terms of those goals.

Other school personnel, the physical education teacher, the music teacher, the school nurse, may be included in the discussion when there are talents and skills or special problems for which their evaluation or advice is needed.

The individual conference provides the opportunity for the teacher to discuss all phases of the child's development, social and emotional, as well as intellectual, to help the parent understand the interrelatedness of all aspects of their child's growth.

Joint Responsibility of Teachers and Parents

It provides the chance for the parents and teacher to explore together the possible causes of difficulty or of behavior which is detrimental to the child's greatest welfare. They can give their undivided attention to the child, his abilities, his needs, his problems and strengths. They can make realistic plans for helping him make the maximum use of his interests and abilities and they can formulate possible ways of helping him alter or eliminate immature or undesirable attitudes and behavior.

The conference provides an opportunity for the parents to ask questions about the school's program, the actual classroom procedures employed in teaching arithmetic, spelling, or art. If they do not understand the teacher's evaluation of their child's progress or behavior, if she uses terms whose meanings are vague or unfamiliar to them, the conference allows an opportunity for these things to be discussed and clarified.

The Child's Attitude

Not the least of the values of the parent conference is the sense of well-being that it can foster in the child. The knowledge that the adults, parents and teacher, in his life enjoy a harmonious, cooperative association, lends a sense of security which is most desirable. The greater understanding of his personality and needs, of the reasons for his success or failure, and the resulting consistency of approach to his problems at school and at home creates a healthier, less emotional reaction to reporting.

The child will often participate in a part of the conference. While the extent of the child's participation will depend largely upon his age and maturity, it is often enlightening to the parents and teacher to know how he thinks and feels about his progress, what he believes would be helpful to him in his efforts to improve. The opportunity to express his views and to set goals for himself which are both realistic and understood can be a source of satisfaction and great motivation.

Opportunity or Ordeal

As with any change involving long established custom, this change to the conference form of reporting pupil-progress encounters some obstacles.

Too often in the past parents were requested to come to the school only when a serious problem or infraction of the rules was encountered. So that, now, many parents approach their first conference with their child's teacher defensively, expecting only complaint and adverse criticism.

Or, because it is a new experience, they do not know what to expect and, so, come to it unprepared to extract from it the maximum benefits to themselves or their child.

How, then, can they approach this meeting for the first or the fifteenth time so that it may be most satisfying and productive? The following observations and suggestions are ones which teachers who have worked with many parents in such conferences have found beneficial.

Anticipate a Pleasant Experience

1. The sole purpose of the conference is to provide an opportunity for the parents and teacher to talk in an informal and friendly atmosphere about the child, to share information about his physical, social, emotional, and intellectual development and to plan as wisely as they are able for his future growth.

The teacher will be eager to share all the fine and commendable things she knows about your child. She will discuss problems involving academic achievement or undesirable conduct only in an effort to find ways to help your child overcome his failures or correct his mistakes.

Keep an "Objective" Viewpoint

2. While it is always difficult, and often impossible, for a parent to be completely objective about the child he loves, the extent to which he is able to do so often determines the success he will have in understanding his child and accepting his own role in helping him. The mother who has recognized that her own concern for neatness and cleanliness, the result perhaps of her training as a nurse, might be the source of her child's refusal to fingerpaint or engage in any activity which she considered "messy", is well on her way to helping her child overcome her difficulties.

The brilliant and overworked father who saw his own reflection in the tired and distraught teacher's description of his son as impatient, argumentative, demanding of attention but thoughtless of the feelings or interests of others, might have gone away angry and resentful of the teacher's judgment of his son. Instead he questioned her closely about the boy's actions and discussed with her changes he might seek to make in his own behavior toward the boy. Not only did that boy make enormous progress toward becoming a kind, considerate, and likable person but the father reported the development of a new and happier relationship with his son.

Have Confidence in the Teacher

3. The teacher is a member of a profession which is

closely involved with people. Because of this she hears many things which are simply none of her business. One of the first things she must learn to do is to reject from her mind everything which is not pertinent to working more effectively with her students. That information which is pertinent she will treat with the respect and privacy due any confidence given into her trust.

For this reason you should feel free to discuss with her any problem which you feel may affect the child, to express your feelings freely. Her questions are not intended as intrusions into your home and life but as seeking information which will help her understand and work successfully with your child. Whatever she learns will be used only to that end.

Be Curious

4. Do not hesitate to ask questions about anything which puzzles or is of concern to you. Many times sources of conflict or discomfort for a child will be revealed to a teacher only because a parent asks a question.

While many questions may arise during the conversation, it is wise to give some thought beforehand to what you, as a parent, wish to know. You may even want to make a list so that nothing important to you will be forgotten.

There have been many changes in the methods and techniques employed by teachers since most of today's parents were pupils in the elementary school. Many criticisms of schools which are heard today are largely the result of the adult's lack of knowledge or understanding of just what is being done and why. Your child's teacher will welcome the opportunity to explain, to answer your questions. If, sometimes, her answers seem too brief or as vague as your doctor's when you ask why he recommends a certain course of treatment, she is not trying to evade answering. She is just having trouble finding the most adequate way to transmit to you in a thirty minute conference, the knowledge and skills she has spent years acquiring. So be patient with her and keep asking!

5. The teacher will have samples of your child's work available. These samples have been selected because they are representative of his overall performance. They should serve to illustrate many points she is trying to convey to you, so look at them carefully. They can tell you much about your child.

Share Your Own Ideas

6. When the time comes to make plans for the future guidance of your child, the teacher will have suggestions as to how she thinks you might help Jane overcome her shyness, or Bobby extend his interest in paleontology, or Jack develop a greater interest in reading. She will be equally eager to hear how you think you can help him. Don't be afraid to offer your own ideas. They are probably excellent and you may have skills or access to materials or equipment of which she has no knowledge. If, for some reason, she feels your suggestions might not be in the best interests of your child, she will try to explain why.

7. Parents often are uncertain about what to tell their child concerning the conference. The teacher may make some recommendation about this. If she doesn't, ask her for one.

Parents are justified in asking, "How is my child doing in school?" But they have the right to know much more than that. They have the right to know why he is doing well or poorly, what they can reasonably expect of him and how they can guide him in developing his potential. They have the right to learn these things in a manner and setting which is not emotionally charged. They, also, have the right to contribute to the teacher's understanding of their child and to share with her the responsibility of working out an effective and realistic program for the child at school and at home in terms of his abilities and his needs.

It is therefore assumed that it will be necessary to utilize every possible agency in meeting the ever increasing need for better education.

PARENT CONFERENCES SUPPLEMENT TEACHING   5

Three decades ago the report card was the primary method used by a teacher for parental relationships. Personal visits were utilized only when serious problems existed.

The situation today is different. It is generally accepted that report cards provide little meaningful information about the pupil. In fact, report cards often obscure the need for personal communication. "Contact before a crisis" is now recognized as important. It is easier to prepare than to repair.

Current philosophy views parents as partners in the educative process. Parents begin the teaching function five years before the child enters school. Parental responsibility continues after the child terminates teacher relationships.

Values and Goals in Conferences

Conference time is an investment rather than an expenditure. By investing time with parents, the teacher is more likely to receive parental support and understanding which will enhance pupil achievement. Teacher success depends upon home cooperation, and teaching goals are more attainable when shared with concerned and cooperative parents.

The parent-teacher conference offers an opportunity to compare ideas on the direction and progress of a child's capacities, interests, and adjustment. This relationship will help each understand the other's viewpoint.

The conference helps a teacher become more aware of the child's home environment and developing personality— even if the parent presents a biased picture of the home situation, for the teacher can learn what the parent would like to be true. While a parent conference will not resolve a disturbed family situation, it may begin to improve communication between home and school.

A parent conference is the teacher's opportunity to learn about the child's reaction to school, family adjustment, leisure-time activities, health history, and home responsibilities. By knowing the stresses and the positive experiences a child has encountered, the teacher can more effectively structure instructional material to individual needs and readiness. The conference offers an opportunity to learn about parental attitudes and concerns which affect child behavior.

Likewise, it is important that parents get to know the teacher as a human being and not see her as an institutional fixture. The manner in which parents discuss their child's teacher at home is important in developing a healthy attitude toward school and learning.

Conference time provides an opportunity for the teacher to funnel parental energy into constructive educational avenues for children. The teacher can stress the importance of parental involvement and interest to promote pupil learning, and can help parents see the values in playing educational games, going on educational trips, or sharing educational television programs. Parents ordinarily want the best for their child. It becomes the teacher's responsibility to help parents know what careful research has found to be best.

Another important conference goal is to help parents

understand that they alone can provide space and time for effective home study. Their role also includes the provision of adequate materials not supplied by the school.

Conference goals include answering questions and concerns pertaining to curriculum, grading, teaching materials, grouping, class projects, field trips, and school rules.

The most meaningful conference goal is that of enhancing the relationship between parents and children.

Understanding Parental Feelings

The teacher who recognizes parental feelings about coming for a conference has an advantage. Since most parents have memories of being pupils, they possess ideas and attitudes about teachers. Hence, the teacher may be a depository for a parent's unresolved early problems. It is important that the teacher accept these feelings without becoming defensive. The teacher must realize that her age, experience, and marital status will sometimes affect a parent's approach to a situation.

Parents may feel strained or anxious in a conference. They come for a report on their success as parents, always fearful that the results will not conform to the desired ideal. The teacher should realize that some parents have difficulty sharing their child with a "competitor," especially in the lower grades.

Some parents expect the teacher to succeed in every aspect of child behavior, in spite of their own difficulty in training their children for adequate self-control. In discussing the performance of a child, it is well to remember that parents are not completely objective about their own child. Parents look to the teacher as one who understands child behavior and can help them know when a degree of deviation should be a concern. Most parents are eager to cooperate because they have much at stake.

Preparing for the Conference

Just as successful teaching must, an effective conference must be planned. Selecting a time and place to avoid interruptions and to ensure a relaxed atmosphere is important. In the telephone call or personal note asking for the conference, the teacher should define the purpose. This may be simply stated "so that I may learn about your child," "to share progress," "to renew our association," "to share common concerns," or "to answer your questions." The purpose "to satisfy our school policy" is not appropriate. Sharing the anticipated conference length is helpful.

It is important for the teacher to plan with parents, not for parents. Parents are helped most when they are involved and when their role to make decisions is respected.

The teacher must determine significant information for dissemination. Sometimes a check-list is helpful—including such areas as work habits, peer relationships, performance levels, and emotional development. A flexible approach is needed as the teacher can not anticipate all items to be covered. The teacher must be aware of information in the cumulative folder assembled by prior teachers. Skill in the proper interpretation of standardized test results is essential.

Sometimes the teacher may wish to post samples of classroom performance so parents may see their child's work in relation to that of the whole class. In other situations it may be best to maintain a file on the child's performance, showing changes that have taken place.

Teachers should tell their pupils why parent conferences are important. Pupils benefit when they realize that the adults who influence their lives are united. A few private words after the conference contribute to the pupil's status.

Conducting the Conference

Rapport should be established at the opening of the conference, before plunging into the planned agenda. This may be an expression of appreciation for the parent's attendance, such as "I'm pleased with your interest in Jimmy's education." It is also helpful to give parents a feeling of pride in their child. A positive beginning will make a lasting impression. A friendly cooperative tone helps reduce parental defenses. The teacher's pre-determined attitudes must be minimized. Parents remember what teachers feel more than what they say.

There are factors which will have a negative effect on even the best-planned conference. If the teacher appears to be rushed, parents will feel uncomfortable. While teachers have status to parents, this is most effective when minimized. Sitting around a table helps the teacher appear less authoritarian.

If there are problems to be discussed, the teacher may wish to absorb some of the concern—possibly by stating, "I'm not sure we're doing our best for Billy; we need your ideas." Parents are happy to share their thinking. This assures the needed communication, and indicates that the teacher is on the child's "side."

The greatest service the teacher can offer is the skill of listening. This is the parents' invitation to share their concerns. Parents will be ready to listen after they have expressed their anxieties and made suggestions.

The teacher must accept the parent's role and respect the parent's sphere of authority. This reduces the parent's anxiety. Parents feel guilty when reminded of what appears as neglect of their child.

True parental feelings are not so likely when the teacher reacts with surprise or disapproval at information being revealed. An accepting attitude encourages parents to continue. The teacher should strive to show that parental feelings are understood, but saying "I understand" too quickly may prevent further sharing.

The teacher should support parents when possible. Parents need recognition for their accomplishments, and encouragement to continue. Teachers should understand that most parents do not want concrete advice. Friends and relatives may already have suggested every possible answer. Instead, parents need discussion to help them see the situation. Some parents do ask specifics. Then the teacher may begin, "Some parents find this helpful," or "You may wish to try this." Such an approach encourages parental initiative and participation.

Teachers should help parents realize that it is the quality, not the quantity, of time spent with children that is important. Family stress and strain will deter children's learning.

Teachers must exercise caution to avoid creating a false impression of the child. An appraisal of both strengths and weaknesses presents a realistic image.

Having initiated the conference, the teacher's responsibility is to guide the discussion into meaningful areas. The teacher should accept the "causes" which parents offer plus an exploration for other causes. It is well to realize that there may be more involvements than parents are willing to share.

The teacher should be alert for clues in facial expression, gestures, excitability, or conflicting statements. Pauses, gaps, or silences may communicate parental feeling or attitudes. Voice tenseness or shifts in conversation may indicate painful associations.

Generalities should be avoided. Arguments, criticism, or

unfavorable comparisons will create resistance and resentment. Problems are encountered when the teacher introduces too many topics in the conference. It may be better to plan a subsequent conference.

The teacher should acknowledge that an absent parent also contributes to the child's well being. It may be beneficial to suggest that the absent parent try to attend the next conference.

The teacher may feel uncomfortable when a parent discussion reaches an intensive level on behavior. A teacher may feel it easier to avoid being frank in sharing school-centered problems. Objectivity is enhanced when focus is kept on helping the child.

A knowledge of self-limitations is important for the teacher. The best approach is one of honesty. The teacher may need to point out, "My area of competence is to guide the learning of groups of children. While I would like to help you on this, I know you would benefit by seeing a qualified person." For some cases, a school social worker or school psychologist may be helpful. If this is not possible, community resources—such as a mental health clinic or family agency—may be consulted.

Some conflicts may not be resolved. This may be due to factors not apparent in surface interviewing. Sometimes a problem is serving an unconscious need for the parent, and psychotherapy may be indicated.

There is a vast difference between intellectual and emotional understanding. Parental agreement is no indication that the teacher's ideas are accepted. Likewise, predetermined attitudes of the teacher will impede results.

The teacher should accept parents as doing their best. Inadequacy in parents is often due to personal tension and unmet needs. Parents should not be condemned for behavior over which they have no control.

The teacher should summarize the highlights of each conference so the parent feels a sense of accomplishment. The teacher may feel it necessary to assure the parent that the information is confidential. The closing of a conference should include some specific plan—an increased recognition of the child's social needs, reassurance that all is progressing well, referral to a community resource, etc.

Through experience the teacher learns how to acknowledge constructively parental defenses. Experience also helps a teacher know when to inquire, when to listen, when to comment, when to take notes, when to include the principal, and when to conclude the interview.

There are no infallible formulas or rules. No one procedure is ever the only approach to solve a given problem. The personality of each parent and each teacher is unique. Hence each conference is different. However, these ideas and techniques may help teachers provide positive benefits for pupils. This, after all, is the only real justification for the parent conference.

PREPARING FOR A TEACHER-PARENT   6

CONFERENCE

The teacher has just seen the notice on the bulletin board. The time has come to brave the "avenging hordes" of parents who will soon be streaming toward the school to await their turn for that moment of truth too often dreaded by both sides—the teacher-parent conference.

What shall I say? How shall I say it? Why? Am I prepared?

The parent sees the letter pinned to Johnny's polo shirt, feels its contents even as the small boy ducks beneath the shower of leaves he has just gleefully hurled into the air. The crinkle of fall foliage makes it easy to guess the contents of the letter. With Back-to-School Night scheduled, the missive from the school must surely announce the first annual joust—a teacher-parent conference.

Why do those teachers ask the questions they do? What do they really need to know from me? What to say? How to say it? Am I prepared?

No, it isn't easy, that two-way conference. Somehow parents and teachers too often approach the appointed time to confer harassed by fear and doubt. Somehow they often leave the conference with all their misgivings reinforced.

Person to person

Yet if ever there was a more effective method of reviewing home and school progress that the face-to-face exchange, it has not yet been reported. Research has shown how inadequate it is to define a child's progress in the traditional way—by sending parents a piece of paper that reduces each child to a set of cold, impenetrable notations (A,B+, or S, VG or I).

Child development specialists now assert what most parents have always known—that no child can be understood so simply and that progress in human relations is tough going when school achievements are analyzed only through an impersonal report card. Teachers know that their classroom job becomes a spiritless task unless there is a more complete picture of the child than his cumulative record card.

Thus reporting to parents is not a one-way street. The proper education of a child cannot be a mere telling by an all-knowing teacher. Rather, it should be an exchange of perceptions. The conference turns parent and teacher into a team and makes possible a thorough examination of the main concern of all of us—children, whether they are our pupils or our sons and daughters.

For each concerned party there is so much to gain that we dare not be held back by the built-in pitfalls of conference holding. If you are a teacher, you might remember that in the last five years voters have turned down more school bond issues than ever before. It just could be that the impersonality of the schools (typified by such things as report cards, notes sent home, one Back-to-School Night a year, one Open School Week) has widened the traditional chasm between the public and its schools and in particular between teachers and parents. The teacher-parent conference can go a long way toward establishing the humanness of teachers. Folks don't like to give money to strangers!

If you are a parent, the conference with your child's teacher may fill in gaps left by the barrage of letters or numbers on the report card. Let's face it. An S (Satisfactory) in the social studies is something less than satisfactory as a detailed report. How much does your child read in related social studies material? What are the character and quality of his oral reports? Does he show interest in the subject? Has he accomplished any special research? The S says nothing but that he has completed acceptably an unknown amount of work. So the opportunity to meet your child's teacher ought not to be easily dismissed.

If parents and teachers are to be partners in progress, each must prepare for his conference role with full knowledge of the other's purposes. It is time to lift the blackboard curtain and at the same time to open the back door of the home. The few simple but important preparatory steps suggested here should remove some of the obstacles that weaken the impact of the teacher-parent conference.

Pointers for parents

Parents, what should you want to know about your child in school? Here are some possible questions:

How is your child progressing academically? Try to learn something about both the quantity and the quality of his work. Ask to see sample tests and other records.

What are his talents and aptitudes, both evident and submerged? If enough teachers concur in the belief that your child is apparently a genius, that assurance is about as good as an IQ score—maybe better. On the other hand, if they say he's just an average lad they are probably right there, too.

How does your child get along with others? If this question smacks too much of the old bugaboo of "progressive education," don't fret. Solid research in American industry makes it clear that more than 80 per cent of dismissals happen because employees couldn't get on with the people they worked with, not because they couldn't or didn't do their work well.

How good is his mental health? The relation between a child's health, mental as well as physical, and his success in learning is definite and positive. Should your child display emotional conduct that seems to be interfering with his school progress, it would be well for you to know about it. I wouldn't worry about eccentric behavior unless it seems to be inhibiting progress in school.

Parents frequently ask some questions that are really not vital to the success of the teacher-parent conference. If you avoid these, the success of your visit will be measurably enhanced. For instance, it is not important to know:

The IQ score of your child. Like a report card, a number is often a fairly meaningless symbol. For the most part the traditional IQ tests administered en masse to children report only the extent to which they have mastered the kind of thinking and information from which future school success can be predicted.

The teacher's opinion of another teacher, student, or parent. Professional ethics require that teachers support colleagues and students and, at the very least, make little comment about nonprofessional matters. You will save the teacher some embarrassing silences by making no inquiries he oughtn't to answer.

Where your child stands in relation to another student. Questions about *relative* standing in the group are appropriate, but when that early English poet said "Comparisons are odious," he was so right. Except for sometimes bolstering your ego, information about the academic progress of your neighbor's child is anything but profitable.

Tips for teachers

And now, teacher, how best can you prepare for the teacher-parent conference?

Let the children know you welcome the opportunity to confer with their mothers and fathers. Discuss in class some of your ideas about conferring with parents. This will stimulate the children's interest and assure them that the conference is not a tattling session. (How well I remember waiting, tense and almost suffocated under the blankets, on nights when my mother went to talk to my teacher!) On the contrary, the teacher-parent conference gives you an opportunity to find out more about your pupils and to discuss with parents how to make school more valuable for their children.

For each child, gather records, samples of work, anecdotal comments, and other tangible evidence. Were you to consult your physician and discover that he really had no record of your past history but rather relied on his memory, you would probably change doctors. Parents usually can't change teachers, and they do deserve to see evidence that you are carefully noting their child's school progress. May I suggest that you start keeping a loose-leaf record for each child, so that on the eve of the teacher-parent conference you won't have to rely on an already over-burdened memory.

Jot down some pertinent questions or comments you want to ask or make about each child. Again, don't trust your memory. To avoid feeling later on that the conference was simply an exchange of ignorances, you'll need to reflect about each youngster and prepare comments and questions which will guarantee that he will profit from the conference.

Prepare your classroom. Let your room reflect the educational environment. Are there samples of written work, art, committee activities, co-curricular interests, special projects on view? Does the room express the thrust of your class?

Prepare *yourself.* Clear the decks. Put away your home

worries and personal problems. You are about to enter into the lives of a great many people. The last thing you want to do is present to parents the timeworn view of an exhausted, purple pupil-eater. Get some rest and relaxation for the demanding but exhilarating hours ahead of you.

Clearly the teacher-parent conference cannot be just a casual way of passing the time for either parents or teachers. If each understands the functions, restrictions, anxieties, and problems of the other, then this method of evaluating the progress of children in school will cease to be a traumatic experience.

Let us never forget these words of John Dewey: "Children are people. They only grow into tomorrow as they live today." To fulfill our dreams for youth as we discuss their lives in school, parents and teachers must surely become partners in preparation.

CONFERENCE TECHNIQUES   7

How to improve meetings
with parents

THE IMPERSONAL NATURE of an increasingly complex society brings into sharp focus the need for more face-to-face relationships. The teacher observes this phenomenon in terms of exploding knowledge, demands for increased achievement in schools, pressures exerted by parents, and anxieties exhibited among children. Trained personnel, school counselors, were employed in the schools to meet some of these needs. However, the unique position of the teacher, the relationship of the student's problems to learning, and the numerical size of the task still make the teacher the key to direct relationships in the school.

Face-to-face relationships are provided through the conference technique. A conference provides the direct contact between the teacher, parents, students, and other interested individuals. Subjects of a common or mutual interest may be discussed.

Types of Conferences

A. *Telephone Conference.* The telephone conference is used for initial contact with parents, for quick and easy follow-up contact, and for emergencies. The telephone conference should be brief, should not go into great detail with complicated school matters, and should be pleasant and positive. The telephone conference should never be used in lieu of a formal or face-to-face conference.

B. *Informal Conference:* The informal conference usually consists of a casual meeting which develops into a discussion of a mutual need for understanding of a student or part of his school program. These usually occur during PTA meetings, encounters on the street or in a store, or social occasions. The informal conference, too, should be pleasant and positive, and the professional teacher should avoid going into great depth with technical matters relating to the child and the school. If the need for a discussion in depth is indicated, plans should be made for this type of conference. The teacher should be careful to avoid allowing the informal conference to substitute for a formal conference when a need exists.

C. *Formal Conference:* The formal conference is a prearranged appointment which brings the interested parties together in the school setting. Generally, one or both parents are in attendance. The student may or may not be included. The teacher should make extensive plans prior to the conference. Information and materials which might be available include: (1) materials which clarify the purpose and operation of the specific phase of the program about which the conference is held; (2) the student's performance in this program; (3) the student's ability; (4) the student's health record, including attendance data; (5) the student's extracurricular activities; (6) the student's performance in other phases of his program; and (7) other related information selected by the teacher or requested by the parent.

D. *Case Conference:* The case conference is generally a detailed study, followed by a meeting of all parties involved, concerning a student who is having difficulty in adjusting to the school program. A case conference is generally initiated by one or more teachers who sense a need for it, developed and organized by the counselor, and participated in by parents, teachers, administrators, and other persons concerned.

Structure of the Conference

The telephone conference and informal conference require little structure. In the telephone conference the parent should be greeted by the teacher and, without being abrupt, the purpose of the call should be indicated. If further action is necessary, plans should be made and the call should be terminated rather quickly. Long telephone calls should be avoided because of imposing on either the teacher's or the parent's time. The informal conference has literally no structure except that of greeting and showing concern for each other's mutual interest. If items are interjected by either the teacher or the parent that indicate a need for a conference with structure, the teacher should move immediately to provide an opportunity for this need to be met. The teacher should avoid getting into long discussions in this informal setting when he has not made preparation for the conference and does not have his materials available.

A suggested structure for a formal conference follows:

(1) The parent should be made to feel at ease and welcome or wanted at the school.

(2) Positive factors relating to the student should then be mentioned. These factors should emanate from the true feelings of the teacher or else this approach should be omitted. Parents as well as students are very sensitive to the expression of insincere feelings.

(3) The parent should be allowed to express himself on matters relating to the student. The parent should be encouraged to discuss the child, the home, or the family at random and should be interrupted only in ways that indicate an interest on the part of the teacher.

(4) The teacher should outline the purposes of the conference and present the factual information concerning the purpose.

(5) An opportunity should be provided for the parent to talk briefly and positively regarding the information provided by the teacher or the problem being discussed.

(6) The teacher then might follow up with a few pertinent questions to which the parent would be asked to respond.

(7) The teacher should move to close the conference by summarizing the purpose of the conference, the relevant facts and factors that have been discussed, and plans or decisions that have resulted from the conference.

The case conference follows a more definite structure. The primary participants in the conference are persons who have been included because they are in a position to contribute specialized information on the case. After each specialist has responded, decisions and plans are made. Counseling with parents or students is provided by the counselor after the specialists have been dismissed.

Conference Record

In the case of the formal conference or the case conference, the teacher or the counselor should keep a record of the conference actions. This record is becoming more and more important each day, with additional people working in the school to assist with the large variety of concerns that students have. The records should be brief but should contain enough information for another teacher, counselor, administrator, or case worker to benefit in future conferences if they prove necessary. The record might contain the date, participants in the conference, specific purpose of the conference, important information presented during the conference, and decisions or plans made during the conference. This record should be maintained in the student's folder, but should not become a part of the permanent record in the sense that the academic record, health record, and standardized test scores usually do.

Values of the Conference

Among the conference's values are these:
A. The conference enables the school, the home, the teachers, and the parents to coordinate their efforts to help in the student's development.
B. The conference develops good rapport with parents.
C. The conference enables the teacher to understand and deal with the student.
D. The conference provides the medium for additional conferences when needed to have the parent and teacher working together for the best interest of the student.

Summary

This complex society with its demands and its impersonal nature has created a need for more face-to-face relationships in the educational process. The conference is the appropriate technique for providing this contact. Personal relationships may be provided by the telephone conference or the informal conference with little structure or they may be provided by the formal conference or the case conference, both of which are highly structured. Appropriate records of conferences should be maintained. The conference can be of inestimable value in building rapport and coordinating the efforts of the home and school in educating the child.

EDITOR'S NOTE

Ask any rising young executive and he will tell you how important it is to develop proper techniques for conducting conferences. In fact such instruction frequently is an essential part of an executive training program. Teachers similarly need to become proficient in applying these techniques. Therefore we suggest you test the guidelines presented by the authors the next time you have face-to-face conferences with parents. These meetings may be more gratifying—and even shorter.

HOW TO CONDUCT PARENT CONFERENCES   *8*

to Benefit Child and His Education Most

The sole justification for the existence of a school is the child and his education. The two agencies most interested in that child, ideally, are the school and the home. These agencies can best provide for a child's growth in mind and body by working together toward the same goal. Paul Woodring* in his book, *A Fourth of A Nation*, defines it as follows: "In a society of free men, the proper aim of education is to prepare the individual to make wise decisions."

Perhaps one of the most important duties that school personnel have is that of meeting with parents to discuss the various problems which arise in connection with the education of a son or daughter. Certainly the teacher who can meet and talk with parents wisely will go far toward bringing about the closer cooperation between the home and the school which we all desire.

The parent may come to the school for a conference: (1) upon his own volition, or, (2) because the school has asked him to do so. In either instance, and depending upon the

---

*Woodring, Paul, *A Fourth of A Nation*, McGraw-Hill Book Company, Inc., New York, 1957, page 111.

circumstances, he will arrive at school filled with one or more of the following: anger, fear, anxiety, concern, curiosity, suspicion, hope, discouragement, but most certainly, interest.

THE TEACHER may not know that the parent is to pay him a visit, or he may have time to prepare himself. In any event, the teacher knows that, as a matter of course during his career as a schoolman, he will meet with all types of parents, under all kinds of circumstances. It behooves the teacher then to know some guiding principles which he can apply and which will help him in this very important area of public relations.

In the following, an attempt has been made to state a number of these principles which will serve as guides to the successful fruition of the parent conference. No attempt has been made to list principles in the order of importance.

1. **The teacher should never let such an important occasion as a parent conference become mere routine.**

While the conference may be routine to the teacher, it is exceedingly important to the parent. Frequently the teacher will confer with one or more parents. It is evident that because of the repetition of similar problems the teacher may come to feel that certain things should be self-explanatory to the parent. This is far from true. The average parent will visit the high school for a formal conference but one, two or possibly three times during the course of his child's schooling. To him the problem is unique, important and disturbing.

Each parent must be made to feel that he is welcome, that the school is genuinely interested and that every attempt will be made to work out a satisfactory solution.

2. **The conference should be held in a place free from distraction and interruption.**

A successful conference must be private. It should not be interrupted by ringing telephones, pupils or teachers with other problems. True, a busy teacher cannot spend his entire time talking with parents; the conference in most instances need not be lengthy, but while he is in the conference, his time should be devoted entirely to the problem at hand.

3. **Time enough must be allowed to cover the situation thoroughly. The parent must be made to feel that he has had ample time to present his problem.**

Under no circumstances should the teacher rush the conference. If he is so busy that he lacks the proper amount of time to devote to the parent, he should schedule the conference at another more propitious time. If the parent comes unannounced at an inopportune time, the principal should hear the immediate problem but schedule a conference as soon as possible when time can be devoted to do a thorough job.

4. Records, facts, figures, anecdotal accounts and other pertinent material should be easily available and complete.

It cannot be stressed too strongly that it is absolutely essential to the efficient operation of a school that all pupil data be complete, correct, understandable and filed in such a way as to be available for immediate scrutiny. A school found in the embarrassing position of not maintaining complete records brands itself as inefficient and, very possibly in the eyes of the parent, as untrustworthy.

5. If possible, the teacher should have prior knowledge of the conference in order to brief himself adequately.

It follows as a matter of course that the teacher will often need to enter into a parent conference "cold." If, however, he has the opportunity, prior knowledge of a pupil, his background, scholastic record and other information will not only save time but will convince the parent that the school has an intimate interest in him and his children.

6. In the case of an angry, excited parent, the teacher must maintain his equilibrium.

It is advised that an angry, excited parent be allowed to talk himself out, to "get it off his chest" without counter-argument. Eventually he will "run down"; then the teacher can calmly and reasonably present the school's thinking. An angry, excited person is usually in no condition to listen. It is best not to argue with the parent; try to remain calm and objective.

7. The parent must be dealt with honestly.

Honesty is still the best policy. It is a great mistake to "soft-soap" a parent just to mollify him. The parent will not always be right any more than he will always be wrong. It will be better for the school to have him leave a conference period not completely satisfied or only partly convinced than to allow him to leave with the impression that everything has been satisfactorily solved, only to find out later that he has not been dealt with truthfully. Loss of respect is not easy to overcome. Respect is much more important than popularity.

8. Be yourself; avoid "pedaguese."

Unless both parties understand each other, there can be no adequate solution to a problem. Any effort on the part of the teacher to be a "big shot," to try to impress his visitor with his vast knowledge and importance or to overwhelm him with lofty phrases and high-sounding words will completely destroy all rapport. The science of semantics becomes increasingly important. Without understanding, there can be no satisfactory communication between individuals or groups. Simple, clear-cut language, stated in a friendly way, and with warm interest, will lead to far more satisfaction for all concerned.

9. Learn to listen.

By careful listening, one can learn not only what his visitor is trying to express but also he may often be able to discern emotions and prejudices which the individual is trying not to express. Taking notes will help the teacher to retain pertinent information and will also make the parent feel that what he is saying is receiving attention. The notes that a teacher takes during a parent conference can also be used in relaying information to other interested parties when the conference ends.

10. Others involved should join the conference if it will aid in resolving the situation.

Most parent conferences, since they revolve about the scholastic achievement or the conduct of the child, will involve all his teachers as well as the principal. The teachers who have intimate contact with the child will have information about his work and attitudes and will more often than not be able to provide the personal details of his problems. If the administrator deems it inadvisable for the teacher or teachers to be present at the conference, then he should ask the teacher, or teachers, to provide him with written statements concerning their knowledge of the pupil involved.

11. The administrator should beware of allowing an irate parent to confer alone with a teacher, especially an inexperienced teacher. He should insist upon being present.

The administrator is responsible for the best interests of the school. Since this is true, he must retain command of any situation which involves public relations. If an irate parent and a teacher, especially a young, inexperienced teacher, are allowed to confer alone, the results may be unpleasant. The administrator must see to it that the school, its policy and philosophy are properly presented and protected; and too, he should be available to protect the teacher from abuse or even physical violence.

12. While there are times when the pupil involved should not

be present at the conference, he should most often be available if it be necessary to include him.

Most conferences will progress more satisfactorily if the child himself is not present. Usually a point will arrive in the proceedings where his presence may be desirable. When the child is to be involved personally in the talk, he should be assigned to a place where he will be easily accessible, but where he cannot hear the conversation until he is called.

13. The administration should back its teachers right or wrong, publicly.

It is essential that the school present a united front. The administrator should not blame his teachers for the situations which have arisen, even though he may not approve their actions. If the school is wrong, then the administration should be willing to assume its share of the blame. This does not mean that the administrator cannot criticize the teacher privately; it does mean that he should not do it publicly, or, when talking with a parent in the teacher's absence. Any other course will destroy staff morale.

14. Beware of the content of written communications to the parent. Be careful what you put in writing.

The written word once delivered cannot be recalled. Unless written communications are carefully worded, they can be misunderstood or misconstrued. It is safer to delay the details of a situation until those directly involved can meet. In most instances written communications should be limited to advising that a problem exists and that the parent is requested to come to the school for a conference. Very often even this can best be done by a telephone call.

15. Try to put yourself in the parent's place.

So many times we have heard the statement. "Put yourself in my shoes." In the case of the parent conference, the role-playing method can be utilized in a limited way. The teacher who honestly tries to view a situation as the parent views it can often help himself to find a better solution or perhaps a better way of explaining a situation. It is possible in some instances for the teacher to ask the parent to do some role-playing himself by asking him to try to put himself in the school's place. Mutual understanding is the necessary aim of the conference; a little modified role-playing can help.

16. The school is obligated to keep the parent advised as to any change, good or bad, resulting from the conference.

Once the original conference is concluded and a method of approach or attack agreed upon, then time for implementation must elapse. One conference may not be enough. The school is obligated to keep in touch with the parent to advise him of changing conditions. Often this can be done through a telephone call. However it is done, the point to be stressed is that the follow-up is an important part of the conference.

LET'S NOT TELL PARENTS THEIR CHILDREN'S I.Q.'S 9

So you are going to tell parents the I.Q. of their children!

In principle, I heartily agree with the idea that parents should know the capabilities of their children. It would make it so much easier to plan for their future. After all, there is not much point in spending years of heartbreaking struggle trying to prepare for college if a young person is not capable of doing college work.

For the slower students—shall we say those in the lower quarter of the population?—it is best that they get on with the job of finding a comfortable niche that will not be too taxing and that can be the basis of a pleasant and worthwhile life. Pushing these young people into aspirations to be college presidents, lawyers, and school teachers can only lead to frustrations and eventual mental ill health. It is better to be a good ditchdigger than it is to be a poor doctor; better for the person and better for society.

Conversely, is it not desirable that the bright be identified early so that they can be encouraged to work a little harder to enable them to fulfill their promise? We need all the good minds that we can locate and develop. Why, then, is there any question about telling parents the I.Q.'s of their children?

I think there are two good reasons. The first one is that we do not know the I.Q., and the other is that, if we did know the I.Q. of an individual child, there is no way of communicating this information to the average parent.

I shall elaborate. I have before me the I.Q. scores for a small class, selected because the students in it were well above average in ability. These scores were obtained at different times from kindergarten through grade 8. Let us look at them:

Intelligence Tests and Grades in Which Administered

| Individual | K | 1 | 2 | CTMM* | | | | | SRA† | WISC+ |
				3	4	5	6	7	8	8
Student 1					140		136		130	139
Student 2	129	129	112		122		130		119	131
Student 3			116	134	115		130		105	133
Student 4					94		131		98	133
Student 5		125	127		126				123	143
Student 6	119		136		123				116	133
Student 7	124		107		131				107	117
Student 8						117	128		129	134
Student 9	122		130		128		130		118	118
Student 10	125		126		120	109	135		127	112
Student 11									117	122
Student 12	147				135		134		123	125
Student 13	136		127		131		133		119	131
Student 14					118		129		102	130

*California Test of Mental Maturity
† Science Research Associates Primary Mental Abilities Test
+ Wechsler Intelligence Scale for Children

Portrayed in this array of figures is the first major dilemma of the conscientious administrator who wants to inform a parent about the ability of his son or daughter. It makes quite a difference to the parent of Student Number 14 whether he is informed that his child has an I.Q. of 102 or of 130. Both of these scores were obtained within a very few months of each other. Looking over the array, it seems as though the WISC test yields scores consistently, and sometimes substantially, higher than the SRA test. About the time that this fact begins to dawn, Student Number 10 shows up with a score of 127 on the SRA test, the second highest score in this particular list. However, this student obtained a score of only 112 on the WISC test, lowest in the group by a good five points. Over the years, the record for Student Number 10 would seem to indicate that the 127 score is the more accurate of the last two. In his case, analysis of his WISC results indicates that he had a high verbal score but quite low performance on four of the five tests. Is this information important in the interpretation of this youngster's intelligence? (It may be a clue to the fact that he was in a gifted but non-motivated group of students.)

Which Test Will You Use?

When you decide that you are going to inform parents of the scores their children earn on intelligence tests, which test are you going to use? Are you going to explain to the parents that these scores might have been either higher or lower if different tests had been used? Are you going to base your results on one test only? (To use only one test obviates many difficult decisions, of course.)

From this problem of choosing which I.Q. you tell the parent about, let us turn to the problem of communicating with the parent.

You have been trained over many years to understand the meaning of the I.Q. It is only natural that you assume that everyone is almost as conversant with the concept as you are, at least with the vocabulary. But everyone is not. If you wish to test this statement, ask a number of your teachers—not counselors or test experts—to explain to you the meaning of the standard error of measurement as it relates to an I.Q. test. Unless you intend to report the test scores in bands such as those that the SCAT test uses, you are almost certainly going to have to explain to the parents the concept of the standard error of measurement. The I.Q. score is not sufficiently stable to permit you to avoid this concept, even though you might avoid the name. If your teachers cannot tell you what this means, even though they have recently had to pass an examination which presumed such knowledge, how do you expect the parents to understand you?

The parent who wishes to push his youngster will interpret your explanation as meaning that there is a real chance that his child is actually two standard deviations above where his score places him. On the other hand, the punitive parent will interpret your report as meaning that his child really did well on the test, but that the test results were probably a fluke and that his child is probably not as intelligent as the score given would indicate.

Some Horrible Examples

I have seen the harm that I.Q. information has done to individuals who have been informed of their scores. I am sure that you have also. The following example will illustrate the point I am trying to emphasize: A friend of mine, while in the junior high school grades, was told that he had an I.Q. in the 90's. This bit of information haunted him through the years, although he must have been aware that the information was erroneous, for in a university noted for the quality of its graduates, he earned a degree with distinction, completing a joint major in mathematics and physics. He went on to graduate school and earned a master's degree with straight A's. He is currently the superintendent of a large school district and handles the job very capably.

Another example will describe a different danger to which people supposedly intelligent enough to know better are subject. There were three partners in a business, all university graduates who had taught school. One of them had been a school principal. By one means or another, they had all learned their I.Q. scores, which were 135, 133, and 132. The man with the score of 135 quite seriously pointed out that he was smarter than the other two partners and that the partner with the I.Q. of 133 was smarter than the one with the score of 132. It was bad enough to have this conversation take place, but it was worse to find that none of the men would accept the fact that the scores were so close that there was absolutely no basis for feeling that one partner was more capable than the others. These people were gifted, yet unable to understand the significance of the scores.

How Well Do Teachers Understand?

My students would be quick to point out the danger that is inherent in using isolated cases to prove a point. They would be entirely correct. Therefore, before authorizing your teachers to give I.Q. scores to parents, try a little experiment to learn just how well the teachers understand the meaning of the scores. If this test is passed, test the same subjects to see how well they can pass on their information to a *thoroughly biased* individual.

Having said all I have about the danger of giving I.Q. scores to parents, some of you will probably come to the conclusion that the scores are so unstable that they are meaningless. This is not so. They are just a bit more difficult to interpret that it at first seems.

If you are willing to make the necessary effort to verify the accuracy of scores by checking them against other tests and against performance, and if you have the patience and the skill to work carefully with the parent of a youngster who needs the kind of a push that this kind of information might supply, by all means go ahead. Most of you have been working on this basis with parents of the mentally retarded already. You have used individual scores to confirm teachers' judgments and group scores. You have conferred with the parents and have explained the nature of the program for the slow learner and the advantages of his being in this special class. It does not always mean that the parent accepts your evaluation of the situation, but usually he does.

Similarly, if you are willing to go to the same lengths with the bright and the average pupil, if you are aware of a real need for a course of action that is dependent upon the parent understanding the level of intelligence of his child, and if you are willing to verify the teacher's judgment and the results of the group test with an individual test properly administered, then by all means go ahead. Tell the parent what he should know, but tell him in such a way that he can understand and follow up the information with action.

If you are going to give out scores of a routine group test to parents so that they can play with them at the bridge table, using the information to maim each other in subtle ways, then it would seem to be inadvisable. Remember that I.Q. scores are one of the most dynamic status implements obtainable. This is particularly true in certain socio-economic groups, usually the ones that would like to have the information made available. It is an implement that can damage as well as aid. Please make sure that these scores, if you make them available, are used to benefit and not to harm.

LET'S TELL PARENTS THEIR CHILDREN'S I.Q.'S   *10*

Every once in a while professional people discover to their surprise that the clientele they serve is much more capable of understanding "professional" matters than they had thought possible.

Physicans are learning they can explain a cardiograph to patients and by doing so secure cooperation in therapy otherwise unobtainable. Dentists find that insight into theory underlying decay will result in improved dental hygiene for the people they serve.

So it is with respect to education: parents are being informed about many matters formerly considered either beyond their comprehension or not within their ability to accept with reasonable objectivity.

Information about their children's I.Q. is one of these matters.

Up to now we have played a hush-hush game with the I.Q. because we wanted to protect parents from what might be bad news to them or from what they might view as good news which in itself is not. They might assume, we believed, that a low I.Q. means that their child is destined to failure in whatever he tries; or, conversely, that a high I.Q. promises success for the asking. They would be wrong, of course, in either case.[1]

Time and again we heard ourselves saying, "Parents of bright children will become overbearing and parents of dull children ashamed." Or, "Parents who tell their children their I.Q.'s will cause those who are high to loaf and those who are low to become discouraged and quit."

But even these frightening thoughts are not justification for keeping the I.Q. secret from parents. The anticipated consequences come about, if they do at all, not from knowledge of the I.Q. level of children but from *attitudes* of the parents toward this information. Some parents boast about their child's ability to climb to the top of the jungle-gym and others are embarrassed by their adolescent boy's squeaky voice. Keeping parents in ignorance of facts which concern their children because their attitudes might be wrong seems indefensible.

Our reluctance to discuss the I.Q. has had much to do with the present unhealthy state of affairs. As in sex education, the more secretive we were the more intriguing the subject became. And as with sex, everyone talked about it but most of what was said was exaggerated. Paradoxically, while we refrained from telling parents we continued to use I.Q. information for the very same reasons that would make it useful to parents.

Which brings us to the most important argument for telling parents the I.Q.'s of their children. It constitutes one additional, significant measure of a set of qualities possessed in varying degree by all people. Parents ought to have

---

1 Cronbach writes, "Some persons of I.Q. 110 make significant contributions and some of I.Q. 160 lead undistinguished adult lives." See p. 123 of Cronbach, Lee J., *Essentials of Psychological Testing.* New York: Harper, 1949.

information if they are to plan the future with their children. They guide children through the "long haul" while we teachers of necessity are concerned only for a year or so in the lives of the young people we guide. Yet teachers feel that this is essential information to have about each child. And so should parents know about the potential of their children in order to plan intelligently for further education and make hundreds of other decisions that affect their children's future.

If there is a cardinal principle of mental health, it is "know thyself." Know your own (in this case your children's) weaknesses and strengths and accept them, governing yourself accordingly. I.Q. information seems to be this kind of essential knowledge, especially during the elementary and secondary school years.

We have been correct, however, in assuming that if parents were told the I.Q.'s of their children without qualification and explanation some misinterpretations would be made. Consequently, explanation and instruction to parents (and to many teachers) is in order.[2]

They can well be told, individually and in workshop groups, that the I.Q. is a measure established by two or more paper-and-pencil group tests. They can be told that, in spite of the general constancy of the I.Q., there can be some fluctuation over the developmental years, and great fluctuation in rare instances. Usually, appreciable change in I.Q. comes about only through rather extensive "interference" with intellectual functioning such as emotional illness, physical illness or handicap, or an impoverished environment such as might prevail at a poorly-operated orphanage. In other words, for most children the I.Q. is relatively constant.[3]

---

[2] Smith writes, "Ideally, parents and teachers should work as a team in sharing information for the welfare of the child. But parents as well as teachers must thoroughly understand the meaning of intelligence test scores before they can use them to the child's advantage." In Smith, Henry P., *Psychology in Teaching.* New York: Prentice-Hall, 1954.

[3] Ausubel states, "Generally speaking, once the I.Q. approaches stability it tends to remain relatively constant ... At the age of nine, for example, the probable error of an I.Q. is about five points. This means that one-half the tested persons do not deviate more than five points on retesting." See p. 593 of Ausubel, David P., *Theory and Problems of Child Development.* New York: Grune and Stratton, 1958.

Another aspect that can be pointed out is that I.Q. does not represent *general* ability, but specific abilities related to the manipulation of verbal-abstract symbols. For example, the I.Q. one possesses does not assure scholastic achievement but contributes to it. Other abilities and attitudes that contribute to school success are at least equally significant: seriousness of purpose, social insight, mechanical aptitude, to mention a few. McDaniel writes, "The student with highest test scores is not always the achiever, nor is the student with a low score inevitably doomed to failure. Many factors other than intelligence enter into scholastic success; and, at best, a test represents only a sampling of the individual's abilities."[4] Ruch supports this point of view when he notes that " . . . a person can be intelligent in one field and not in another, indicating there is not a "general" intelligence which includes all abilities."[5]

Don't Undervalue I.Q. Significance

Just as we should avoid attaching too much importance to the I.Q., so we should not depreciate its significance. We could very well point out that the median I.Q. of college freshmen in American colleges is about 109, but to graduate from a high grade college with average marks and normal effort an I.Q. of 120 may be necessary. We could tell parents that the mean *minimum* I.Q. of students doing average work in the high school academic curriculum is approximately 104.[6] We should tell them that the theoretical average I.Q. in an unselected population is 100, but that this average increases the higher the group on the educational ladder.

When we inform parents about the I.Q. of their children there is no reason why we should not engage in some "directive" group and individual counseling. Just as we suggest to parents that it is unwise to compare school marks of children in the same family (or of any children, for that matter) in the presence of the children, or as we admonish

---

[4] McDaniel, Henry B., *Guidance in the Modern School.* New York: Dryden, 1956.

[5] Ruch, Floyd L., *Psychology and Life* (Third Edition). New York: Scott Foresman, 1948.

[6] Cronbach, *op. cit.*

them not to overprotect, so we should urge them to consider the desirability of using I.Q. information in an appropriate way.

Parents may be told at this time that there is nothing to be gained by using I.Q. data as a "threat" or a "promise" to get a child to work harder or feel prouder. They may be informed that it is probably unwise to tell the child his I.Q. until he is old enough to understand its significance, and that this perhaps should be left to the high-school counselor to do, if he feels it wise. If we handle it delicately enough, we might even suggest to parents that none of this information, whether it consists of scores on standardized achievement tests, school marks, results of aptitude tests, or I.Q., need be shared with other adults but should be used only as valuable background as they guide their children.

Much of the present unhappy misunderstanding between the public and educators has come about simply because many of us in education have failed to recognize that parents must be informed about what is going on in school.[7] Education that moved ahead with changing needs and improved methods was labeled "progressive" and earned a poor reputation, almost certainly because the public (and not a few teachers) failed to understand what it was all about.

Times have changed. Parents are more interested in the problems of education and are more capable of understanding the many complexities involved. They want to know the facts, deserve to know the facts, and should be given the facts. I.Q. information may well be included.

REPORTING I.Q.'S TO PARENTS   *11*

Should parents be given results of I.Q. tests?

Yes, but . . .

Any parent who expresses a desire to know the mental ability of his child gives evidence of some motivation. The school needs to determine the nature of the motivation in order to interpret properly the results of mental ability tests to the parent.

---

[7] If we do not supply the information, the public may demand it. By legislative action, schools in California will be required to show parents the permanent records of their children beginning with the school year of 1960, if the parents request it.

One parent may ask for this information because he is worried about the poor scholastic achievement of his child. He wants to know if the child's achievement is in line with the child's mental ability. Another parent may want to know his son's mental ability test score so that the boy can be compared with the neighbors' children. Still another parent may wish to find out his child's I.Q. to use a verbal whip, to wit: "I know you can do better in school than you have done. Your teacher told me your tests showed you were bright enough to do 'B' work. Now you either get down to business or else."

Just as parents vary greatly in their reasons for wanting to obtain test results, so teachers have various motivations for wanting to give parents test information. One teacher may feel that he can reduce undue parental pressure on his pupil if he lets the parents know that the pupil is "not very bright." Unfortunately, a few teachers believe that if parents know that the child is not working up to capacity, the parents will use that information to coerce the child to study harder. Yet other teachers want parents to have test information for the simple reason that they believe a parent has a right to know about his child.

Parents and teachers, as the preceding paragraphs point out, have good and bad reasons for wanting to receive or to give test information. Likewise, both have good and bad reasons for not exchanging test information—"The test may not be accurate." "You can't be sure the parent will understand." "I don't believe in tests; I know my boy can do it if he will try." "I know he's not very bright, but he has a lot of other good points and these ought to be taken into consideration."

The desire to get or to give test information is not based solely on rational thinking through of how the exchange of information will benefit the child. But the basic question that every person who is called upon to impart test information to parents should be able to answer affirmatively is "Will giving the information help the child?" Before this question can be answered, some judgment concerning the parent's motivation must be made by the teacher.

In practice, this means that a teacher who is asked for test results must do two things. First, he must talk with the parent or determine by other means that the desire for information stems from wholesome and constructive motivations. If he finds, for example, that the parent plans to use the test result in a vindictive or chiding manner, it is better not to reveal the information sought for.

Second, the information must be so interpreted that the parent can understand and use it. For most parents, the I.Q. expressed as a number has little real meaning, although they feign an understanding of it. (Likewise, a few teachers do not seem to understand the concepts basic to an accurate interpretation of an I.Q.) Hence, explanations of test scores in terms of percentile ranks based on local norms, in comparison with the level required for average achievement in school, or predictions of probable success in college are usually more meaningful to parents and also are better received.

A teacher might say, "The mental ability test score of your child places him at about the 75th percentile. That is, his score is higher than that of about 75 per cent of the children in his class." For another parent the interpretation might be, "In view of the mental ability test score of your child, he should earn above average grades but probably will not be in the top group in school." It is never necessary and rarely advisable to report the I.Q. to parents. Rather, the I.Q. should be interpreted in a manner that makes sense to parents.

Should parents be given results of I.Q. tests? Yes, but only if they will use them for the child's benefit. And only if the results are presented in such a way that parents can use them.

APPROACH ENLIVENS   *12*
PARENT-TEACHER CONFERENCES

Smorgasbord? Teacher supermarket? College registration? The array of people, tables and chairs suggested these ideas, but the event actually was an effort on the part of Barron Area Schools to make parent-teacher conference day at the junior and senior high schools more effective.

Taking a hint from industry—from banking, in particular—the administration and teachers set out to prove that parent-teacher conferences at the junior and senior high school level could be meaningful, private and conducted in the time allotted for them.

P-T conferences at the Barron Area Junior and Senior High Schools have not been considered entirely successful in the past. The main objection to the past system has been the amount of time required for parents to confer with their children's various teachers.

Barron Junior and Senior High Schools have a combined enrollment of about 900 students and a faculty of about 45 teachers. Often it is necessary for one parent to see a dozen or more teachers if they have children at both buildings.

To overcome this objection, a new idea in parent conferences was initiated. The high school gymnasium served as the conference area. Teachers from both junior and senior high classes were seated at tables spaced throughout the gymnasium. To facilitate locating the teachers, the various departments were grouped together. Each department and each teacher had a sign.

Parents were invited by letter to come to the school on a Thursday evening from 7:00 to 9:00 and all day Friday from 9:00 a.m. to 5:00 p.m. The letter, which explained the purpose and mechanics of the new system, asked parents to register their attendance outside the gym door. Coffee and doughnuts were served in the home economics rooms throughout the conference period.

Parents moved from table to table and conferred with their children's teachers. Centralizing of the teachers, ease of locating the departments, informality of moving from teacher to teacher and the friendly atmosphere that prevailed throughout the gymnasium helped to make the conference highly successful.

The project was not undertaken without a few misgivings. However, those who had feared that the massing of the teachers in the gymnasium would discourage parents from discussing their children's work or problems were surprised to discover that privacy was almost as complete as it had been in their own classrooms in previous years.

People busily conferring on either side gave a surprising amount of privacy to each teacher's table. In fact, the informality of the conferences encouraged the parents and teachers to open up to each other—to center their attention on the individual in whom both have common interest—the child.

Comments from both parents and teachers were 100% in favor of the new system. The turnout was large, about 700 registrations, including about 200 fathers.

We feel that we have initiated a sound, feasible plan, and plan to continue with some improvements.

In the future we shall use both Senior High School gyms,

one for junior high and one for senior high faculty to get more spacing between tables.

To facilitate parents' finding teachers, we plan to draw a master floor plan of the gym, locating each table. This will be duplicated and handed out at the door. Student council members will be made available to act as ushers.

GRADE CARD

Subject:

Parent-Teacher Conference

Comments:

Generally contributes much information relative to the welfare of the child.

Teacher—Principal Responsibilities
for

PUPIL PROGRESS

Of experimentation with systems of reporting, one of the promising methods of this century is the parent-teacher conference; a two-way communication that generally contributes much information relative to the welfare of the child.

Teachers and principals have a personal responsibility in gathering, assimilating, recording, co-ordinating and reporting information concerning pupil progress. Although certain functions require action of principal and faculty, there are those areas of responsibility for which the two groups have distinct assignments.

Responsibilities of the Principal

An elementary principal provides the foundation upon which the framework of the conference will be built. His concern is with the development of policy, mechanics of organization, and general welfare of pupils, teachers, and parents.

The principal also makes special provisions for:

1. *Administrative Conferences.* If classroom teachers are to have time for reporting effectively, some plan should be initiated which relieves them from certain teaching duties. An

administrative conference is often necessary in order that the superintendent, principals and board of education can formulate policy which regulates the released time made available to teachers for conference purposes.

2. *Staff Meetings.* Staff meetings should be used to ascertain the kinds of information and ways of reporting it in conferences. In addition, the faculty should discuss the sources which might be used to obtain this selected information.

For example, it is questionable as to the importance of reporting certain intelligence test data to parents (John's IQ is 130). The group may decide that a better way of reporting John's intelligence would be through the use of generalizations (In view of the mental ability test score of your child, he should be in the top group of our class).

Detailed conference guides could be developed as an outgrowth of these staff meetings.

3. *Informing the Pupils.* Grade level meetings should be held with all children so that practices used in reporting about their work would become meaningful to them.

4. *Informing the Parents.* Several effective methods used by principals to inform parents of conference programs are: (1) newspaper articles (2) citizen committees (3) PTA meetings (4) brochures handed to pupils.

5. *Personal Orientation and Planning.* The principal should prepare an informative letter and a schedule sheet for conferences with the letter outlining purposes of the conference method of reporting, and providing guidelines for completing the schedule sheet.

Included on the schedule sheet would be days selected for conferences, sessions available (morning, afternoon, evening), a signature space for the parent, and a place for the names and grades of his children.

Upon receipt of all schedule sheets from the parents, it is a routine matter of scheduling first, those parents who have children in more than one grade. This will prevent, in most cases, the necessity of the parent making extra trips to confer with the several teachers.

The principal is usually responsible for setting the dates for the fall and spring conferences. Several Missouri elementary principals hold their conference sessions during the months of October and April.

Prior to conference sessions, the principal may assign older children as ushers. These ushers escort parents to designated rooms at the appointed time, or in accordance with the bell schedule set for ringing at intervals of 15 or 20 minutes.

Conference procedures provide excellent opportunities for the showing of class projects and teaching aids. The principal may want to provide displays and exhibits in the auditorium or waiting room during conference sessions.

The PTA often serves coffee and tea to parents who are waiting in these areas.

A plan should be developed by building principals to facilitate the transmission of pertinent information from clinical services and special teachers to the classroom teachers so that it could be combined with other information to be imparted to parents. In addition to the above mentioned responsibilities, the principal should be available to help his teachers confer with parents who have children with special problems.

Responsibilities of the Teacher

1. *A Thorough Study of the Materials Used in Evaluating the Pupil's Progress.* Workbooks, daily class papers, art work, and class charts are included in this category. Results of standardized achievement tests, intelligence tests, teacher made tests, and socio-metric devices should be reviewed prior to the initial conference.

2. *Preparing Briefs and Outlining Ways Selected Information Might Be Discussed with Certain Parents.* By teachers failing to study the ways in which information might be imparted, parents may fail to obtain accurate and precise meanings.

Giving concrete examples and allowing parents to draw their own conclusions is one way problems could be reported; e.g. "Billy left his papers for arithmetic at home yesterday, and lost his language work on the way to school today."

Another procedure is citing descriptive phrases and examples to parents which indicate certain reasons for the lack of performance on the part of the child; e.g. "Jim's achievement is limited because of poor habits in practice and drill sessions."

3. *Adjusting Conference Practices in Time of Great Change.* No longer are parents satisfied with information limited to a child's academic progress. They are concerned about the child's social, emotional and physical growth and development and growth in aesthetic values.

As an example, look at creativity. Many elementary school activities involve originality, inventiveness, ingenuity, experimentation and initiative. The ways of reporting information include:

1. Showing projects in art and shop craftmanship with emphasis on originality; 2. giving examples of a child's efforts in striving for original answers to questions rather than to accept the conventional; 3. showing forms of creative communication; 4. discussing the quality of a child's performance in dramatic activities; 5. discussing the way in which the child did imaginative thinking; and 6. citing the special talents the child is developing and the uniqueness or style in which he performs them.

4. *Summarizing Conference Data after the Initial Conference.* A summary record would be valuable to the teacher for future conferences, and the completed record will be especially useful if the child is transferred from one school to another.

Specific suggestions made by either the parent or the teacher should be recorded so the method of attack and progress on a child's problem might be followed with accuracy and consistency.

REFERENCES

1. From Celia B. Stendler. "Let's Look at Parent-Teacher Conferences." *Educational Leadership.* February 1949. 6:292-98. Reprinted by permission from *Educational Leadership.*

2. From Charles A. Nicholson. "Parent-Teacher Conferences—A Positive Approach." *Ohio Schools.* December 1965. 43:32. Reprinted by permission of *Ohio Schools.*

3. From Barbara W. Merrill. "Under the Surface of Parent-Teacher Conferences." *The Instructor.* November 1965. 75:35. Reprinted by permission of *The Instructor.*

4. From Catherine L. Davis. "Getting the Most from Parent-Teacher Conferences." *Targets in Education.* October 1961. 3:1-4. Reprinted by permission of *Targets in Education.*

5. From Virgil Murk. "Parent Conferences Supplement Teaching." *Illinois Education.* March 1965. 53:302-4. Reprinted by permission of *Illinois Education.*

6. From Elliott D. Landau. "Preparing for a Teacher-Parent Conference." *The PTA Magazine.* November 1965. 60:13-15. Reprinted by permission of *The PTA Magazine.*

7. From Harold T. Johnson and Lester R. Herman. "Conference Techniques—How to Improve Meetings with Parents." *The Clearing House.* December 1965. 40:239-41. Reprinted by permission of *The Clearing House.*

8. From David S. Cunningham. "How to Conduct Parent Conferences to Benefit Child and His Education Most." *New York State Education.* March 1961. 48:26-27. Reprinted by permission of *New York State Education.*

9. From John A. R. Wilson. "Let's *Not Tell* Parents Their Children's I.Q.'s." *Phi Delta Kappan.* June 1959. 40:343-45. Reprinted by permission of *Phi Delta Kappan.*

10. From Robert Topp. "Let's *Tell* Parents Their Children's I.Q.'s." *Phi Delta Kappan.* June 1959. 40:342-345. Reprinted by permission of *Phi Delta Kappan.*

11. From Clifford P. Froehlich. "Reporting I.Q.'s to Parents." *Nation's Schools.* April 1955. 55:8-10. Reprinted by permission of *Nation's Schools.*

12. From Robert Kempkes and David Darsee. "Approach Enlivens Parent-Teacher Conferences." *Wisconsin Journal of Education.* 98:9, March 1966. Reprinted by permission of *Wisconsin Journal of Education.*

13. From R. C. Bradley. "Teacher-Principal Responsibilities for Pupil Progress." *School and Community.* May 1964. 50:8-9. Reprinted by permission of *School and Community.*

Critical Issues Meriting Special Handling by Teachers in the Interview Situation

Introduction

Many parents have their own special needs regarding their children. A parent of an *exceptional child* may need a special type of conference. He wants to know, for example, —How much should I do for my child? How can I better accept his fate? What special talents can be use to compensate for his weaknesses and inabilities? What are his special needs? Is he like all other children while at school? Is he accepted by his peers?

Some children are *learning disability* cases. What do you tell a parent about children with such handicaps? How much do you tell them about their problems as identified by the schools? What does an interviewer say to the parent about a child's emotional needs?

New programs of *sex education* are becoming adjuncts to the school curriculum. What should the teacher tell the parent that makes sense about sex education and its effect on their own child? How can the parent assist the school in the sex education program? What do children learn at school in

11

class about sex? Where might a parent go to get more materials on sex education for his age-level child?

The work in this chapter is geared to expose clearly what parents need to know about *special* reading problems, the needs of *exceptional* children, and problems to be reported regarding *learning disability* cases. Moreover, orientation to problems encountered in reporting information about *sex education* is presented and parental involvement in decision making regarding the implementation of sex education programs is discussed. It is a wise teacher who knows what to say to both mother and father who might query at conference time, "Specifically, what do you deal with when offering my child instruction in sex education?"

The article entitled, "The Behavior-Guidance Tools of the Classroom Teacher," is included to remind all teachers who confer that the picture of what they are as persons in daily contacts with children far outweighs what one might seek to reveal through verbal communication in the conference. From what the teacher has already said and done with a parents' children over a course of weeks has much to do with how comments are accepted or rejected at conference time. Just as "no tool is any better than the 'intent' with which it is used," likewise, conferences are of little value if a person does not measure up to parental and professional standards at times other than during conference sessions.

REPORTING TO PARENTS— *1*
WHY? WHAT? HOW?

For some 25 years now, there has been widespread experimentation with newer types of reports. Reporting to parents has changed in many respects, mostly to the good. More information than percentage marks in the subjects is now commonly given in reports. Much effort is devoted to exchange of information and advice between parents and teachers. Many teachers try very hard to use the whole marking and reporting system as a means of helping their pupils to carry on self-appraisal and improvement.

But have those who are zealous to improve reporting sometimes confused parents, pupils, and even some teachers? In trying to communicate better with parents, are teachers sometimes making it more difficult for parents to understand later on when their children encounter other reporting practices? Have some fine efforts to aid pupil progress made it more difficult for pupils to judge their progress?

I would answer yes to these questions, because some teachers and interested parents have frequently overlooked two relevant if unfortunate facts:

1. Differences in reporting practices from level to level and school to school are not easily understood by pupils and their parents.

2. Try as many teachers and parents may to guide learning for learning's sake, there has been far more guidance of learning for the sake of grades and good reports.

Perhaps further improvement in reporting would be aided by more common understanding of the logical answers to three questions: Why report? What to report? How to report?

Why Report?

Any boy and girl can tell us why schools send reports home: so that parents may know how their children are getting along in school.

The newer practices have not reduced parents' basic interest in their children's progress. Indeed, informative reports may have whetted the interest of many mothers and fathers. Reporting systems that fail to convey to parents information they understand about their children's progress (or, perhaps more factually, their class standing) invite trouble.

Marks or grades have long been accepted reporting symbols. These marks found their way into school records as well as school reports, and so into college transcripts. From numerical marks or from point equivalents of letter marks, rank in class could be computed for high-school seniors and used by college-admission officials.

Marks could also be reported to prospective employers. Thus, marks and reports became inextricably related, and their purposes were somewhat broadened, especially at the secondary level, to include prediction of college success and even of success in a job.

But the central purpose of informing parents about their children's school progress, and even the related purposes of informing colleges and employers about prospective students and employees, has frequently been subordinated to other purposes: Marks could also be used to decide on promotion and graduation.

Reports become the signposts of passing or failing. Although retardation has been drastically reduced in the past half century, marks still separate pupils by achievement in those schools in which a pupil's previous record determines his assignment to homogeneous groups or tracks.

In recent years, school people, pressed by many needs for better public support of the schools, have awakened to the public-relations aspects of reporting. Here is one place, it was realized, where teachers and parents have a common interest and a reason for getting together. Therefore, reporting systems have been geared in many communities to their potential for interpreting the school and its needs to parents.

However, reports to parents were and are so widely used by both parents and teachers as clubs over the heads of children as to make the report card—and school in general—hateful to many. Are today's parents, whose own parents granted or withheld privileges on the basis of marks on the report card, likely to perceive their child's report as a happy symbol of the parent-teacher partnership?

Undoubtedly, one purpose of reports to parents has been to provide pupils with the incentive to do schoolwork that neither parent nor teacher knew how else to supply. However, indiscriminate clubbing through marks is known to have quite different results from those which well-meaning parents and teachers seek for children.

Of these various and frequently conflicting purposes of reporting systems, two seem clear-cut and justifiable:

1. Parents should have information about their children's progress and standing in school. If this information can be given in a way that promotes understanding of home and school, all the better. But the information needs to be sufficiently factual, even if disappointing, so that the mother and father can use it to understand and help their child. Certainly such information at the high-school level should also be available to college-admission officials and prospective employers.

2. Ultimately, it is even more important that boys and girls have the best information available in understandable form about their own progress. To understand themselves, to capitalize on their strong points, and to remedy, if possible, their weaker ones, they need to know what these strengths and weaknesses are. Many types of evaluative data are needed for this purpose in addition to a six-or-twelve-weeks' set of marks, but the accumulation and summary of facts at

reporting time may be very useful in the pupil's own plan for continued, improved progress.

What to Report?

Differences of opinion and practice about the purposes of reporting seem almost minor as compared to those which exist about the content of reports. Great variations occur in the items on which information is reported and in the marking symbols. These variations are both vertical, from level to level, and horizontal, from school to school at the same level.

The educational philosophy in a school or system and especially in the classrooms concerned would be expected to control the nature of the instructional program and the content of the report.

If achievement in subject matter is a central goal, the report card would report pupil's standing in knowledge of subjects of the curriculum. If behavior according to stated criteria of growth and development is a goal, then a description of relevant behavior would be reported. If progress in various work skills and habits is desired, then the report would indicate pupils' status or progress in specific skills and habits.

Since the instructional program typically serves more than one of these goals, the report may give a mark in the subjects and a check on various behavior traits and work habits. Sometimes, however, the philosophy is not clearly stated in the report or understood by either parent or teachers, and what the report is trying to report on is not really defined.

The dominant philosophy relates also to the basis on which standing and progress are determined:

Does an A, for example, mean that the pupil is doing top work with respect to his own potential or to the norm for the class? And if the latter, is the norm determined as an average of the distribution of marks in the class, or by the teacher's expectation of some standard of achievement, or by the norms of some standardized test? And does it describe the pupil's present standing or his progress since some previous time?

An A may mean any of these things in different communities, in different schools in the same community, or perhaps even in different classrooms of the same school.

Confusion arises, at least among some pupils and parents, when the items and underlying philosophies vary from level to level. The transition from elementary to secondary schools in many communities includes introduction to the use of letter marks for achievement and perhaps elimination of reports on behavior characteristics and work habits.

Even at the same level teachers may, and sometimes do, disregard in written forms the check lists or other spaces for reporting on items other than subject achievement. In oral reporting there may be even less uniformity in the items about which teachers and parents converse.

Lack of parent understanding may be increased by varieties in the symbols used in written reports and records. Elementary schools may use S and U, and perhaps also an E (excellent) or O (outstanding), or other symbols; and secondary schools, the traditional A's, B's, and C's. Or 1, 2, 3, 4 may replace A, B, C, D.

Ability grouping introduces still another problem: Does an A in the low section mean the same as in the high? Indeed, can A's be given in the low section? Actually these are problems only if the report is focused on relative standing rather than individual progress.

I am not alarmed by these variations or even by the confusions they create for parents and pupils. Instead I see them as encouraging signs of genuine concern by American teachers for finding better ways of reporting to parents in the interest of helping individual pupils.

Although further experimentation with what to report is critically needed, would it not be well meanwhile, to stick to the two central purposes for reporting mentioned earlier?

Should not the school faculty be certain, first, that parents understand what their children's reports are intended to tell, and second, that the reports summarize data which pupils can use, and indeed have already used, in self-appraisal and improvement? If so, should not the report clearly distinguish between marks and comments related to present standing and those related to recent progress, and also among goals such as subject-matter achievement, work habits, and behavior traits?

How Report?

Where teachers are certain of the purposes of reporting and of what to report, the form of reporting seems to follow logically. Other articles in this feature show how careful studies of reporting by faculty groups help. Perhaps the great differences in reporting procedures are created by varying degrees of understanding by school faculties on the *why* and *what* of reports. School leaders might reduce confusion as well as the range of practice by providing for more thorough study of the problem.

Certainly our knowledge of communication methods brings into real question the use of written reports alone, especially when these consist of letter symbols and check marks only. Face-to-face communication seems to be as effective in reporting to parents as in other matters. My belief—which has been strengthened by many comments from parents and others—is that the single most effective reporting medium is the teacher-parent conference.

But whatever the method of reporting, there is still the question of how to express that which is to be reported. Marks and checks are simple to write but hard to explain.

The single hardest question to answer—and the one for which most parents would probably settle—is, "How is my child doing?" The complete record, plus samples of work, helps the teacher to explain Johnny's progress but may still fail to answer this question. The teacher, therefore, needs to explain two things to parents: First, how Johnny is doing in relation to his potential, as best it can be estimated (and teachers estimate it very freely among themselves), and second, how he is doing in relation to the class norm.

A satisfactory answer to the basic question in which parents are interested really means a two-way or dual marking system. In the elementary school, this system may be fairly simple. It may be enough, for example, to explain that Johnny is doing as well as he is expected to, although he is below the class average in arithmetic. But in the secondary school, marks are generally needed, and Johnny's status will probably have to be expressed by two sets of letter grades—one for progress or effort, the other for relative standing or achievement.

The Dilemma of Reporting

This overview of practices and problems in reporting may suggest that the situation has become hopelessly confused. To the contrary, I see it as having been hopefully experimental. However, we do need more widespread understanding of present variations in the *why, what* and *how* of reports.

The perplexity of parents and others caused by varied reporting systems is real and must be recognized. Just as real and to be recognized, however, is the teacher's desire for better ways of helping individual learners.

This is the dilemma we face in reporting systems: A uniform system of reporting throughout the nation might eventually be more easily understood by everyone, but it might also greatly inhibit effective provisions for individual differences among both pupils and communities. In fact, providing for individual differences has already been adversely affected to some degree by greater uniformity of marking and reporting practices in high schools.

I believe that the following items are essential to improve the reporting system throughout the country: agreement among the teachers in each school as to the purposes of reporting and as to what is to be reported; careful explanation to each parent, both on the entrance of his child to school and repeatedly thereafter, of the reporting system used (and of its relationship to any previous systems the parent has known); and careful planning with parent groups as to the method of reporting most useful and convenient for both parents and teachers.

In addition, more systematic publication of relevant research findings, of results of experimentation with different reporting procedures, and of surveys of practices by local, state, and national educational agencies might help to bring about the understanding and spread of good practices.

WHAT PARENTS WANT TO KNOW

ABOUT THEIR CHILD'S SCHOOL

Schools play a vital role in the child's life. They directly affect the family life. Parents want to know about everyday school happenings, how the three R's are taught, the various school regulations, how the tax dollar is spent. They are deeply interested in knowing their child's teacher and are eager to have the opportunity to talk with her about their youngster's progress. These are a few of the findings from a study we conducted with the help of graduate students at Arizona State College at Tempe in 1955 and '56.

The study was made through personal interviews with parents in 900 homes. About 200 of the interviews were conducted in California, Texas, Nevada, Ohio, Connecticut, New York, Alabama, South Dakota and Kansas. Among the 700 interviews made in Arizona more than 150 were with families who had lived previously in 31 other states, Alaska and nine foreign countries, and their children had attended schools in these places.

Interviews were unstructured and informal. Graduate students, mostly teachers, were trained for this type of interviewing by Dr. Stout. This was part of the instruction in classes in school-home relations. From the student point of view this was training not only in professional relationships with parents and in their awareness of school-home relationships but also in ways and means of research. Parents gave generously of their time and expressed deep interest in the one question the interviewers asked: "What do you want to know about your child's school?"

The time spent in each interview varied from one and one-half to four hours. This in itself furnished evidence of parental interest. The interviewer wrote up each interview with no attempt to organize or edit the material, because it seemed important to keep the responses spontaneous.

In order to study the parents' statements each item was entered on a separate card. As cards accumulated they were sorted into large general groups. As the groups became too large to handle they were divided into smaller groups. In this way categories for classification emerged rather than being preconceived and planned. A frequency table was used to help organize the material. No attempt was made to analyze the statements statistically as for the purposes of this study the main interest was the thinking of the parents. We believe that the value of their statements lies primarily in their thought provoking quality.

All types of homes. In order to get a wide sampling, each interviewer was asked to select the parents to be interviewed. They came from all walks of life. More than 433 occupations were represented. In 233 instances the mothers worked outside the home. The children were being brought up in homes that ranged from meagerness in an almost unbelievable degree to affluence in large measure. As might be expected, the largest number fell in the average class.

Parents in the 900 homes had 2145 children in school. Each grade was represented, with a minimum of 123 in the kindergarten and 108 in the 11th grade. The vast majority of the children were in public schools, although a sufficient number came from parochial and nonparochial private schools to provide a sampling. The schools attended were in rural areas, villages, small towns, medium sized towns, and cities. Some were schools known for their conservative procedures and others for their efforts to keep pace with the latest in educational thought.

What findings revealed. The things parents said they wanted to know grouped around curriculum, methods of teaching, school services, administrative details of school operation, the teacher, and relationships pertaining throughout the school.

The fact that parents said they wanted to know this or that does not of any necessity mean that they did not know these things, or that their school had failed to tell them. It should be kept in mind that the one interview question was: "What do you want to know about your child's school?" Replies properly included anything that, to their minds, was desirable for them to know. In many interviews it came out that the school their child attended had done a thoughtful and thorough job of keeping them informed. Indeed, it often was apparent that they spoke of details that conceivably might not have come to their attention had the school not taken the initiative in making them known. However, this was not always the case, and comments showed that in some schools little or no effort had been made to keep the parents informed.

How the parents feel. The statements and comments offered in the interviews reveal a startlingly clear picture of the way these parents feel about their child's school, the vital role they see it playing in his life, and their feeling of dependence on it to help them in their job as parents. It is a picture of profound belief in the school as an institution, of genuine concern that it fulfill the high function they feel it should, of deep respect for and acceptance of it as an established part of our way of living, a vital and crucial influence in their child's life. Anyone reading these interviews could never doubt that in these 900 homes the parents look to their child's school as a factor of fundamental significance in determining the kind of person he will be, and they want it to be good as they see it. They did raise objections and told of things they wished were different, but the very strength of their feeling accented the depth of their interest.

Back of all the comments, statements, suggestions, complaints, expressions of appreciation, it was easy to catch the feeling that parents see the school as an institution belonging to them. They look to it to provide the learning that will determine their child's success. They wish they might have more say about it.

How school affects home. The interviews reveal the way a child's school in its every aspect affects the entire pattern of family living from the time the youngster is enrolled until he graduates or otherwise leaves school. With the reading of one interview after another, this picture comes into clearer and clearer focus, and one sees with deepening understanding the day-by-day adjustment of family living to school hours, school bus schedules, rules and regulations, services, policies, activities, requests, requirements and demands. It is readily understandable that it is not only for their child's sake but for the sake of family living that these parents want to know so much.

There emerges further a picture of parents who want to know many things, but feel shy about asking; some are uncertain what to ask; many feel doubtful about how the teacher would take it if they did ask. Some confessed a definite feeling that questions would not be welcome. Many spoke of their deep appreciation that opportunities are made for them to talk to the teacher, and asserted that they feel welcome at school. Some said that they would not go to school unless invited. Whatever their individual feelings, these parents almost unanimously look to the school to take the initiative. The gulf between home and school seems to be one that only the school can bridge.

Parents speak constructively. The general tone of the interviews was not one of complaining, griping, or fault finding. It was markedly the opposite. True, there were complaints. Often parents said they wished thus and so might be different. But gripes were so few as to be negligible. There was no playing up to the interviewer, since that person was not connected with the child or his school. There was no tendency to take the interview lightly.

The range of matters covered and the multitude of details mentioned showed both breadth and depth of interest. Parents were unanimous in wanting detailed information both about what is being taught in their child's school and how it is being done. They reiterated that they send their child to school to learn and they want to know whether and how this is being accomplished.

Curriculum questions. Not one interview failed to carry a statement of desire to know about some specific phase of the curriculum. Often there were many areas about which the parents said they want information. High on the list are the three R's. There was general concern and some apprehension expressed lest a child might move through the grades without acquiring what parents believe to be adequate facility in use of the fundamental skills.

Coupled with parental concern about the three R's was equal concern lest, in emphasizing these, their child be deprived of experiences with music, art materials, science and physical education. Even those parents most vociferous in their statements about the three R's spoke also of other phases of the curriculum which they hope are being provided. Many spoke of wanting assurance that human relationships are given full attention. One father who spoke long and earnestly, not to say vehemently, about the importance of the three R's and deplored the lack of attention to them said: "But if people can't get along with other people, of what use are the three R's?"

Mentioned frequently was a feeling of confusion about the newer ways of teaching. Parents wonder about the results of more classroom freedom than they themselves had known; they wish there might be more opportunity to hear from school people how ideas about teaching have changed and why.

Nor was the comment always on the side of wanting to know why changes have taken place in their child's school. Frequently they said they would like to know why changes had *not* taken place and what they as parents could do to bring about those changes they regard as necessary to bring the school up to date. To anyone who thinks of the school as always taking the lead in making changes, and usually trying to convince parents of the desirability of these changes, comments in some of the interviews might come as a considerable surprise.

Support was revealed for thoughtful, well considered, carefully instituted changes in curriculum, in methods of teaching, in school administration, in general school planning that would prove heartening to any school administrator who welcomes such support. It should not be supposed that all of these parents are ready to support change in line with up-to-date educational thinking. Some longed for a return to the kind of school they had known, but they were in the noticeable minority.

Discipline interests all. Discipline was one matter on which virtually every parent had something to say. Parents unanimously wanted to know about it in their child's school. They wanted to be assured that their child was in a school and a room where he would learn to respect authority, law and order; where the teacher deserved and demanded respect; where good work habits were expected and taught. With few exceptions they decried harsh discipline, and they deplored threats, appeals to fear, and corporal punishment. It seems significant that discipline so often was spoken of in connection with the child having enough to do; with the work being interesting and challenging; with a child having a chance to use initiative but with the teacher holding a firm hand; with individual attention from the teacher; with a teacher worthy of respect and with genuine interest in each child.

Homework. The desire of parents to know about homework was virtually unanimous. Some thought there was too much; some too little; some the wrong kind, but all wanted to know about it. A study of the comments, complaints, suggestions, expressions of approval and disapproval gives an enlightening glimpse of how they look upon homework as telling them something of what goes on at school. It gives them an idea of what the teacher is trying to help the children to learn and shows something of how the teaching is being done.

Repeatedly parents said they wished the teacher would let them know how to help at home. Over and over they said they feared that what they do with well meaning intent may prove more confusing than helpful, yet they believe they should help and want to. Now and again it was said that the teacher seems to think they are incapable of helping and asks that they keep hands off. This, they say, puts them in a bad light with their own children.

School attitude toward parents. The school's attitude toward parents was spoken of again and again as something these parents wanted to know about. Frequently there was the statement, and more often the implication, that they would welcome being looked upon as an asset but that they felt it to be otherwise. They would like to be of more help than they feel is welcome. They would like to be told specifically how they can help and would welcome an opportunity to offer suggestions.

Implicit in the parents' suggestions is the wish for open lines of communication. It is not to be supposed that in many of the schools represented these do not exist. On the contrary, it was evident that they do exist and the parents bespoke their appreciation for them. Nor is it to be supposed that all of the parents have a yearning to be of help to the school. Some said that it was the business of the school to see to it that the child learned and all they wanted to know was that he did. They did not feel the school should look to the parents to do its work. These, however, were in a small minority.

Grading, reporting, promotion. Among the parents in these 900 queried families only a few failed to mention grading, reporting and promotion as matters about which they want to know. They spoke of wanting grades that let them know with certainty how their child is doing. Most of those who mentioned the system of grading that uses S for satisfactory and U for unsatisfactory are definitely and emphatically opposed to it. They complained that it gives them only the vaguest idea of their child's achievement. Instances were cited of feeling comfortable about a child's rating of S only to find out too late that he would not be promoted. The consensus was in favor of the 1 2 3 4 5 or A B C D E system, which to them seems more definite. In a few instances parents spoke of meetings in which the administrator explained the S U system in advance and gave reasons for the change. In these cases objections were more moderate, but even so the system was looked upon unfavorably. When the 1 2 3 4 5 or A B C D E system was mentioned the wish was often expressed that the teacher would tell how grades are determined. A few of these parents spoke up in favor of the percentage system. Always the comments and objections pointed to the same thing. They want to know what their child is doing in school and they want some system that tells them. Many spoke in appreciation of the teacher comments on the report cards. Teacher reporting by interview was mentioned by many and always with approval, although the 15 minutes allowed for each interview was considered woefully inadequate.

The promotion system ranked high among things these parents said they wanted to know about. Those who spoke of the social promotion plan, and many did, tended to be either unfavorable in mild degree or violently opposed. Those whose child was in a school where it is in use almost unanimously deplored the plan and wanted none of it for their child. Objections included the charge that it leaves both parents and child in the dark as to the youngster's real achievement or lack of it; that it is unfair both to those who learn readily and to those who do not, with the gap between them widening as they move on together. This makes it, they pointed out, difficult for the teacher.

School services. These parents wanted to know about much more than the happenings within their child's classroom. They spoke of wanting to know about school services as they affect their child, about the administrative details of the school, about the over-all school setup and planning. Composite comments and suggestions pointed to arrangements which the parents envision, arrangements which some knew about in their child's school or in others, arrangements which would keep teachers accurately informed about many details of school administration so that they could pass the facts on to the parents; time allowed for conferences with parents; effort on the teacher's own part to keep informed about the entire school operation; meetings with the administrator; bulletins from the administrative office; regular school news notes to parents.

School finances. A large percentage told of wanting to know about school finances; what the school tax money goes for; on what basis budgets are set up; what planning is being done ahead to provide adequate space and up-to-date equipment; how district lines are determined, and so on. Scarcely an administrative detail could be thought of that wasn't mentioned a sufficient number of times to have significance to the administrator who looks upon giving information to parents as a vital part of his public relations program.

Teacher is key. These parents again and again pointed to the teacher as the most important single factor in their child's school life. The statements related to the teacher and the teacher's relationship to the children outnumber all other groupings, and the statement was made many times that "the teacher is the key to it all." Pursuant to this was the reiterated concern about knowing not only the kind of person their child's teacher is but knowing his attitude toward teaching as a profession. Often it was the teacher who was mentioned as the first and most important matter on which they wanted information. By statement and comment they set forth, in a way that would be enlightening to teachers, administrators and those charged with training teachers, just what it is they would like to know. This included how teachers are chosen; what qualifications the school sets up as requirements for employment; what salaries are paid; if these are not sufficient to attract a high quality of teacher why they are not raised; what the arrangements are for retirement.

Retirement arrangements constituted the subject of widespread comment, the parents setting forth their wish to know with certainty that their child has a teacher who is well, vigorous, interested, up to date. While some spoke of wanting a teacher who is young, many spoke in favor of experience; the general emphasis was on youngness of thought and interest rather than concern with actual years. Again and again mention was made of love of children as one of the basic qualifications without which they believe no person should be in the classroom. Others were adequate preparation for teaching and skill in teaching so that the child would have every opportunity to learn.

Opportunity to know teacher. The possibility of knowing their child's teacher and having frequent opportunity to talk with her alone and long enough to get some satisfaction out of it was a point many mentioned. They expressed themselves freely as to their feeling about the importance of such contacts and their wish that they could feel assured that the teacher would be honest with them even though the facts relative to their child's progress might be disappointing to them. There was frequent expression of appreciation for the time and thought given by certain teachers their child had had, an interest often carried beyond anything they had expected. The comments showed that, in many of the schools represented, opportunity for conferring with the teachers is confined largely to casual meetings at P.T.A., which parents said affords them only little satisfaction.

Best public relations. It seems reasonable to believe that the parents in the 900 homes covered in this study are sufficiently typical of parents the country over to suggest that what they have said may well be given serious consideration by administrators and teachers. What they have said is simple. They want to know about their child's school from the broad aspects of philosophy and curriculum to the minutest details of classroom procedure and method. They want to know what their child is taught. They want to know how he is getting along. They want to know his teacher and what kind of person he is. They want to know what the administrator and the teacher think of them as parents.

The administrator who realizes that this is what parents want to know and who wants to have them know it will find ways not only of talking with them himself but also of helping his teachers know what to tell and how to tell it and, above all, to realize the importance of doing it. This is public relations at its best.

HELPING PARENTS TO ACCEPT   *3*
THEIR EXCEPTIONAL CHILDREN

If you, as a teacher of exceptional children, had three wishes that could come true, what would you wish for most? I'm sure one wish would be that the parents of your pupils would really accept these youngsters emotionally. Another wish might be that the parents do their homework in helping your pupils to be their own best—not their parents' best. A third wish would probably be that the parents of your pupils would work closely with you and with one another in helping their children to achieve individual happiness and responsible citizenship. In other words, you know that you're in danger of being defeated in what you wish to do for your pupils unless you can develop wholesome attitudes in their parents. You know that you must enlist the active cooperation of parents in the best possible development for your pupils.

PARENTS MUST ACCEPT THEIR CHILDREN
EMOTIONALLY

Your experience will have impressed upon you that often it isn't the handicap that really matters, but how the individual feels about his handicap. Bonaro Overstreet says, "The weight of a problem is the significance it has for the person who carries it." Parents of an exceptional child can help him effectively only by accepting him as he is, without embarassment, resentment, shame, guilt, or resignation. The only way that parents can do their proper job as parents is to accept their child as a loved and treasured human being in his own right, and to recognize that he deserves their best help in realizing his possibilities. It is also the only way in which a child can be helped to accept himself as a worthwhile human being, and to work effectively at the development of his own potentialities.

HELPING PARENTS ACCEPT THEIR CHILDREN

You may be so fortunate as to work in a community where you have the help of psychiatrists, psychologists, social workers, or visiting teachers in getting parents to accept their exceptional children in wholesome fashion. However, even in that case, you, as the child's classroom teacher, have an important part in helping the parents of your pupils. You are the parents' most active partner in the development of their child. Together, you and the parents plan for the child and meet concrete problems in his development. On your shoulders, then, must fall much of the responsibility for helping the parents of your pupils to accept their youngsters with the love and respect which is the right of all children. The question is: How are you going to do it?

Your own attitude will help form the parents attitude. You, yourself, must accept these children emotionally as worthwhile, treasured human beings. Pity is not a good basis for acceptance; respect is much better. Genuine affection based on the child's inherent worth is much better than a coldly scientific attitude. Your own attitude is catching. Any inner feeling that the exceptional child is basically inferior as a human being to other children will communicate itself to the parents—and to the children. You can't cheat. The exceptional child, like all other children, must be accepted emotionally by his teacher as well as his parents so that he may develop the sense of trust which, according to the Mid-Century White House Conference, is the cornerstone of a wholesome personality.

NO ONE CAN ORDER A BLOND BABY

The second step in helping parents is to get them to realize that all parents have to accept their children. Many who wanted a girl-baby must accept wholeheartedly the boy who arrives instead. All parents must accept their child's characteristics—be he short or tall, plain or beautiful, blue-or brown- eyed, long or short nosed. The father who dreams of his son as a great football—or hockey player may have to accept one whose physical equipment doesn't fit him to compete. Parents of physically handicapped children need to understand that their problem is only one aspect of the problem that all parents have to meet.

Then, too, parents have to take the mental abilities of their children as they come. Parents who want a gifted child may have to accept one of average intelligence who will never be a scholar or, perhaps, even a professional man. A mother who wants her daughter to be a great musician may have to admit the fact that her child has neither ability or interest in music. The man who wants his son to enter his business or his law office may find that the boy is interested in art, and not in business or professional life at all.

We do not set up impossible standards for friends and acquaintances. We take them as they are. In choosing wives, husbands, and friends, parents of exceptional children and the rest of us don't choose angels, but human beings, all of whom have definite limitations. Certainly they aren't all great athletes, or great musicians, or outstanding scholars, or public figures. Few are really outstanding for their beauty. If a human being were to reject family or friends because they weren't perfect, he would soon be all alone in the world. We love relatives and friends in spite of their imperfections. In living on a realistic basis, we all have to accept human frailties and put them into the right perspective. Parents of exceptional children must do likewise. Of course, no one will try to persuade either parents or children to adopt the Pollyanna attitude that handicaps don't matter. But parents can face the problem, see it in perspective and say, with courage, "Yes, it's a handicap to be deaf, but how can we develop the child's other abilities?"

THE DEMOCRATIC VIEW OF LIFE

If we are to pay democracy more than lipservice, we must believe that every human being (including exceptional children) is entitled to the best possible opportunity for "life, liberty, and the pursuit of happiness." One of the great pitfalls for teachers is to consider that the slow-learning child or the otherwise handicapped child is less worthy of professional skill than the gifted child. True democracy means attempting to give all children (including the gifted, for that matter) the best possible opportunity to develop to the limits of their own possibilities. Teachers who really feel this, not merely accept it intellectually, will be successful in helping parents to see that their exceptional child is entitled to the best possible chance to develop as a wholesome personality and an effective citizen, in the same way as their other children, who happen to be typical in abilities and development. Parents need help in realizing that the objectives of education: selfrealization, happy human relationships, economic efficiency, and civic responsibility, are the same for all children, but the means used to attain these are different, as is the degree to which pupils attain the objectives.

Religion May Help

Parents who have a religious view of life can be helped to

understand that every human being is equal in the sight of God, and that all God's children are of infinite worth. It follows that exceptional children are entitled to respect and to the best help that homes, schools and communities can give them.

Feelings Of Guilt Handicap Parents

Many parents of handicapped children are prevented from doing their best for their children by a sense of guilt. They may feel responsible for the child's handicap—that if they hadn't done so-and-so this wouldn't have happened to their child. Or they may seek for reasons in their own general sinfulness, or in heredity. Their thinking is reminiscent of Dean Inge's article on "The Ifs of History," where he speculates, "If Saint Paul had been caught when he was being lowered down the walls of Damascus in a basket, would we now be Christians?" Too much indulgence in such interesting intellectual exercise is not wholesome for any human being. All of us learn to accept past events, past decisions, and even past mistakes, and go on from there. In most cases the parents of exceptional children cannot be blamed for their child's condition and, even if they could, feelings of guilt would hinder them from doing a good job for the child here and now. Teachers can often help parents to a more practical and realistic attitude. The more serious cases of parent guilt fixation should be referred to a psychiatrist.

Exceptional Children Have the Same
Needs as Other Children

Teachers can help parents to realize that the exceptional child has the same needs as other children. Any child wants to be loved, to feel that he belongs in his home, and that his parents and family value him. Any child who feels emotionally insecure with his parents has two strikes against him. Parents who reject or resent an exceptional child increase both the child's burdens and their own, and jeopardize his chances of developing to the limit of his capacities.

Like other children, the exceptional child needs gradually to learn to make his own decisions and to do things for himself. False pity and sympathy may lead to overprotection which will destroy any child's emotional independence. The Mid-Century White House Conference stressed the child's need to develop a "sense of autonomy"—the feeling that he is an independent being with a will and mind of his own. This attitude is at the basis of selfcontrol and selfconfidence. Teachers can help to show parents how important a part they play in the developing of this independence.

The parents of exceptional children need help, too, in understanding that their youngsters, like all other boys and girls, need achievement, recognition, and selfesteem. They need the chance to accomplish things in work and play, to receive recognition from others for what they are, and do, and to know from the reactions of parents, teachers, or playmates that they are treasured and valued human beings. A child's feeling about himself is apt to be the mirrored-back reflection of how others feel towards him. Teachers can help parents to find ways of giving their exceptional children the feeling of accomplishment, approval and sense of worth which all children need.

While no attempt should be made to minimize a child's handicaps, attention should be focused on the youngsters possibilities. Probably no human being makes complete use of his resources of mind, body, and personality. All parents need help in realizing what goals are possible ones for their child, and what can be done to promote his best development. Too many expect impossible things from their child— either at his present stage of development or eventually. Others entirely overlook many of their child's resources. Teachers can help the parents of an exceptional child to be realistic about their child's possibilities for development, and to work patiently and consistently in promoting that development.

Parents Groups

Four sets of teachers guide the development of all children: home teachers (parents or other relatives), school-teachers, playmate teachers, and community teachers (which include all community agencies—church, recreation, welfare, and the like). It is vital for the development of exceptional children that this partnership be made effective. Not only can the schoolteacher and parents do joint planning for the exceptional child, but the teacher can help parents to extend this partnership to clinics, rehabilitation centers, social workers, and the like. The teacher can encourage the formation of parents groups where parents of exceptional children share their problems and give each other mutual support and help. Such a group may be made up of parents of children in one special class, or may be a city, county, state, or national body. Group study of problems releases tensions in parents, frees them from a sense of isolation, and helps them to do concrete planning for their children. Teachers should remember that fathers are parents too, and that every effort should be made to enlist them in group study and activities. An uninformed or uninterested father can readily undo all the good a mother may be trying to foster in a home.

Gifted Children Need Acceptance Too

In case it may be inferred that what has been said above applies only to physically and mentally handicapped children, it might be pointed out that gifted children are often rejected by parents and teachers. A gifted child is often not understood. His needs for emotional security, independence, achievement, recognition, and a sense of worth may be frustrated even more greatly than are those of the handicapped child. Democracy demands for gifted children that they be given every possible opportunity to develop to the limits of their abilities. Parents need help in accepting their gifted child, in recognizing his peculiar problems of adjustment, and in understanding the methods by which he can be helped to achieve his high promise.

Make Your Own Partnership With Parents Effective

If you are a teacher of exceptional children, one of your primary jobs is to improve your own technics of working with parents. This may involve a study of ways of improving the individual parent-teacher conference, or it may involve a study of group dynamics, so that group meetings of the parents may yield the dividends they should. In any event it is well to realize that your help in assisting the parents of your pupils to accept their youngsters emotionally may well bring returns a hundredfold, in the development of the boys and girls with whom you work from day to day.

COUNSELING PARENTS OF CHILDREN WITH *4*
LEARNING DISABILITIES

Many members of the helping professions have mixed feelings toward parents and their aid in a child's remedial program. There are a number of forces at work in producing the negative feelings many professionals harbor toward parents of patients.

First, all are heir to the legacies of the environmental school, which seeks to explain people largely in terms of parental influences. Most professionals realize the negative things parents can do to their children. Yet few have worked out the relationship between causal, deterministic explanations on the one hand, and notions of "accountability" or "blame" on the other. Hence, consistency is rare in these matters, and while one "explains" behavior among those toward whom one feels positively inclined, the tendency is to "blame" and "condemn" these same behaviors among those toward whom one lacks positive regard.

Second, professionals often project their own self-anger at parents. It is not unusual for a professional to blame himself or herself for not helping the patient to a greater degree than has been possible. This all-too-human anger often ends up directed at the parents, who are seen as the "real" reason the patient is not making more progress.

Third, all professionals and non-professionals harbor ambivalent feelings toward their own parents. These feelings are often confused with feelings toward other peoples' parents, including those of patients.

Fourth, many professionals believe that since it took them so long to master their helping skills, it is unlikely that others less trained than ourselves could contribute anything of importance to a helping process. Stated bluntly, many professionals are unwilling to believe a lay person can be therapeutic and/or helpful.

Fifth, likewise, those impressed with the role of the unconscious in human behavior are sometimes unwilling to acknowledge that help can be had from the uninsightful. Professionals of this persuasion seem to believe that because a good bit of behavior occurs outside, so to speak, the purview of conscious intention, that therefore *all* significant behavior is outside the influence of conscious will.

Lastly, many professionals seem to believe that *since* some parents are motivated *in part* by a desire to *sustain* their children's problems, this desire constitutes the major force in *all* parent-child relationships.

Thus while it is true that parents *are* in fact responsible for some of their children's problems, and while it is true most parents lack insight into the why's and wherefore's of their children's problems, and may even desire, at least in part, that their children stay sick, it does not follow that these negative forces define the whole of parent-child relations. Nor does it follow that all or even most parents cannot be depended upon for active help in a remediation program.

Thus professionals such as Barsch (1961)[a] Ginott (1961)[b] and Rappaport (1969)[c] have emphasized the utilization of parents in remedial programs. Prior to this emphasis (or in its absence) parents felt even more guilty than was necessary, left out, impotent, and decidedly angry, consciously and unconsciously, at the professionals who stood between them and their troubled youngsters.

The parents of a child with a learning disability have usually lived through several years of doubt and confusion in relation to their child. They have probably been given much conflicting advice. They have tried many things—pushing, not pushing; yelling, not yelling; helping with homework, not helping. Nothing has worked—at least not for long. It is no wonder that they approach the interviews of a diagnostic study with fear and doubt.

When a special school is recommended, some parents breathe a sign of relief: "Now someone else will do the job." Then they withdraw. Others, although willing to follow the recommendation, continue to hover anxiously. For all, there are unasked questions, unresolved feelings and much doubt about the future.

When a child enters Parkway Day School his parents also enter a parent counseling group composed of about six couples who meet weekly with a group leader. The Counselor also meets weekly with the teachers. The philosophy under-lying these sessions is that parents have very important and specific roles to play in the helping process, that remediation is a twenty-four-hour-a-day affair (not just a matter of a schoolday or a therapeutic hour), and that parents as well as their children have both the capacity and underlying desire for positive change.

PURPOSES AND CONTENT OF THE SESSIONS

The most obvious purpose is to provide the parents with

information concerning learning disabilities, to define the entity, not only in a broad general way but specifically for each family. This is a prelude to helping a parent-pair face the problem, its true implications, and their feelings about it. Much anxiety grows from a lack of knowledge. Too long some professionals have felt information should be kept from parents or else have couched the information in complicated terminology. This was done either because the professional doubted the parents would or could do anything positive with the information, or because of some other irrationality on the professional's part.

The first time a parent has his child's problem explained to him he usually misses a great deal. The information is perceived to emotionally. His own hopes and fears get mixed in with what is told him. There is no time to assimilate the information. He does not want to hear. This same parent comes to the (later) counseling sessions with three important questions on his mind:

1. What is this learning disability my child has?
2. What caused it? (He really means: Who is to blame?)
3. How long will it take to overcome it?

Initially sessions are spent discussing the varying types of learning disabilities, identifying the problems of particular children, showing similarities and differences among different children and categories, spelling out and defining characteristics, and listing things that can be expected with the passage of time. The question of causality is handled honestly in terms of current professional knowledge.

Parental anger and guilt emerge rapidly. Almost at once parents begin blaming themselves (or others) for their children's problems. They are helped to see the utter futility (but understandableness) of this approach—that not only is it unlikely any one person or thing caused the difficulty, but that "blaming" solves nothing anyway. The focus then becomes: what can we do to help?

The matter of the time necessary for remediation is handled concurrently; however this is impossible to answer directly, but it does make sense to talk of sequences children go through as they improve. It is via observed movement through these stages that improvement is gauged. How long a particular child will remain at a particular level is difficult to predict in advance.

The second purpose of the sessions is to provide a liason between home and school. What are the child's reactions when he arrives home? What has the teacher seen? Has the child seemed especially tired, unhappy, out of control? Such matters can be explored with the parents. Information about the child's reactions at home and school can be pooled, to better plan a coordinated program. Within this context it is important that the need for both honesty and confidentiality be stressed. It is important for the counselor to be able to assess accurately how a parent will use information about a child's behavior in school. It is important, also, that the children do not see the parent sessions as "tattling" or "blaming" meetings, but rather as one more essential part of the remedial program.

Parents have many questions about a special school program and many feelings to express. "Why does my child have no homework?" "My child *has* homework, but why is it so easy?" "Why do you tolerate bad behavior?" "Why is my child allowed to talk in class?" "Were you punishing him when he had to work alone today?"

In other instances it is easier for parents to express their negative feelings about certain aspects of a school program to some one whom they see neither as their child's teacher or as a member of the school administration. (This should be established at the outset, along with the groundrules.)

It is essential that both school and home be aware of the importance of a twenty-four-hour-a-day coordinated approach. It helps parents and teachers not to feel so frustrated or impotent. Neither feels alone. The importance of knowing someone else understands how you feel can never be overestimated, for parent or professional.

The third purpose of the meetings is to help parents understand the behavior of their children and to understand the feelings in the child which generate certain kinds of behavior. Along with this, parents work on understanding their own reactions and feelings to the child's behavior. The aim here is to realize that a child's total behavior is important in the remediation of his difficulty. The way in which limits are set or the way in which independence is encouraged or subtly not encouraged may have a great bearing on how the child learns in school. In the course of the school program the child's behavior may change markedly. A formerly inhibited, tightly controlled child may suddenly begin acting out. A parent needs to be prepared for these changes and offered suggestions on how to cope with them.

Some parents approach any discussion of their child's behavior with "We're sending him to school to learn to read.

Other than that, leave us alone." Some come looking for gimmicks. "What magic words can I use to get him to do his homework, clean up, come in for dinner?" Occasionally this kind of parent will attempt to parrot the counselor's words in response to a child's behavior. Sometimes it works and the child responds appropriately. But it may not work the second time, and the parent becomes disillusioned.

The aim then is to get away from gimmicks or the "What do I do when?" question and *develop a total approach* to the child's behavior. In order to do this, it is necessary to discuss behavior both in the context of typical child development and within the context of a particular child's specific problems. Several things are important here. The parent needs to learn to really listen to the child and become an accurate observer, so that he can find out what the child is trying to communicate through his behavior. Parents begin to understand that before the child can change they must accept him as he is with all his problems. This is a very hard step. They also begin to understand that children with learning disabilities are usually angry children who are very much afraid of this anger. They begin to accept too that they are angry parents. Again these are very hard steps. They start to learn to accept themselves as they are, to be honest with themselves and gradually to reduce their anger both at themselves and their children. They work on effective ways of setting limits and encouraging independence.

The sessions by their very nature are child centered. Feelings and actions have been discussed in relation to the children and the total family. The final purpose of the sessions applies to some but not all parents. Occasionally as the sessions develop and the child progresses in school, a parent will realize that a readiness has been developed for deeper personal exploration. Such parents may seek psychotherapy for themselves.

ORGANIZATION AND IMPLEMENTATION
OF THE SESSIONS

In setting up groups of parents an effort is made to group parents of children with similar problems and age. Thus parents of "acting out" children, "tightly controlled" or "overly dependent" children might be in different groups although the children themselves might be in the same classroom. Grouping is flexible and may be changed during the school term. Parents of children new to the school are usually seen individually, then as a group, and only then gradually worked into an existing group.

The degree of structure the leader gives to the session and the amount of leader participation varies considerably. In the beginning when basic ground work is being developed and the importance of conveying accurate concepts is considerable, the sessions are well structured. Leader participation is great. As the sessions progress to areas involving feelings and reactions to children's behavior, leader participation diminishes. During this phase the leader accepts and acknowledges feelings, keeps the discussion child-centered and problem oriented and serves as a sounding board against which various solutions to problems can be tested. The group and the leader together summarize each session.

Mrs. S., the mother of eight year old Billy whose learning disability involved number concepts, arrived at one of the sessions very upset. Her younger son Johnny, six, had just begun first grade. Johnny had always seemed happy and self-confident. Since the beginning of school Billy, the eight year old, had followed first-grader Johnny around after school asking him, "How much is 300 plus 400? 600 plus 200? 25 plus 50?" Johnny seemed increasingly less and less happy. He ran to his mother for answers. Even after the boys were in bed at night, she could hear the quizzing continue. She was upset because she was unsure how to respond to Billy. Billy had had great difficulty with number concepts, and now, although he knew and understood the answers to the questions he was asking, still lacked confidence in himself. Billy sought to bolster his own confidence at Johnny's expense. How much of this should you tolerate? Is it fair to allow Billy to build his confidence at Johnny's expense.

The group's initial and uncensored response to Mrs. S's problem was: "Tell Billy to keep quiet." But they rapidly decided this would be unwise. They agreed this was a difficult thing for Mrs. S., and began to discuss the possible negative outcomes if Mrs. S. lost her temper with Billy, her immediate impulse. Should this happen the group decided: 1] both children would learn that this was a good way to upset Mommy, 2] Johnny, the little one, might define himself right into a helpless dependent role, and 3] Billy, the eight-year-old learning disability child, might confuse his mother's condemnation of his testing his younger brother, with condemnation of him for knowing something his brother didn't. The group then decided that the real problem was how to respond to both children so as to help both.

Further discussion revealed that all the parents had observed this behavior in second and third graders toward first graders and agreed that it was typical of children this age. They also agreed that in Billy's case it was occurring in excess. This served to place the behavior in appropriate perspective.

After further discussion it was decided that responding positively to Billy's new-found skill in adding and not responding at all to his questioning of his brother might be helpful to him. Mrs. S. decided that she wanted Billy to know she was pleased at how well he could add, that she knew it took a lot of hard work and that he must be very proud of himself. These were the things that she and the group felt were important in what Billy was saying.

To the younger child, Johnny, who had always seemed self confident and happy, they decided that when he came to his mother for the answer she should tell him the answer and add: "This is something that you are not supposed to know now. You will learn it later in the year." From this they thought Johnny would learn 1] "I'm not supposed to know it now so I'm not dumb if I don't," 2] "Mommy will help me when I need it," and 3] "I'll soon be able to do it myself."

Summarizing, it was pointed out how what seemed like such a simple piece of behavior turned out to be quite complex—that it was extremely important to find out what the child was really saying to you through his behavior. Even more important, however, each parent had to decide what he wanted the child to learn *before* he responded. Too many times one responds to a child thoughtlessly and the child learns an unintended message—a message one would never want conveyed. Many parents, at the outset, worried about the exact words they would use in communicating with their child. The more practice they had in thinking through just what they wanted to communicate, the more easily the words came.

REACTIONS OF PARENTS AND TEACHERS

A recent discussion with a group of parents who had attended sessions for two school years, and a separate discussion with the teachers, revealed some striking similarities.

1. Members of both groups felt their ability to see the child from different perspectives was very helpful. A given child may have been provoking at home, but not at school, and vice-versa.
2. Parents and teachers both thought it helpful to know everyone was struggling for the same things—that there were no easy magic answers, known to others but not a particular person.
3. Everyone found it helpful to know more about sources of daily stress.
4. The teachers felt greater empathy for the parents, and no longer saw them as "critical" outsiders.
5. A greater understanding was gained by all that each adult was not totally responsible for a child's actions. "When a child has a difficult day, it may not be my fault, or anybody's for that matter."
6. Both parents and teachers were better able to evaluate the truth of the child's utterances. In the beginning, parents and teachers accepted as gospel the children's tales: "My mom won't give me breakfast." "All we do is play all day in school." Now much needless anger was avoided.
7. Parents and teachers were both able to set more effective limits. Parents and teachers appreciated the consistency of an approach that attends better communication.
8. One parent summarized the feeling of being better able to ask the right questions: "Remember when I used to ask you every week when he'd be ready to go back to public school and he couldn't even read a pre-primer? It might be more useful for us to talk about all the bragging he's been doing lately. It's so unrealistic." That particular session then moved to a discussion of ways children have of coping with their fear of failure. Each parent had examples and they exchanged ideas on the best ways to respond.

CONCLUSION

In a school for children with learning disabilities parent counseling sessions serve a number of functions:
1. They provide information concerning learning disabilities and help parents understand and cope with their feelings about their own child's problems.
2. They coordinate home and school activities so that the approach to the child is relatively consistent.
3. The sessions help parents understand their child's behavior as it relates to typical child development and to sort out those behaviors growing out of his learning disability. They learn to recognize and accept their own feelings as well as those of the child.
4. The sessions help parents set more effective limits, accept and acknowledge feelings and develop appropriate independence in the child.

Much that is asked of parents during the counseling sessions is difficult. It is hard to look at things differently, to explore feelings and to change ways of responding to children. Parents, however, just as their children, have the capacity to change. To the degree that parents are already basically healthy from an emotional standpoint have they been able to profit from the sessions. Some, however, have realized that many of their problems with their children stemmed from deeper personal needs and have sought individual psychotherapy.

SEX EDUCATION:
PARENT INVOLVEMENT IN DECISION MAKING

Although it is axiomatic in curriculum theory that those affected by a decision should be involved in its formulation, the pragmatic administrator often tends to regard the axiom as impractical.

When it comes to including sex education in the curriculum, however, there are compelling practical reasons for involving parents in decisions to be made. After all, the area is so charged with emotional dynamite that if the parental community is not consulted, the administrator can be dynamited right out of his job. In this article we report an involvement experiment; it includes some suggestions for administrators contemplating change in the sex education curriculum of their schools.

Many elementary schools have a "Fathers' Night" at which presentations are made about the new math, the reading program, discipline, federal aid, and perhaps sex education. Frequently these meetings end with a question-and-answer period, and all go home until the next fathers' night.

In the situation described here (Henry Ford Elementary School, Redwood City, Calif.) the desire on the part of the school for community involvement and sharing in decision making is evident.

Although other curriculum areas at Ford's Fathers' Night sparked questions and discussion, it appeared that the fathers felt a more direct involvement and concern with what the school was doing about sex education. They queried and probed about existing programs and available materials. Fathers wanted to know about the program and material used. The principal explained that traditionally the school provided films on menstruation for girls, and the classroom teachers provided some "sex instruction" via science and health units. The principal pointed out, in response to a father's question about the contents of this material, that "the human body as far as the textbook is concerned ends just below the navel."

Some fathers asked why. Others wondered if this might not be an extension of the "dirty and secret" syndrome characteristic of sex discussions in Victorian days. Other questions were asked: What should the school do in this area? How can we help teachers and mothers? What materials are available for boys as well as for girls? What do they talk about in films on menstruation? Do the films discuss masturbation?

It was evident from the questions that fathers wanted something more than what the school was providing. They wanted to see the films their daughters see. They wanted to see the few films available for boys. Finally, they wanted the staff to select such materials to be presented at a follow-up meeting. The principal clearly pointed out that he wanted them to help make decisions with respect to curriculum material. The fathers agreed.

An overcrowded library provided a theater in which the fathers viewed the films and other materials selected by the staff. After intensive discussion five major decisions were developed:

1. *The Story of Menstruation and Human Growth* became a part of fifth-and-sixth-grade curriculum.

Fathers decided that the school principal should lead the

discussion rather than nurses or doctors in order to avoid, in the words of one father, an "antiseptic atmosphere."

2. The film, *Boy to Man*, would be shown at an evening meeting at which fathers would bring their sons.

The major reason this film was selected for a father-son showing was the attitude it takes toward masturbation. Although there were differences of opinion of an ethical nature, most fathers agreed that this problem could be overcome. One father wondered whether the program might encourage "bad behavior." Others reacted by saying that the presentation of facts alone would not assure proper behavior. This discussion led to agreement that there should be communication and dialogue between fathers and their pre-adolescents based upon the facts of the film.

3. Boys and girls would see and discuss the films together.

The fathers decided that the opportunity to view the films and ask questions in a mixed group could help develop a mutual respect for physical differences and perhaps initiated an openness to communication about sex. The fathers were determined *not to extend the "dirty-secret" notions* if at all possible. It was also decided that the principal would guide the question-answer period for the mixed group.

4. Boys would have an opportunity to ask questions of the principal, girls of the school nurse.

Fathers felt that certain questions might not be asked in the mixed groups. Working to develop openness in relation to sex, these "special questions" might be best answered in segregated groups.

5. The mothers would have an opportunity to see and discuss the films.

The films and materials were viewed and discussed. The fathers' decisions were enthusiastically supported by the mothers. They expressed pleasure in having their husbands become involved both in school matters and the children's welfare.

It is important to note here that these decisions were made by consensus. Parents did not feel threatened or pressured because *they* were involved in the decision-making process. They admitted the need, wanted to do something, and had trust in the school. Given the opportunity for honest involvement in matters which have an impact on the family, parents will, we discovered, come to school and make important decisions.

The principal prepared himself for the programs by viewing the films several times, jotting down ideas, vocabulary, and potential questions. He consulted with teachers and reviewed questions and comments resulting from the various meeting with parents. He studied several articles and pamphlets on sex education. He reviewed material in textbooks at various grade levels, noting what was provided and what gaps, misunderstandings, or omissions existed. Actually, through self-education, the principal became something of a specialist.

Each meeting (one with fifth-graders, the other with sixth-graders) lasted almost two hours. The principal showed both films (*The Story of Menstruation* and *Human Growth*) and spent about one and one-half hours in discussion. Following this two-hour session, the principal took the boys out on the lawn area of the school and spent another hour answering questions in a free and open discussion. The principal had prepared for this by informing the parents that if they wanted their youngsters to venture into the area of sex education every question was to be answered honestly and intelligently. He also indicated to parents that they should be prepared to follow up on the questions asked.

The school nurse and female teachers reported that the girls were equally open in their discussion. Both the principal and school nurse found that fifth- and sixth-graders asked the same kinds of questions. There was little difference in the quality and depth of these questions, although it appeared that the fifth-graders were more open, willing to explore every area of the subject in the mixed group.

The following five questions served as an example of what was asked. Do people mate just once? If you masturbate, do you get diphtheria and go crazy? How do sperm cells know which way to do? Why do people have to learn about mating when other animals don't? My aunt takes pills to get pregnant. Why?

A fathers-sons meeting followed by one week the students' meeting with the principal, school nurse, and teachers. At this meeting fathers and sons (some of junior college and high school ages) viewed the film *Boy to Man.* Few questions followed, but this may be the result of the incident which occurred at the beginning of the discussion period. One boy raised his hand shortly after the discussion began and asked: "What is masturbation?" Before the principal could answer the question, the boy's father indicated that he would appreciate the opportunity to discuss this question with his son alone. This seemed to set the tone. Most fathers wanted to take their boys out of the meeting and talk "man to man."

It is difficult to provide conclusive evidence of the worth of such a program. Evidence of increase in knowledge gained was not statistically evaluated. Yet the experience seemed worthwhile on other grounds.

First, the climate and relationship between the principal and fifth- and sixth-grade boys seemed to change in a positive direction. The school nurse and teachers also felt a change in attitude, something conveyed in the phrase, "Oh, you know too; thanks."

Both the principal and nurse felt extreme pressure from the provocative questions asked by pupils and the push for meaningful answers. But because of the involvement of parents and the careful preliminary planning they did not hesitate to answer these questions to the best of their ability.

It was exhilarating for the staff to see how fathers involved themselves in school planning and curriculum decision making.

Teachers indicated to the principal that they had to go back to old biology notes and read college textbooks to continue to answer questions on cell division, twins, heredity, and the like.

Parents were quite enthusiastic about the program. They enjoyed becoming involved with school personnel in designing and implementing the program. About 75 percent of the families were represented. We believe that acceptance of the program is directly related to the fact that *parents were involved in the decision-making process from the beginning in this curriculum area.* Parents did not feel that outside "do-gooders" were going to set things straight. Nor did they feel that their privacy was being invaded in the very private matter of sex.

Parent attitude towards the program is perhaps best illustrated by the following incident: Two days after the formal presentation had been completed, the principal received an anonymous phone call at school. The mother calling indicated how appreciative she and other parents were that the program had been inaugurated. She concluded by saying, "What you did caused my husband and me to sit up until two o'clock in the morning talking about sex as it relates to us and the kids. This is the first time in 16 years of our marriage that this had ever happened."

SEX EDUCATION THAT MAKES SENSE   6

People are becoming increasingly aware of the need for sex education for their children. Episodes running the gamut from permarital pregnancy to adolescent homosexual play strike terror in the hearts of parents and accelerate the pressure on the schools to hurry up and get a sex education program going.

What often results from this crisis climate is one or two lectures about menstruation and reproduction. Usually the school nurse or a doctor is brought in to help the teacher in this "sensitive" area of education. The teacher or the expert proceeds to give the children all the correct terms, using slides and anatomical charts. Sometimes a movie depicting the development from girl to woman and boy to man is shown. The students are permitted to ask questions, but the answers they get are often limited to the anatomical and functional aspects of growth, development, and reproduction.

What is wrong with this kind of sex education? Aren't the youngsters being taught the "facts of life" in an objective, unemotional way, with the correct use of terms, and aren't they receiving vital information about their bodies?

Let me answer on the basis of 14 years of professional experience in dealing with sexual and family living problems of children, adolescents, and married couples.

The short answer is that the information they are learning is necessary to the development of healthy sex attitudes, but this is only one aspect of such development.

It is sexuality, not sex, that is crucial. Human sexuality is what is personally important to the growing child, the adolescent, and the adult. Sexual identity is an important part of the self-image and affects every aspect of life. For example, sexuality involves the name we are given at birth, the toys we play with as a child, the clothes we wear, the friends we have, the things we like to do, the courses we take in high school and college, the careers we choose, the way we see our roles and responsibilities in our homes, and last but not least, the ways we satisfy and cope with out sexual needs and urges as responsible and committed human beings.

Asking other questions may reinforce the point: Is it enough to teach a sixth grade boy how one becomes a father without teaching him what it means to be a respected man?

Don't we also need to teach him attitudes and behavior that will help him, on reaching manhood, to be a sympathetic, kind, and understanding husband and father? As upset and panicky as we get at the thought of youngsters' having premarital relations, how much more critical and upsetting is the crisis that will be caused later on if they marry and have children only to end up with divorce and family disintegration.

During adolescence, when youngsters need to discuss their conflicts and concerns with adults other than their parents, it is particularly important for them to have teachers who understand their emotional and social problems. During the transitional ages, particularly in early adolescence, children have trouble accepting their sexual identity. Some girls feel no pride in their sex and actually fear being women. Many boys, especially when they are smaller than their contemporaries, fear that they may not be able to be real men because they associate masculinity with physical size and development.

Some questions that youngsters frequently ask reflect the real worries of youth and indicate that it is mainly their attitudes about sex that constitute a problem for them, for their parents, and for teachers.

How can we help them with their bewilderment as to whether the sex urges they feel mean they are in love? How can the young boys or girls sort out the various emotions that accompany sexual desires to hug, to kiss, to pet? Are their tumultuous feelings the real thing or just puppy love? Is there a way to work out sex needs, other than in sex play? What are young adolescents to do about the fantasies, fears, and dreams that they experience along with their sex urges?

Human sexuality includes the social roles that men and women play. Many young children have difficulty understanding and learning these roles. Those most enmeshed in the dragnet of uncertainty are usually children brought up in a one-parent home, especially where they have little contact with adults of the sex of the missing parent or where parents are passive, resentful of the children, or unable to accept the responsibilities of parenthood.

In recent years, many leading sociologists have stressed the need for young boys to develop a strong male image early in life in order that they can later take on their role as head of the house. Psychologists and sociologists have emphasized the importance of providing male substitutes for absent or rejecting fathers. Whenever possible, male teachers, coaches, relative, older brothers, recreation leaders, and scoutmasters should be encouraged to act as models and substitute fathers.

Since over 75 percent of our population marries at one time or another, the teacher should give young people an opportunity to discuss dating, going steady, engagement, marriage, and family life. A trained sex educator can help students explore the pros and cons of going steady and the sexual behavior appropriate in dating.

In a ghetto school, during an eleventh grade class in personal and family living recently, the students, a boy and a girl, spontaneously role played a problem that the class was discussing—should a girl ask the boy into her house after her first date with him? The scene was set at the door of the girl's house and the young man, age 17, asked whether he could come in. The girl, also 17, said she was tired and would like to say goodnight. She added that she had enjoyed being with him.

The young man looked forlorn and disappointed. In an awkward but angry manner he mentioned that the least she could do was to invite him in because he had taken her to the movies and for a hamburger and coke later and that this cost him $5. He felt he wasn't getting his money's worth from her.

The girl wisely answered that she thought the good time they had and the progress they had made in becoming friends were more important than paying back by kissing and necking.

The class talked over the issues involved in the scene enacted and concluded that a "real man" respects his girl friend's wishes.

The class discussed the fact that the sex urges of boys and girls are quite different in nature and degree—for example, that girls should be aware that their behavior can sometimes be painfully provocative to boys. Boys are readily stimulated by a girl's figure, her flirtatious remarks, and the way she wears her clothes, while girls are stimulated more by romantic feelings of love, an atmosphere of tenderness, and music and soft lights.

With what has been discussed thus far by way of background, let us turn now to practical considerations.

How, what, and by whom should sex be taught in the schools? No ideal model will fit all schools, neighborhoods, or cities. However, a few general guidelines may be helpful, especially those that have proved useful in a variety of school situations.

As a first step, the school should enlist parental support and involvement throughout the planning and operation of the program. [See "Planning for Sex Education: A Community-Wide Responsibility" by Mary S. Calderone, M.D., in the January 1967 NEA Journal.] With parental consent and involvement, the school can proceed with confidence in developing a sex-education program.

Educators should be sensitive to parents' concerns. Many parents are fearful that new values, standards, and behavior patterns contrary to their own will be taught their children. In the process of cooperating in planning a program, educator and parent can learn to trust and understand each other—all to the benefit of the children under their care.

Regardless of the length of the program for students, parents need to be involved in separate group discussions, study groups, lectures, or seminars on human sexuality while their youngsters are receiving sex education. (Involving ghetto parents is hard but worth trying. For one hour a week during a whole semester, I worked with a nucleus of four mothers of elementary school children. The next year there were 25 parents, including some fathers. The word had been spread.)

This kind of parallel education enhances communication between the parent and child at home and within peer groups as well. Many a sex education program was suffered because when the children came home with new insights and understanding, they were met by parents who still clung to many outmoded or uninformed concepts and attitudes.

A second step involves developing a sex education program appropriate for each age level and making it an integral part of the curriculum from preschool to college level. Children in special education classes and schools should be involved as well as those attending regular classes. (A principal pointed up this need recently when he reported the pregnancy of a 14-year-old special-education student who is confined to a wheel chair. She had never received sex education at home or at school.)

Sex education should encompass human sexuality rather than merely the reproductive aspects of sex. It should deal with the psychological, sociological, economic, and social factors that affect personality and behavior as well as with human reproduction.

Team teaching appears to be the most effective approach to sex education. In urban centers, opportunities abound for enlisting the help of experts in the community. Even in small towns or in suburbia, the schools can invite a doctor, social worker, or psychologist from outside the school system to supplement the efforts of teachers, counselors, and other school personnel. If the budget will allow it, schools might well bring in paid consultants occasionally to discuss with parents and teachers new trends in and classroom approaches to sex education.

The team approach is used in the Webster Girls' Junior-Senior High School in the District of Columbia, where I was the clinical psychologist and group therapist. This D.C. public day school for pregnant teen-age girls was originally funded by the U.S. Children's Bureau as a pilot project. The school provides continuous education for the girls during pregnancy and returns about 90 percent of them to regular schools two months after childbirth. A multidisciplinary approach is used—teachers, a psychologist, an obstetrician, a public health nurse, a social worker, and a nutritionist participate in the sex education and family life program.

A comparison of girls who attended Webster with those who were unable to attend because of lack of space indicates that those who attended had fewer second pregnancies, did better in their academic studies, found better jobs on graduation, and appeared to have more stable marriages when they did marry.

The project has demonstrated the need for sex education as an integral part of school curriculum beginning in the early grades. (Many of the girls at the Webster School reported feeling that if they had studied human sexuality with understanding teachers during elementary school, they would not have become pregnant. They felt their parents needed help too.) It has also shown that teachers at all levels, but particularly at the elementary school level, need special training in the presentation of sex education in order to make it succeed.

Since a comprehensive school program in sex education should be multidimensional, it needs to involve teachers in all subject areas as well as such staff members as the counselor and school nurse.

Sex and sexuality ought to be dealt with in many courses in the curriculum rather than be confined to one course labeled Sex Education, Personal and Family Living, or the like. It can be introduced in courses in biology, sociology, health, history, literature, economics, and psychology.

The preschool curriculum can deal with plant and animal growth and care of the young.

In addition to providing appropriate information about puberty and reproduction, the elementary school curriculum can deal with family roles and relationships; understanding one's emotions (especially feelings of love, anger, aggression); and how anxiety and guilt affect relationships between family members and friends.

The junior high school curriculum can deal with customs, values, and standards in dating and in boy-girl group relationships; with emphasis on the meaning of masculinity and femininity; and on the economic, social, legal, and psychological factors involved in carrying on the responsibilities of adulthood.

In high school, sex education should include consideration of marriage, family planning, infant care, vocational choices and opportunities, divorce, unwed motherhood and fatherhood, masturbation, homosexuality, and conflicts confronting young men and women in their social and personal relationships.

The course work should be taught by certificated teachers who are comfortable with the material and interested in teaching. Classes need to be tailored to the students' needs, and students should be encouraged to express their feelings and differences. Panel discussions, role playing, group discussions, films, exploration of case studies, and listening to recordings of individual problems help create a comfortable atmosphere where students enjoy participating and learning.

In my opinion, the important thing in sex education is to deal with human sexuality openly and fully in a classroom climate that makes the student feel safe and free to express his feelings of wonder, pride, and concern about his sexuality.

AN ARGUMENT FOR SEX EDUCATION IN THE   7
ELEMENTARY SCHOOLS

While the debate regarding sex education in the junior and senior high schools goes on—even in our more enlightened age—less has been heard about the possibility or desirability of teaching family life and sex education during the more formative elementary school years.

It is hard for many parents, who may have been reared in homes where discussion of sex was taboo and who picked up information from "here and there" to see the need for teaching sex education in the schools, especially at the elementary level, because they claim, "I got along fine without such courses. Why shouldn't my child?"

However, Helen Manley, noted health education and physical education specialist and writer, points out that sex education of a sort has always been present in the elementary schools. "A child notices that boys and girls go to different toilets. Some words make people giggle. A boy pulls up a girl's skirt and giggles. Some books have pictures of naked bodies, and these are carefully examined," she says. "Boys and girls need to be given factual knowledge to counteract the misconceptions and half-truths they often acquire from various sources.

"With today's pressure on children to grow up fast, the emphasis on sex in advertising and the media, and the sex education children get from their group life, boys and girls have good reason to be confused about this important aspect of living. For the most part, sex has been associated primarily with the sex organs and vulgarity. Children need to be made aware of the broader concept of human sexuality as something fine that everyone has, with which he was born, and which he has until death. Through a carefully planned comprehensive and progressive family life and sex education program from childhood to maturity, the school can assist each child in developing this broader concept."

Miss Manley expresses these viewpoints in *Family Life and Sex Education in the Elementary School*, a 26-page bulletin requested and published by the National Education Association's Department of Elementary/Kindergarten/Nursery/Education for educators in elementary schools where there is interest in either improving or establishing programs of family life and sex education.

"It was time for a sensible statement on the subject since so much has been written and so little understood," explains Robert Gilstrap, executive secretary of E/K/N/E. "Family life and sex education should be a natural part of a child's education in the elementary schools as early as kindergarten," he maintains.

According to Miss Manley, sex education should begin in kindergarten because "children often come to school from families into which baby brothers and sisters are being born and are full of questions but have no correct or uniform vocabulary for asking questions. There are many ripe moments for good teaching of family living and sex education which teachers should utilize to help these young boys and girls develop a feeling of the goodness of themselves and their bodies at this early age."

A total sex education program in the schools should be designed to "produce socially and morally desirable attitudes, practices, and behavior," she notes. "The over-all program should be more than merely presenting the physiological facts of reproduction and warning against venereal disease. Rather, in its totality, such a program should help children and youth develop ideals, attitudes, and practices which will increase the probabilities of their establishing happy families of their own. The scope of activities involved in this extended program includes all human relationships with all persons of all ages, not only relationships between peers of the opposite sex," she adds.

The bulletin gives suggested curriculum guidelines for kindergarten through grade eight. To be most effective, according to Miss Manley, curriculum guidelines should be prepared by a committee of teachers with the help of appropriate consultants who know the needs and interests of children at the specific age levels, the existing school curriculum, the subject matter of family life and sex education, and the processes of introducing change.

Miss Manley says that steps in staring a comprehensive sex education program include developing community understanding, developing curriculum, developing well-prepared teachers, and evaluating the program.

She suggests a community council of outstanding citizens from the churches, service clubs, and medical and education professions to study the need for sex education after school authorities believe that the community is ready to sponsor such a program and that they themselves approve and back it. The committee could help develop and explain the program at PTA and community meetings, she says, and could point out the following:

Parents have five of the child's most formative years in which to develop his values and standards. The school then supplements the home while the family continues to transmit values throughout the child's life.

The school teaches the whole child. Omitting family life and sex education casts sex relationships in the sub-rosa atmosphere of vulgarity.

Sex education permeates many activities. It is not a separate subject and must be planned as part of the entire school curriculum.

Research has proved that factual knowledge of sex and sexuality lessens experimentation. Children may receive inaccurate information and may even be stimulated sexually by the mass media. The school program will attempt to clear up such misconceptions and encourage factual understanding.

Miss Manley strongly emphasizes in the bulletin that the success of the entire program is dependent on the development of well-prepared teachers with a positive attitude toward the subject. She notes that many teachers feel insecure about teaching sex education since pre-service health curriculum is generally inadequate. She suggests in-service workshops and curriculum guides and other materials for classroom teachers, the ones who should present the program in the elementary schools. Toward this end, Miss Manley cities resource materials for both teachers and youngsters for such a program.

> *"There is something appropriate to be taught at every age; it is a matter of keeping pace with development and of being alert so that pupils may approach teachers when they feel the need to do so.*
>
> *"Sex education should be given sometimes to classes of just boys or girls and sometimes to mixed classes, but always to the end that the sexes will be able to understand and respect one another. Children enter school with widely varying amounts and kinds of information about reproduction, having learned, for example, that they came from 'Mommy's tummy' or a stork or a cabbage. They also know there are sex differences between boys and girls. In the early grades, the teacher's task should be to welcome unexpected questions and answer them truthfully in a warm, calm manner. Later on, during the fourth and fifth grades, when children enter puberty and become aware of the social implications of sex differences, sex education should become more intensive, for this is the ideal time to provide all the basic factual material possible. The approach must be scientific—human reproduction can be studied along with that of plants and animals, but the primary emphasis should be on friendship and human relations."*
> *—From "What Parents Should Know About Sex Education in the Schools," a leaflet published by the Publications Division, National Education Association. Price, 35 for $1 (Stock No. 051-02066). Order from Publications-Sales Section, National Education Association, 1201 16th Street NW, Washington, D.C. 20036.*

SEX EDUCATION AND
THE TEACHER*

8

Around the thought and the act of sex there hangs a confusion and a danger, a tension and a fear, which far exceeds those hanging around any other normal and useful part of life in our culture.

We regard our sexual lives as private, important and potentially explosive in a way we regard no other part of our lives.

The reason is not entirely clear for isolating, cutting off, demarcating and labelling as "special corner" that area of our lives where physical desire and fulfillment have their functions. (1)

It appears that since ancient times, activities that appeared to interfere with the stability of marriage and the home, including sexual activities which led to the begetting of children outside of marriage, were pictured as socially undesirable. Similarly, members of communities felt that the social interest of the Judeo-Christian traditions would be threatened by those pleasurable sexual activities in or outside of marriage, which did not satisfy the procreative function of human sexuality. Masturbation, mouth-genital contact, homosexual contacts or other types of pleasure-seeking acts, became labelled as undesirable activities for members of the community.

Orientation To Sex Varies

The roles played by parents, teachers, clergy and others in teaching children and adults the "acceptable" forms of sexual behavior have been strongly determined by the existing value orientations to human nature of the various historical times.

In the past, the human being has often been viewed as innately evil and filled with animal-like sexual desires which could be controlled only through strict discipline, moral education and rigid social controls. It appeared then, as it appears today to some people, that to decrease the chances whereby sexual curiosity or sexual desires might be aroused, the members of the community should not speak of sexual pleasures in public; that activities considered to be shameful, sinful, immoral or animal-like should be controlled by law—or at least by rejection of misbehaving individuals from society.

Orientation to human nature has been gradually changing as the importance of learning and the significance of environmental influences in personal and social growth has been recognized. Today, there is a trend to view the human being as an individual who is neither good nor bad, whose nature can and does change, and who, when in the possession of adequate information, is able to select a behavior pattern from alternatives offered to him without necessarily endangering the welfare of society. (2) Although value orientations have changed over the years, and with it the public moral attitude, official moral codes have not changed appreciably over the last 2,000 years. The official institutions of the community have not kept up with currently changing or acceptable human values, and many members of the community are left confused,   puzzled, uninformed—yet prone to experimentation.

Sexual Problems Related To Lack
Of Information

As an example, sexual problems of youth are often related to the fact that the human male and female become biologically adults some years before the law or the social customs of the community recognize them as such. The attempts to ignore and suppress the physiological needs of the sexually most capable segment of the population has led to more complications than the community is willing to recognize. Most unmarried males and females would like to know how to resolve this conflict between their physiological capacities and the legal and social codes of the community. They would like to know whether masturbation will harm them physically, or interfere with their subsequent responses to a marital partner; they would like to know whether they should engage in petting; and part from the moral issues that may be involved, they would like to know what premarital petting experience may actually do to their marital adjustment. Should they or should they not have coitus before marriage? What effect will this sort of experience have on their subsequent marital adjustment? In any type of sexual activity, what things are normal and what things are abnormal? What has been the experience of other youth facing these problems?

The problems of sexual adjustments in marriage represent another public need for information. There are probably few married persons who have not, at least on occasion, recognized the serious need for additional knowledge to meet some the sexual problems that arise in their marriages. On the solution of these problems, the stability of marriage may sometimes depend.

Yet another set of needs is emerging out of the growing concern of the public about population control, family planning, contraception and abortion, and the fate of those whose sexual activity may be contrary to ancient yet still operating laws.

Parents Recognize Need For Information

Within the last 30 years or so, many parents have come to realize that suppression of information or threatening of children about sexual matters have not brought about the happiness which it was supposed to create. Increasing demands have become voiced by individuals and organized community groups to change the community's approach to sex education, and instead of withholding information about sexual matters, to now make information available widely.

Confusion About The Meaning Of Sex

The why, how, when and who of sex education has become perhaps the most discussed educational topic of the last decade. Hardly a week goes by without an address to a church group, a youth movement, or a PTA by a speaker who expresses an opinion on education in sex. Many misconceptions about sex education arise because of disagreement on what sex actually means, the multiplicity of expressions about the aims of this venture, and differing definitions of education.

Definition Of Sex

The major problem lies in the definition of "sex." The rigid, clear-cut relationship between reproductive fertility and sexual responsiveness so characteristic to lower mammalian species, is obliterated in the human. Evolutionary changes occurring over the course of millions of years have resulted in a relaxation of hormonal control over human sexual-oriented behavior. Although tendencies toward sexual activity are still genetically determined, evolutionary changes have brought about an increasing dominance of the cerebral cortex over human sexual practices.

From a popular point of view, therefore, all the physical rituals and activities of courting, from hand-holding to sexual union, are included within the meaning of the word. From a scientific point of view anything from the careful study of the union of the male and female germ cells to the investigation of the male and female relationship in various cultures may be included.

It is apparent that sex cannot be defined in precise terms. "Sex" involves conception, gestation and birth with all their emotional and social consequences. It involves premarital, marital and extramarital relationships, both heterosexual and homosexual, not only in this society but in other societies as well. In involves certain aspects of religion, law, custom, economics and politics, and thus it is really inseparable from any discussion of the life processes and the activities of people. All this might be summarized by defining sex as the process of becoming and being a female or a male, with all the duties, responsibilities, rights and privileges which this may imply. Like other roles, the male and female roles change as the years go by; they change according to the forces of economics, technology and the social scene—and herein lies the educational problem.

The Aims Of Sex Education

Each person wants to be and needs to be in possession of at least some of the knowledge, some of the attitudes and some of the skills that are necessary to fulfill the male or female role. Knowledge may include such variety of things as the detailed understanding of family relationships, the ability to recall the names of the parts of the body, or the history of the people of certain societies. Attitudes may include love, hate, pride, desire and many other sentiments, while skills may range from the ability to put together a shelter for one's family to the ability to perform the sexual act.

Over the span of history, each culture has made provisions for all of its members to learn their role. In this sense, sex education is not a startling invention of the twentieth century.

Ways Of Education

Today, as in the past, sex or role learning occurs through two somewhat related—yet different educational processes. One is the process whereby the traditions and the pattern of behavior of a people are passed from one generation to the next. This is often referred to as the enculturation of an individual, because this form of education depends largely on the assimilation by a member of society the elements of the culture around him. It is reinforced by periodic, informal instruction, which is often in the form of moral exhortations or examples of behavior. Since the beginning of the human race, much of the knowledge, attitudes and skills for the roles of the male and female, have been acquired through the mechanism of enculturation. This has been, and still is, the process whereby a family's basic moral codes concerning human interpersonal relationships are passed on to children. This has been, and will continue to be, the primary educational domain of the family and the community.

The other process of education takes place in schools. Schooling is a convenient educational arrangement which is carried out at predetermined times, at predetermined places for definite periods, by persons especially trained for the task. In general, schooling takes place without too much regard for the individual's specific emotional or social needs, and there is usually greater emphasis on achievement as reflected by exam results than on the fulfillment of human needs. (3)

Many parents tend to believe that educational decisions in schools are always pondered ones, and that all educational interchange constitutes a purely rational affair. (4) Inherent in this belief is the idea that, given a perfect sex education course, children will learn wholesome sexual habits.

Somehow parents have failed to acknowledge that whatever influence the school does have on the child, depends to a large extent on the teacher, and that the classrooms are miniature communities where, even discounting all other factors, the maleness or the femaleness of the teacher is in itself a potent sex educational experience for the students. It is a curious paradox that the public is ready to entrust its children for over 25 hours a week to close personal contact with the teacher, yet it does not recognize him as a moulder of the male and female roles of children. It appears that the school teacher is not regarded by the public as one of the helping or health related professionals, and he is not looked upon as a person who might be knowledgeable about contemporary acute human concerns. Whatever parents or teachers themselves may believe, it is a fact that a teacher of any subject does contribute in one way or another to the student's gradual learning of the male or female role. Teachers must accept the fact that they do have several roles in sex education, even though this may be unrecognized by all concerned.

Teachers' Roles In Sex Education
1. The "Available" Teacher

The one role that is a must for a teacher is that of an available, enlightened individual who is able to engage in a conversation with young children or growing teenagers. In this role, the teacher is expected to look upon the young person as a human being of worth; one who is existing within the framework of a family, and who is coping with life with the means available to him. The teacher in this role, recognizes the right of his pupil to learn about events of life as they may arise, and he takes steps to offer evidence to show relevance—if any—between events of life and the rules and regulations of society. In this role, then, the teacher provides formal education in a challenging, curiosity-arousing and curiosity-satisfying atmosphere, utilizing moments appropriate for the introduction of certain socially sensitive issues for discussion. The teacher in this role recognizes that wise educational programs must be rooted in an understanding of the nature of man and of the nature of society. As an example, the teacher fulfilling this role, would introduce to the student Romeo and Juliet not only as a masterpiece of literature, but a story with great relevance to today's young people.

2. The "Complete" Teacher

The second role would be expected of those teachers who assume responsibilities for the transmission of certain specific areas of knowledge. The biology teacher, who until recently was not permitted to deal with human reproduction; the social science teacher, who could never discuss the problems and possible solutions of such far-reaching world problems as overpopulation; the guidance teacher, whose potential discussions about the psychology or sociology of sexual pleasures have never been sanctioned; and others may fit into the category. In their "sex educator" role, these teachers provide educational experiences to their students in accordance with available knowledge about sexuality related to their field of expertise, rather than according to the opinion of school boards or governments.

3. *The "Forecasting" Teacher*

The third and perhaps newest role might be allotted to a few teachers who would not necessarily work in the classroom. These especially trained teachers would develop a system which might supply information about the various behavior patterns demonstrated by students in and out of the schools, and adults in the community. Using this information, these specialists might be able to forecast emerging trends in the school and community behavior of pupils, and interpret these to the school authorities, other teachers, parents and community agencies. These teachers may assist community groups and the students in the utilization of available knowledge and skills concerning relevant issues, by obtaining resource materials and resource personnel from the community in accordance with the emerging needs of all.

Specialist In Sex Education Not Needed

None of these three roles reflect the need for a specialist in sex education: the whole school system must help young people to achieve some measure of emotional, physical and social well being in the course of their growth and development. Topics related to sex will have to be integrated with—rather than separated from other subject matters.

Elements Of An Integrated Curriculum For Students

Combining the educational potentials arising out of the three proposed roles for teachers, it would be feasible to inject into the existing kindergarten to Grade 12 curricula of schools, a continuous, interlocking series of learning experiences tailored for individual schools which take into account the needs of the pupils and the needs of changing times and fashions. Since the curricula of public schools are usually established by a central agency, efforts must be made to ensure that individual local school districts may have sufficient freedom to introduce into the school program material which is relevant to community life. If such safeguards to maintain flexibility are neglected, the innovations themselves may become so rigid and outmoded within a few years, that they become further blocks in the education of children.

Anxieties of Teachers

Many teachers may have deep anxieties about fulfilling any one of the three suggested roles. Some teachers worry about parental disapproval, peer criticism or rebuke from the principal. Others feel insufficiently informed on the subject areas referred to or deficient in skills of communication with children. These are realistic concerns, for which simple solutions do not exist. The worry about community or school originated disciplinary action against a teacher reflects on the apparently low professional status of the teacher, and on the insecure position of principals, vis-a-vis, the community and the school boards on the one hand, and the religious or governmental educational authorities on the other hand. In general these concerns mirror the lack of understanding of the relationship between life in society and the place of schooling in preparation for that life.

Teachers Have Strong Background
For Proposed Roles

The teachers' concern about lack of knowledge or skill is the easier problem to deal with. The teacher is not stepping out of a vacuum into these suggested roles. He comes equipped with the human experiences of his own past history, including a rather substantial experience in sexual activities. The teacher has rather extensive training in interpersonal communications, experience in pedagogical methods, and has personal qualities which are characterized by warmth, understanding and the ability to establish rapport with his students.

To fulfill the "available" role, the teacher does need up to date information of a type not usually presented to him in institutions of teacher training. This material includes the biology, psychology and sociology of human sexual behavior. He also needs practice in the identification of what "relevant" teachable moments might be, and how they might be utilized; and he does need certain general guidelines relating to the manner of his response to students who bring problems to him in or out of the classroom.

Information

The amount and type of information which the teacher should acquire is rooted in the research efforts of Kinsey (5, 6), Ford and Beach (7), Masters and Johnson (8), Schofield (10), and others on human sexual behavior. From these sources and others already present in the reference materials usually available to teachers, a sociologically, psychologically and physiologically oriented body of knowledge should be assembled and presented to teachers in training. In the course of such learning opportunity, the student teachers might attempt to follow the life of human beings from birth to death, alternatively bringing into focus biological, sociological and anthropological data to demonstrate various aspects of human behavior—and particularly human sexuality. Within such a series of studies the student teacher might recognize a frame of reference to life which assumes that all behavior involves interaction among biological, psychological, environmental, social, cultural and other factors (11).

Skills

Special educational techniques are needed to help the student teacher to recognize teachable moments for sexually oriented subjects and to develop his courage necessary for the utilization of this skill and the knowledge appropriate for the moment. Small group discussions, demonstration periods, role playing exercises, expression of reactions to selected classroom situations are all valuable methods to reduce tension, to increase self-confidence and to acquire the skills necessary to fulfill this role of an enlightened teacher.

Guides

There are perhaps three guiding lines which may assist the teacher in moments when problems are presented to him. First, the teacher should not be caught up in the emotions of a person or a group. Individuals or groups deeply disturbed over the misfortune of others, often fail to see the implication of certain problems and become the enthusiastic supporters of activities which they believe to be the cure of the problem. Second, the teacher should maintain an open mind toward the various aspects of problems presented to him and avoid premature judgment based on preconceived opinions or prejudices. Third, the teacher should recognize his own limitations, whether they might be due to his personality or the lack of his knowledge, and acknowledge and utilize the resources of others.

For teachers who are preparing to assume extended roles in teaching of biology, social sciences, guidance and other areas, extra educational opportunities must be offered for the study of anatomy, physiology, biochemistry, psychology, history, sociology and of the other basic sciences related to human reproductive and sexual functioning.

The teacher who wants to assume the proposed new role of the measurer of social and cultural climate of the community as it relates to the school's educational program, must become an expert in the arts and sciences of social measurements and in their interpretation to fellow teachers, principals, members of school boards and parents.

Evaluation Of The Program

Just as the curriculum must not become rigid, so the results of this type of educational venture cannot be expected to be reflected in any conventional measurement of success. Evaluation of a program's success should not be in terms of the number of venereal disease, illegitimacy or arbitrarily defined public disgrace which can be counted up in any community, nor in the number of marriages registered or babies born. Perhaps the measurement of the program's success and the success of the fulfillment of various roles by teachers should be in terms of the change in social and health legislations of the future, as they pertain to the recognization of the basic, unconditional worth of the individual human being. How the proposed roles for teachers, the outlines of educational programs or any other experiences suggested here, would affect the sexual behavior and attitudes of students now òr in the future, is not yet known. Neither is it known, of course, how the new math, physics and other courses or the reappearance of open schools, or the introduction of no-grade systems will affect the present and future generations.

Sex Education Essentially
"Emotional Education"

It is perhaps evident by now that sex education as proposed here, is essentially an emotional education, more preventive and remedial medicine than moral training. An increasing understanding of human problems by the various professional groups, but especially by the educators in our society, might help in creating an atmosphere in which members of communities may re-examine their value systems and come to some reasonable conclusions about the accepted limits of various forms of behavior, including the sexual one.

The process of education cannot be divorced from the personal commitments and hesitance of individual teachers; and it will be in those private worlds that the true response to what has been proposed here, will be formed (12).

SEX EDUCATION AND THE TEACHER REFERENCES

1. Young W.: *Eros Denied.* Grove Press Inc., N.Y., 1964, p. 17.
2. Knutson, A. L.: *The Individual, Society and Health Behavior.* Sage Foundation, N. Y., 1965, pp. 261-291.

3. Chisholm, B.: *Can People Learn to Learn?* World Perspectives, Volume 8. Harper and Brothers Publishers, N. Y., 1958, pp. 95-125.

4. Smith, C.E.: *Educational Research and the Preparation of Teachers.* A report prepared under a grant from the BCTF, 1962-63.

5. Kinsey, A. C., Pomeroy, W. and Martin, C.: *Sexual Behavior in the Human Male.* Philadelphia: W. B. Saunders, 1953.

6. Kinsey, A. C., Pomeroy, W., Martin, C. and Gehbard, P.: *Sexual Behavior in the Human Female.* Philadelphia: W. B. Saunders, 1953.

7. Ford, C. S. and Beach, F.A.: *Patterns of Sexual Behavior.* Harper, New York, 1951.

8. Masters, W. H. and Johnson, W.R.: *Human Sexual Response.* Little, Brown and Co., Boston, 1966.

9. Vincent, C. E.: *Unmarried Mothers.* The Free Press of Glencoe, New York, 1961.

10. Schofield, M.: *The Sexual Behavior of Young People.* Little, Brown & Co., Boston, 1965.

11. Juhasz, Anne McCreary and Szasz, George: *Adolescents in Society.* McClelland and Stewart, Toronto, 1969.

12. Eliot, C. W. J., *et al.:Discipline and Discovery.* The Vancouver Stationers Ltd., Vancouver, 1965, pp. 43.

A PARENT-TEACHER SPEAKS

At a meeting designed to acquaint the parents of children participating in the school's corrective reading program, the question arose, "What can I do to help my child with his reading?" This question was quickly focused on by many other parents and an animated discussion ensued. The faculty members who were present were looked upon to supply the formula for success.

As the introduction of the topic had been spontaneous, the teachers were not prepared with a formal answer or even a unified approach. Each teacher made suggestions, but interest waned as many parents mumbled, "Oh, I do that" or "That doesn't work!" After the meeting, several parents mentioned their frustration at the outcome of the discussion and the inability of anyone to suggest anything specific he felt the parents could do to really help their children. The teachers, too, were disappointed at their failure to provide concrete answers. They felt they had missed an important opportunity to actively involve the parents in the educative process.

ESTABLISHING A HOME READING ENVIRONMENT

As one of the teachers present, the author pondered what might have been said and decided to give the matter of parent involvement in reading much consideration. One reason for this concern and drive to act on this concern was the fact of being a reading teacher. Another and perhaps more compelling reason was empathy for these parents— empathy arising out of being a parent. The following suggestions were presented to the parents. It is hoped that at another meeting, the parents can evaluate the suggestions and their results.

1. *Parents should act as models.* Children have to learn that reading is not only an important part of life in the sense of economic advantage but also a pleasurable pastime. Parents can help them learn this by demonstrating the fact that they themselves read frequently and read a variety of things, not necessarily books. Adults can read the newspaper, magazines, pamphlets, directions for making and assembling things, train and television schedules, etc., in front of their children. Many times they can share parts of what they are

reading with the children, such as an interesting animal anecdote in the newspaper, an amusing joke, or tricky riddle. They can stress the idea that they often have to reread directions when they are cooking or assembling a bicycle.

2. *Parents should read to their children.* Many parents make it a habit to read bedtime stories to their infants and toddlers but depart from this activity when their children go to school and learn to read themselves. Often, the parents try to help their children by listening to them read and supplying the missing words. This frequently results in frazzled parental nerves and tearful, embarrassed youngsters.

A more pleasurable experience would be the continuation of the childhood ritual, with mother's or dad's reading to the child. This would not necessarily be a bedtime activity nor would it have to be a nightly occurrence. Instead, whenever the parent reads something especially entertaining or interesting, he could share it with the child. This would sometimes be a newspaper clipping, magazine article, or segment of a book.

The reading should be varied to enforce the concept that reading is not limited to books. The parent could read the directions to the child while he constructs a model or before he plays a new game. The parent could read the ingredients and instructions while the child makes pudding, etc. The parent could read the names of TV programs and their description while the child decides what he will watch.

3. *Parents should provide a variety of reading material for children.* Again, it must be stressed that reading need not be synonymous with books. Many beginning readers do not have the confidence to attempt a book independently. Many reluctant readers have achieved so much failure they deter further frustration by avoiding reading, especially the reading of books. In addition, many children do not have the ability to read the books they would like to read, so they attempt none.

To encourage reading, the home should be filled with all varieties of printed matter. Some of the material should be geared to the children. There are many inexpensive and interesting paperback books written for children. There are numerous magazines designed for children. Card games, puzzle books, box games are available for all reading levels—from beginning readers to more advanced readers.

Other materials, not designed for children, should be readily available. The newspaper offers a wealth of interesting reading: pictures, cartoons, puzzles, weather forecasts, motion picture and television schedules. Adult magazines contain interesting illustrations and captions in addition to the ever fascinating advertisements.

4. *Parents should provide children with varied experiences.* Reading is the meaningful connection between symbols and what those symbols represent. Teachers help pupils to recognize those symbols and establish patterns whereby the children ultimately can identify symbols unassisted. Parents can aid the teacher by providing the experiences for their children.

These experiences can take many forms: family vacations, neighborhood and country walks, trips to museums, planetariums, historical shrines, concerts, plays, sporting events, parades, zoos, ad infinitum. Whatever form these experiences take, however, their value depends on parent involvement and supervision. Before embarking on a trip, etc., discuss: where they will be going, what they might see, what they wish to see, and anything else to make the trip meaningful. While there, answer any questions and point out and discuss what they see. Collect postal cards, photographs, brochures and pamphlets to serve as reminders and to provide further information about what was seen. After the trip, talk about what was discovered, what was unusual, and what the children liked the most.

A well thought out trip can be more meaningful and enjoyable than a cursory visit. Let the children's interests and studies suggest possible trips.

5. *Parents should suggest entertainment for children.* Television provides many meaningful and entertaining experiences for children. Parents should take the opportunity to study the schedules, select and suggest those programs which might be beneficial. Oftimes, children balk at watching anything they might view as "educational;" but if a parent watches with real interest, the child's reluctance generally becomes "miraculously" transformed into genuine interest. As with the trips, television viewing has more value when the children discuss and question what they see.

6. *Parents should encourage pets and hobbies.* Raising a hamster and collecting stamps are meaningful learning experiences which provide numerous opportunities for reading. The children frequently must read in order to learn how to care for a pet or how to organize their stamps, etc. As a parent, avoid the easy way, assuming responsibility for directing the

hobby or pet care. Instead encourage children to be independent, even though it may consume much more of your energy.

CAUTIONS

Before parents embark on establishing a home reading environment, certain points should be stressed.

1. Parents are enrichers of experiences and not teachers of skills. Teachers have studied various techniques of developing skills and abilities in word analysis and comprehension. If a child has difficulty reading a word, tell him what it is and leave the teaching of "why it is" to his teacher.

2. One or two of these suggestions is not enough. The development of a fertile environment for the growth of interest in reading requires a full and varied program that is consistent, patient, and long-term.

THE BEHAVIOR-GUIDANCE TOOLS OF THE   *10*
CLASSROOM TEACHER

Every teacher soon discovers that the interpersonal relationships within his classroom group markedly affect the impact of his teaching. It is not until a teacher has actually faced a class that he fully realizes how much of his time must be spent in behavior guidance, just so that he can create an atmosphere for learning. A frequent and justified complaint of young teachers is "I've spent four years learning how to teach my subject only to find that I must handle the behavior problems in my classroom before I can teach."

Most well-conceived programs of teacher education anticipate this behavioral role of the teacher and make concerted attempts to provide some of the psychological and social understandings that are the foundations for pupil-behavior guidance. Unfortunately, no program of preservice training can entirely effect this preparation. The infinite variety of human personalities, along with combinations of, interactions that a teacher may encounter, is much too diverse to be fully anticipated in a college curriculum. Much of what must be learned about pupil behavior has to be learned on the job, when the teacher is confronted with specific situations and is highly motivated to learn.

Fortunately, much practical information about classroom behavior guidance has been learned. The accumulated wisdom of thousands of hours of classroom experience is one of our most important resources for this information. In addition, the contributions of psychology, psychiatry, child development and the other behavioral sciences help to supplement and organize this experiential data into meaningful concepts and plans. Let us remember, however, that this process of developing a workable understanding of children's behavior is a two way street. The specialist can help the teacher and the teacher can help the specialist. Many experienced teachers have translated scientific principles into practice and have accumulated a body of invaluable practical experience that deserves evaluation and communication.

What are the constructive approaches experienced teachers use? Before listing some of the behavior-guidance tools, it is important to remind ourselves that no tool or technique is good in and of itself. Techniques can easily become "gimmicks" that substitute manipulation for understanding. No tool is any better than the "intent" with which it is used. One of the most important factors in the success of these ways of relating and helping children lies in the motivation and sensitivity of the teacher. I strongly suspect that most of behavior-guidance tools we know are mainly different ways to communicate that we understand (a little) and we value children as persons.

The behavior-guidance methods observed seem to fall into four main categories:

1. Emotional climate setting methods.
2. Behavior education.
3. Environmental management of relationships in the group.
4. Emotional support to individual children.

Here are some of the patterns used by teachers to prevent behavior problems, promote better behavior, and ameliorate poor behavior.

Emotional Climate Setting

Many experienced teachers interviewed spoke of the importance of preventing behavior problems by "setting the tone." They felt a teacher sets the emotional climate for the whole day at the beginning of the day, and can reset the tone before each activity. Many felt that this greatly affected the class' general behavior.

The key factor in this intangible thing called emotional

climate seems to be in *the nonverbial communication* of the teacher. Not only in her voice tone and the look on her face, but also in the pace of her talking, her walking, and her teaching. Children are little mirrors that soon reflect which side of the bed the teacher got out of that morning. Tough days seem to happen on the day the teacher comes to school feeling rough and hoping that the children will be good.

The feeling tone for the day is not only set by the teacher's general demeanor but also by the "drama" or *emotional* meaning of what she does. For instance, we all know that walking around with a grade book provokes a quick negative impact.

Compare the children's feelings and reactions toward the teacher who greets them at the door as opposed to one who is very busy setting up books for the lesson as the day begins. One communicates "I care about children the most" while the other demonstrates her preference for topics, content, and books.

Many master teachers seem to be intuitively aware of the emotional meaning of their behavior to the children. For example, there is an important difference, felt by all the children in the room, in the nonverbal drama that may accompany a disciplining. When Johnny, who sits halfway down the middle aisle, sails a paper airplane surreptitiously during study time, what do you do? Marching straight down the aisle and towering over him only deepens the insecurity and need to rebel against adults. The intuitive teacher calmly signals her awareness of the misbehavior to Johnny, and a few minutes laters comes slowly down the aisle checking the work of several children before she talks quietly and privately to Johnny. Her very demeanor dramatizes, "I know what you did, Johnny, but I still believe you and I can get along better than that." Instead of angry confrontatiop, she is showing respect and belief in Johnny, aware that thirty children are watching her handling of Johnny. Her pattern of handling Johnny communicates nonverbally to the whole class whether she cares about children as people. The pattern of handling shows whether this room is a place for cooperation by understanding or a battleground between adults and children.

The day of a teacher is filled with a dozen such "tone setting" opportunities or nonverbal dramas like this. From these almost intangible cues, the children's sense of being respected, valued, and safe with their teacher is being built.

The emotional climate is highly contagious and is primarily set, not by using the right words, but by the nonverbal communication of the teacher.

Behavior Education

Sometimes we get so tangled up in negatives that we miss the fact that most children want to do the right thing. We also get so tangled up in deriving the psychological causes of behavor that we often overlook the fact that some misbehavior arises out of plain ignorance, just not knowing what is the right thing to do, or what is expected. Perhaps one of the best set of tools to prevent poor behavior lies in the principal strength of the teacher, her ability to educate. In short, wise education ahead of time can prevent many so-called behavior problems.

The experienced teacher usually has a well-developed program of educational prevention of poor behavior. The best teachers observed had noticed that year after year certain problems come back again. Others noted that if a certain activity was started, certain children will over-react. The very predictable repetition of these behavior problems makes anticipation and prevention possible and has led to the term "anticipatory guidance," to describe measures taken in advance to prevent problems.

For example, the new freedom and excitement of a field trip for the class can be expected to produce an outbreak of minor behavior problems. Much of this can be minimized by a little anticipatory educational guidance. The wise teacher usually goes over the plans for the trip ahead of time. By class discussions, talking through the plans, putting a map on the board, pointing out when and where drinking fountains and toilets are available, and sometimes by group role playing she communicates the expected behavior. A psychologically trained person watching her do this in three or four different ways soon identifies that she is desensitizing them day-by-day to the new situation anxiety as well as using the processes of identification, imitation, and reinforcement. No matter what words you call it, it works.

What is the heart of the procedure? A teacher sets down a list of regular recurring problems that come every year—playground problems, lunchroom misbehavior, situations that happen in going to the library, while seeing a film or changing from one activity to another. Each year she identifies for herself the children who excite too quickly or who just do not know how to handle some situations. Armed with that knowledge, the teacher then plans learning experiences that will anticipate the problems and minimize them by educating for the expected behavior. As simple as this may sound, our observations picked up the fact that some teachers fail to use teaching, their most familiar tool in behavior guidance.

Environmental Management of the Relationships Within the Group

Perhaps the most varied behavior guidance methods are those things the teacher does to influence how and when children relate to another. We are all familiar with the old device of splitting up two boys who need "to poke each other" by seating one of them far away from the other. This simple environmental change recognizes that some relationships spark too much feelings and interfere with class learning. Such devices might be labelled as attempts at "spatial management of relationships." By seating a certain child close to the teacher's desk or by the development of compatible neighborhoods in the classroom, a teacher tries to minimize conflict and increase cooperation. Recent years have seen the introduction of sociometric techniques which help the teacher obtain a more sophisticated and objective picture of the various functional subgroupings in her class. Such studies give clues toward building compatible work groups, as for helping socially isolated children find the sense of belonging they need so they join others in learning tasks.

In addition to a number of spatial management methods, the teachers observed seemed to be using a battery of "redirection techniques." One teacher's top drawer contained a list of fifty important necessary jobs she kept handy to assign to children "with too much steam." Another teacher had every child assigned to a well-defined group government role. These roles were rotated monthly and were used judiciously as channels for children to work out unmet emotional needs. I shall never forget the grade book of one South Carolina teacher where, after each name, occurred such items as: Alan Beckman—cub scouts, turtles, string catapults, New York Yankees; or Sally Howell cut outs, musketeers, ice cream, and hates boys. She explained simply: "These are my handles. I pick them up every morning at the door as the children come in. I use them to tailor my teaching to their interests, but most of all as conversation pieces to end poor behavior." A list of these so-called redirection techniques would fill a book.

Wise use of these environmental management and redirection methods seems to be dependent on the teacher's sensitivity to the emotional meaning of the relationships within her class. "How does Adele feel about Esther?" "What feelings does Harold provoke in Max?" Beyond this, their wise use rests on the recognition that all children have needs for love, attention, belonging, safety and recognition; and that legitimate healthy channels of endeavor need to be provided to meet these emotional needs. When a teacher looks behind the surface behavior at its cause, especially at the feelings, and the unmet emotional needs at work, she then finds cues that can guide her provision of the relationship opportunities and healthy channels of expression that children need as the emotional foundations for the educative process. The management devices alone are not enough. It takes sensitive teachers to use them appropriately.

Emotional Support to Individual Children

One of the quiet strengths found at work in the classrooms of teachers visited is known in the mental health field as "emotional support." It is almost an intangible thing, but nevertheless very real. It often happens so spontaneously and quickly that it would be easy to miss this very potent, positive contribution that some teachers make to the mental healthiness of their children.

In its essence, emotional support occurs in those moments when a teacher "feels with" a child; senses the hurt and anxiety in the child, and nonverbally or verbally communicates to the child that he feels the feeling too. Words cannot adequately describe such poignant moments for they are felt more than thought. Note that this is a phenomenon of sharing, not advice giving. It is the teacher sharing of himself as a person.

Once we fully recognize how all of us want to feel loved, liked, valued, and safe with others, we begin to take off our emotional blinders and become more sensitive to others. We soon see that much of the poor behavior in our classrooms really represents unhealthy attempts to substitute attention for love or notoriety for popularity. We discover that children who are hungry for affection, recognition, and safety are so bound up in their search for these things that they have little energy to devote to learning. Some of them, unawaredly, are emotionally running away from teachers and classroom defeats in order to keep what little sense of significance they have left. Others seem to be scrapping, fighting, demanding, bullying—trying to reach out for a sense of belonging, being liked, or being safe because they are in control. All of us have some unmet needs, but in some children the emotional deprivation is deep enough to cause insecurity, and in some deep enough to cause anxiety or anxiously driven behavior.

Anxiety is man's most common ailment. It is more common than the common cold. It occurs frequently and in many forms in every classroom and school. Most of it is mild and transient, and will respond to emotional support by teachers or other children.

How is emotional support given? Let me illustrate from a real life occurrence in a Southern school.

"It was two days before school opened. A worried mother came down the hall pulling and dragging a shy, crying, six-year-old child. Just then the principal walked out of his office into the hall.

"He took a quick, perceptive look at the mother and child. Instantly, he was down on one knee smiling quietly at the child. The mother was nonplussed. She had opened her mouth to speak but the principal was down there greeting her daughter. He lifted his face and read the feeling in her face. 'Coming to school for the first time is kind of hard on families, isn't it?' In the silence that followed, the mother's face colored, then relaxed. With tears welling in her eyes, she knelt down, gathered the little girl in her arms and said: 'Oh honey, this is going to be a good school, they understand little girls here.' "

The time it took? Fifteen seconds. What happened? In fifteen seconds a principal nonverbally dramatized that this school was a safe place where children came first. In fifteen seconds a mother's feelings were understood and verbalized. In fifteen seconds a mother turned from her own fears and was able to give reassurance to her daughter. Here is an example of this intangible thing called emotional support. What are its elements? (1) Sensitivity to the feelings of the other persons, (2) freedom and willingness to empathize or feel with, and (3) ability to verbally and nonverbally recognize and express the feeling; to share it, and talk about it. Notice again, its essence does not include advice giving. The empathy, the sharing, the going the "second mile" for a moment are enough.

Professionally Sound

Many of the teachers we observed intuitively and unawaredly moved toward their children in an emotionally supportive way. No teacher can do this toward all children. There are some children, who, for reasons often unknown to us, build up in us feelings that block our being empathetic. In every class, however, there are children, who, we sense, are insecure and anxious, toward whom we can empathize and give emotional support. To give this very important gift of oneself is not only the human thing to do, but also the professionally sound thing to do.

INDIVIDUAL SIMILARITIES   *11*

Much has been written by authorities on the subject of "individual differences" in children. Child variability is a fact. From birth children differ. These differences do increase in most instances with an increase in age. It is said that the teacher who doesn't make provisions for these differences makes little difference, individually, to a child. Children differ in almost every conceivable characteristic—biologically, sociologically, and psychologically. Yet though they differ immeasurably, children have basic needs that they seek to fulfill. It is with one major idea most often overlooked by educators that this article purports to deal.

What are the "basic needs?" Maslow in his book, **Motivation and Personality** (Harper & Row, 1954), postulated the needs of man as being physiological, safety, belonging and love, esteem, self-actualizing, knowing and understanding, and aesthetic powers. Maslow's theory suggests that a child's needs are instinctive and are arranged in a hierarchy of prepotency. That is, the child begins with physiological needs and reverts to lower-ordered needs which are more demanding of fulfillment. Once some physical needs (such as hunger) are served, then the child, having been partially gratified, is allowed to have rising to the foreground the natural need of wanting to know and understand.

As the needs of the child arise, then societal and cultural demands begin their effect. Havighurst (**Developmental Tasks and Education:** University of Chicago Press, 1948) has defined a developmental task as "a task which arises at or about a certain period in the life of the individual, successful achievement of which leads to his success and to success with later tasks, while failure leads to unhappiness in the individual, disapproval by the society, and difficulty with later tasks." (p. 6). Hence, the teacher must recognize that basic needs of a child are always tied in with societal demands. His responsibility is one which calls for sound judgments to be made as to whether or not the curriculum is providing ways of satisfying basic needs arising from maturation, cultural demands and personal values developed by the child.

What is the major similarity of children that is most often overlooked? Children have this one commonality: they have "intra-individual variability." That is, individual variation within themselves. Research indicates that children who are high in one subject, tend to be high in others. If they are low academically in some areas, the tendency is to be low in another. It is the author's contention that for the most part, schools concentrate their efforts upon working mainly upon the "weak spots" of youth. What happens when a child is found to be a poor or non-reader? He is given more reading. We give him more of what he doesn't want. Certainly, we want to strive to gain some balance between his strengths and weaknesses. However, there are many other avenues to compensate, correlate and provide for some intra-individual differences. One thing is for certain, we don't want to give all of our teaching power to working on his weaknesses—some time must be given to extending his strengths.

Similarly, at the other end of the scale we find those children who are academically talented 'top" all of the tests and generally are "well-rounded" pupils. All too often they receive the "A's" with very little effort. Shouldn't our grading system be somewhat reversed to care for these differences? For example, a typical case in the elementary classroom is something as follows:

> Joe, of average ability, works steadily, strives hard, doesn't give up and manages to obtain a grade of "A".

> Jim, of above average ability, works little, hurries along and makes an easy "A".

Joe is using nearly all of his ability; Jim is using little of his. Aren't children really rewarded for their efforts by the measurement coming from the results of some end product (same questions, identical objectives, etc.)? Isn't it possible to judge some children not so much for obtaining the same answers, but by juding the way, technique, or means by which they arrived at them? Shouldn't a different value be placed upon Jim's work, since he got there first, with minimum effort? Isn't one similarity becoming more evident about a pupils work today—more pupils will soon find out that true education is taking place when they can do a task with minimum effort, rather than to be judged by how long they stay at a task?

Curriculum in our schools is planned for groups, but it must be defined and imparted in terms of the individual. If it is true that a major similarity found in children's makeup revolves around the fact that they are not developing an "even front"; they have serious peaks and falls; not likely to be at the same level in all areas developmentally or academically; then it must also be understood that nature does not compensate for weaknesses in some characteristics by providing strengths in others. Therefore, the idea of pupil differences must be considered in this light. What strength of a child is it that we want to foster? What evident weakness is the one that needs to be resolved? What weaknesses must he learn to live with?

Although the focus of most educators must be upon individuality of youth, one should not overlook the essential demands for some common understandings. We have been looking at the curriculum as something which can be reduced to that which can be learned by each and every child. When the facts are faced, it may be found that we have neglected to see that a child has certain weaknesses which can not be solved by rearranging the curriculum. The teaching method may need to be supplemented by several methods and techniques. Moreover, the child's learning power, its depth, breadth and rate must be allowed to vary between and within individuals.

Basic needs' theories provide and afford a basis for formulating educational objectives; whereas, developmental tasks are useful in timing the educational effort needed for fulfilling predetermined objectives. Though there are common learning requirements vital to all cultures and ways of obtaining those goals, there is a need for teachers to concern themselves with the task of selecting the learning activities which are the most useful to a specific child. Then, and only then, will there be reasonable assurance that a child is meeting some successes.

The ideal teacher experiences an accurate, emphatic

understanding of the pupil's periods of anxiety and satisfaction. He senses the pupil's work, fear and confusion as if it were his own, but without ever losing the "as if" quality. More often, conditions exist in which a pupil is expected to succeed, than are found educational settings wherein significant ideas have been communicated successfully to the pupil. A teacher might think a pupil is succeeding, when in fact, the feeling is not shared by the pupil. It is one thing for a pupil to "think" he is doing a good job, and another to "know and feel" it.

REFERENCES

1. From William M. Alexander. "Reporting to Parents—Why? What? How? *NEA Journal* (now *Today's Education*). December 1959. 48:15-18. Reprinted by permission of *Today's Education.*

2. From Irving W. Stout and Grace Langdon. "What Parents Want to Know About Their Child's School." *Nation's Schools.* August 1957. Reprinted by permission of *Nation's Schools.*

3. From S. R. Laycock. "Helping Parents to Accept Their Exceptional Children." *Exceptional Children.* February 1952. Reprinted by permission of *Exceptional Children.*

4. From Patricia M. Bricklin. "Counseling Parents of Children with Learning Disabilities." *The Reading Teacher.* January 1970. 23:331-38. Reprinted by permission of *The Reading Teacher.*

5. From A. Gray Thompson and Edward F. Deroche. "Sex Education: Parent Involvement in Decision Making." *Phi Delta Kappan.* May 1968. 49:501-03. Reprinted by permission of *Phi Delta Kappan.*

6. From Patricia Schiller. "Sex Education That Makes Sense." *NEA Journal* (now *Today's Education*). February 1968. 57:17-19. Reprinted by permission of *Today's Education.*

7. From "An Argument for Sex Education in the Elementary Schools." *Illinois Education.* November 1969. 58:115-16. Reprinted by permission of Francine Richard, *Illinois Education.*

8. From George Szasz, M.D. "Sex Education and the Teacher." *The Journal of School Health.* March 1970. 40:150-55. Reprinted by permission of *The Journal of School Health.*

9. From Arlene Wartenberg. "A Parent-Teacher Speaks." *The Reading Teacher.* May 1970. 23:748-50, & 765. Reprinted by permission of *The Reading Teacher.*

10. From William G. Hollister. "The Behavior-Guidance Tools of the Classroom Teacher." *Virginia Journal of Education.* May 1966. 59:11-13. Reprinted by permission of *Virginia Journal of Education.*

11. From R. C. Bradley. "Individual Similarities." *Arizona Teacher.* Copyright 1967 by The Arizona Education Association. March 1967. 55:16, 48. Reprinted by permission of *Arizona Teacher.*

---

a. Barsch, R. "Counseling the Parent of the Brain Damaged Child." *Journal of Rehabilitation.* 1961. 27:1-3.

b. Ginott, H. *Group Psychotherapy with Children.* New York: McGraw—Hill Book Company, 1961.

c. Rappaport, S. *Public Education for Children with Brain Damage.* New York: Syracuse University Press, 1969.

Evaluative Criteria Against Which to Judge One's Current Parent-Teacher Interview Plan

Successful parent-teacher conferences are characterized by clear-cut purposes which everyone involved understands.
—Joseph P. Rice, Jr.

Introduction

12   Evaluation is central to the whole process of educational change. No matter what new proposals are inaugurated, the parent interview system will not change materially unless the methods of evaluating results are changed. And if these methods *do* change, it is impossible for the persons who interview not to change.

Although there is no universally accepted yardstick designed for measuring the interview system of a school district, certainly there is some valuable information which should be considered as one seeks to compare the extent to which his program of reporting measures up. The criteria which follows has been placed in brief, concise terms so that those who are concerned with evaluating the effectiveness of interview programs would have sound criteria against which to make comparisons. Certainly some school systems will want to go beyond this criteria, such a move would be commendable. The criteria presented here, however, is to help the evaluator determine if the interview system under scrutiny measures up to the requisites of a good means of conferring face-to-face with parents.

CRITERIA TO BE USED FOR COMPARATIVE PURPOSES

I. WITH RESPECT TO THE NATURE OF THE CON-FERENCE PROCEDURE:

1. Conferences should be conducted in order that information might be given parents about the school's philosophy and curriculum program; information might be obtained from parents that will aid the teachers; and, information might be imparted to the parents regarding their child's progress in school—socially, emotionally, physically, mentally, esthetically, and academically. The report of pupil progress by the conference procedure should provide a comprehensive picture of the child's sum total of educational experiences.

2. Public relations is termed a result of parent-teacher conferences rather than its aim. However, a segment of conference time should be given to explaining school policies.

3. The success of the conference procedure is directly related to the foresight and capability of the one who is conducting it. The utilization of pertinent school records and the professional "tools" of instruction greatly aid the interaction and communication within the conference session.

4. Although the teacher should compare the academic achievement of the child with his classroom group, norms for the school, and national norms; the major emphasis should be given to comparing an individual's achievement with his own potential (normal progress theory). This procedure permits individualized reporting without threat to the individuals involved.

5. The conference setting provides an opportunity for the parents and teacher to discuss both good and poor types of behavior of the child. Realistic plans can then be

made to alter or eliminate undesirable attitudes and behavior.

6. The success of the conference procedure depends in large measure upon the relationship that is developed during the conference between the parent and the teacher. The relationship must be one which permits the parent to express his thoughts and his emotions with the knowledge that the teacher will be receptive to his comments and sympathetic to his feelings.

II. WITH RESPECT TO THE ESSENTIAL FEATURES OF THE PARENT-TEACHER CONFERENCE PROCEDURE:

1. Conferences should be scheduled on a regular, periodic plan rather than on an informal "as needed" basis. Preferably, a conference for each child should be scheduled for both Fall and Spring Semesters.

2. Conferences should be held on school time with the exception of an evening conference session held for the convenience of those parents who are employed in activities and cannot attend during day sessions.

3. The time allotted each conference should be no less than twenty minutes and a provision for up to thirty minutes is more desirable.

4. Teachers should be relieved from teaching duties during the scheduled Conference Sessions.

5. The conference plan should be a cooperative venture (parent-teacher-administration) from the time of its inception to its evaluation for purposes of refinement.

6. Provision should be made for orientation of those parents who move to the school community if they are not familiar with the conference procedure of reporting. This could be done on a large group scale with some time given to discussing other matters of general interest to all parents.

7. A faculty should continuously study the effectiveness of the conference plan. Provisions should be made for some re-orientation work in conference procedures during in-service training periods prior to school convening each Fall. These activities should include discussions conducted by the child psychologist, reading specialists, and other special service personnel.

III. WITH RESPECT TO MATERIALS AND EQUIPMENT:

1. A variety of materials should be used when conferring with the parent. These would include: samples of the child's work; health records; cumulative record folders; individual charts and graphs from the several subject areas; and other such materials which yield valuable information.

2. Tape recorders should be used when one needs to reveal specific problems of speech during reading and speaking activities.

3. Over-head Projectors should be utilized when transparencies are needed to depict handwriting difficulties, graphs of school norms, and the like. Often these materials need to be shown quickly in order to make a point during the actual conference setting.

4. For those schools having closed circuit television, certainly television "tapes" which have recorded the behavior of pupils are most valuable to show when one needs to review the characteristics of a child's regular classroom behavior. Particularly this is important if the behavior is of such a nature that it is seriously deterring him from classroom responsibilities.

IV. WITH RESPECT TO EVALUATION OF THE CONFERENCE PROGRAM AND ITS CONTRIBUTION TO PUPIL ACHIEVEMENT:

1. There should be one hundred percent contact of parents through conference procedures for all classrooms in the elementary schools. A follow-up of the parents who were unable to attend the scheduled conference session should be made so that contact with each home is made and future conferences can be initiated.

2. A written record should be kept of the parent-teacher conference and placed in the school files. Such records can be used as a referral for future conferences.

3. A follow-up conference should be held with pupils as seems necessary when it is advisable to discuss specific findings and conclusions that are a direct outgrowth or a result of conference agreements. In some cases it may be necessary for the child to participate a portion of time during the initial conference with his parents.

4. The manner in which the parents and the teachers have accepted the conference plan in various situations is indicative, to some degree, of the success of teachers in

this educational endeavor.

5. An attempt should be made to determine if parent-teacher conferences resulted in fewer cases of misunderstanding between home and school than was the case when report card methods were used alone.

6. At least every two years the administration should survey parents concerning their opinion of the effectiveness of the conference plan.

7. Updating guides, manuals, brochures, and other conference tools should be a continuing process. The procedure regarding such a practice should be a matter of written school policy.

8. A faculty meeting should be held at the conclusion of each conference session to determine the problems that teachers encountered in reporting at the various educational levels.

9. A school system should seek out detectable differences in the growth and development of children where the conference method of reporting is used as compared with measurable outcomes observed through the use of the grade card method. A part of this evaluation might include an attempt to discover if any aids to better mental health for the child has accrued from the use of conferences.

Summary

The practice of inviting parents of elementary school children to come to school to discuss their children's progress is becoming more common. By making such arrangements, it is hoped that discussions can be held with both parents that will revolve around the past development of the pupil, his current performance, and the ways in which all concerned can work cooperatively in the future toward mutually acceptable goals.

If a parent-teacher interview is to succeed in this worthy endeavor mentioned above, there must be an attempt to put more substance into the interview report. The criteria presented in this chapter provides one with a yardstick to measure how well his own interview system meets minimal standards set for acceptable interview methods. Last, but not least, administrators, teachers, and parents should use interviews if but for only one purpose—*to help us remember that each child is a real human being and not just a member of a group.*

EPILOGUE

The Case of Johnny Reportcard—His
Multiple Personality*

In most elementary schools you will encounter an unusual psychological case, called *Johnny Reportcard.* Johnny's last name comes in many forms—Report Card, Report to Parents, or Progress Report; he may have even other aliases. He may speak in any of several languages, but no matter which he uses, he mumbles so that parents do not understand him well.

In addition to his language difficulty, Johnny Reportcard has a multiple personality. Personality No. 1 is the *messenger.* Its function is to combine and condense several months of life experiences into a few stark, cold symbols.

---

*Adapted from Orval G. Johnson. "A Case of Multiple Personality." *NEA Journal* (now *Today's Education*). December 1959. 48:18.

Johnny Reportcard is handicapped by a pitifully small vocabulary. So small, in fact, that it is unequal to the task of relaying a complicated, subtle message.

Consequently, this personality never makes it clear to parents that Johnny Reportcard speaks a relative language so that E, for example, doesn't necessarily *mean* E (whatever E *really means*), but that the meaning of E often depends on the child. Many parents, however, think it depends on the other children, yet most parents, teachers, and principals know it also depends on the teacher.

Personality No. 2 is the *motivator.* The notoriety of which has come for its reputation for stirring children to work at times to ridiculous proportions. There are those who say that it motivates parents instead of children. It has been known to send parents digging into their wallets and purses for reward money. Some parents are motivated by it to go rushing to their schools with wails of protest. Johnny Reportcard may be a motivator, but most people don't know if he moves youngsters to work or more to give up trying altogether.

Less often discussed is Personality No. 3, the symbol of *family heritage.* In this guise, Johnny Reportcard becomes a symbol of the family honor, representing the bloom, blight, or blotch on the family tree.

Since Johnny Reportcard confuses and befuddles both teachers and parents, neither aids high schools nor employers in the world of work, some forward looking people think it's time to force him to retire from his job in the elementary school. What do you think?

IN RETROSPECT . . .

. . . the author of this textbook admonishes that the teacher's task is to contrive each day so that the probability of success in a child's life clearly outweighs the probability of failure. By mastering the day at hand the child in principle, becomes much more capable of the mastery of all days which follow. The parent is still a major cog in an elementary school child's spin of his educational wheel of fortune. Therefore they should learn firsthand from the teacher the extent to which they are contributing to their child's success at school. This type of information cannot be placed on a report card.

An analysis of data showing how most schools are currently organized for report purposes will reveal that measures are taken intermittently throughout the school year with assessments arrived at released in some written form (grades primarily) to parents. There seems to be some incongruities between the philosophy that says in effect, "at school we insist on you becoming the best person you can be," and the gradecard method which is used to invoke such feelings as, "you didn't measure up, you know this, but we'll make doubly sure by making it a public record." One cannot measure the difference in attitude, the increased interest, the growing pride in self-improvement, but a good teacher is aware that they exist. He can *tell* parents about it.

In thinking of an individual's self-structure and the school's responsibility to its enhancement, a system of evaluation and reporting is needed which serves to show a child's "self" as something to be created rather than as something to be discovered. While gradecard systems are prone to cast a shadow of doubt on a child's abilities by reflecting his faults, weaknesses, and handicaps in terms of statistical comparisons to contrived "norms", by contrast a sound interview procedure will enable a teacher to keep the school spotlight upon a pupil's own assets, strengths, and personalized commitments. Consequently, one of the better answers to the question of, "How can I best report to parents?" is, ... The PARENT TEACHER INTERVIEW.

Appendix A

GUIDELINES TO ACTION FOR EFFECTIVE CONFERENCES

1. Conferences are held primarily to inform parents about their child's growth and development, to increase their knowledge of the total school program, and to develop mutual understanding for the better welfare of the child.

2. Parents are often unsure and uncomfortable in the conference setting. The teacher can put them at ease at the beginning of a conference by defining her role in relationship to them as well as making clear the purposes for which the particular conference is held.

3. The papers collected for showing to the parent at conference time reflect the child's own ability; not his standing with the group. The teacher should make preparation to show how the child stands according to his own potential, the classroom group, and national norms. Personal comparisons of individuals, . . . relatives or neighbors . . . should be avoided.

4. Room displays can be used to tell some of the experiences of the children during the parental visit.

5. A neat, orderly room will be noticed by most parents.

6. A review of the child's records immediately before the initial conference will refresh a teacher's memory of that child.

7. When the parent arrives, the teacher should extend a cordial welcome and place the parent at ease.

8. The conference will be more personalized if parents are asked about their child's experiences in the home, neighborhood, scouting, and other significant activities. The child's likes and dislikes might also be discussed.

9. The teacher will give some answers and suggestions to be used in the solution of the child's problem; some solutions will be sought from the parents.

10. An attempt should be made to answer questions posed by the parents.

11. When necessary, allow the child to tell his side of the story during a portion of the initial conference.

12. A reasonable plan for the strengthening of a child's skills and for meeting his immediate needs in a satisfactory manner should be presented during the final stages of the conference.

13. A second conference should be scheduled when several problems seem to merit additional time and effort.

14. The atmosphere of the conference should be so friendly that the parent will feel he can visit a class session for the observation of his child in action should he like to do so.

15. For special problem cases as progress is noted (or lack of it), a contact by phone or letter is very much in order so that the parent may be always clearly informed on the matter.

16. A chart showing the daily program might be prominently displayed somewhere in the classroom.

17. The teacher should have on display textbooks, workbooks, and certain selected aids used in teaching. She should stress application of these materials and suggest how the parent might help.

18. Test scores should be reported in terms of percentile scores, profile charts and the like. Raw scores from IQ tests should be reported only by drawing generalizations (above average, below average, and the like).

19. Confidential records should not be left on the classroom desk as parents often want to pick these up and look at them.

20. Educational vernacular should be chosen carefully. Beware of negative expressions such as: trouble maker, stubborn, sloppy, clumsy, immature, rude, bashful, lazy, uncooperative.

21. Once the conference is begun it should not be interrupted. Insure privacy.

22. One should remember that the conference is a means of exchanging certain types of information. The teacher has something "to give"; the parent has something "to bring" to the conference.

23. Summarize the conference briefly before tactfully dismissing the parent. Strike some agreement upon action needed. Clarify the next steps. Make a written record of the conference after the parent leaves.

24. The teacher should meet with the child as soon as possible after the conference session is completed. Let him know generally what was discussed. Outline his strengths and limitations. This will help him eliminate some of the mystery surrounding modern conference methods and to recognize that both you and his parents are working for him.

25. If one has no suggestions for improving a bad trait or practice, it might be just as well that it is not brought up during the conference.

26. Brochures of "Ways the Home Can Help" might be handed to the parents at the close of the conference. The booklet should consist of information agreed upon by the school faculty. The teacher might make a comment as to the initial purpose of that handbook.

Appendix B

CONFERENCE IDEAS OF A CREATIVE NATURE

WHAT TO SHOW PARENTS AT CONFERENCE TIME CONCERNING THE CHILD'S WORK:

1. Samples of tests (i.e., teacher-prepared and certain standardized tests).

2. Individual charts, graphs, and grids (i.e., individual records; self-evaluation sheets, profiles, health grids, daily class records, and socio-grams).
3. Folders of work (i.e., samples of papers of each child).
4. Projects (i.e., industrial arts, home economics, and art).
5. Special aids and equipment used for instructing their child.
6. Homework Guides (hand out printed booklets containing suggestions for guiding homework).
7. Educational materials (i.e., included here are pamphlets about child growth and development, schedules, and recommended reading lists).

HOW TO EFFECTIVELY USE THE OBJECTS TO BE SHOWN TO PARENTS:

1. Use symbols instead of names. This allows one to show the whole graph or chart. (i.e., On the socio-gram—"Your child's number is six." Or, "On the spelling graph, your child's number is ten.").
2. Discuss the merits of the child's selected samples of work as they are shown for each subject area.
3. Describe the child's projects in the arts as they are shown to the parents. (i.e., discuss beauty of material, form, color, originality, talent, and meaning).

FOR THE CREATIVE CONDUCTOR OF A CONFERENCE:

1. Have the bulletin board "timely" and items displayed neatly.
2. See that chalk boards contain a lesson.
3. Add to the Guidesheet criteria for evaluating Foreign Language, Industrial Arts, and the like.
4. Display a textbook for each subject; include children's magazines and your own professional journals.
5. Have colorful class projects on display.
6. Utilize the tape recorder to emphasize both good and poor characteristics of the child's voice. These brief recordings might illustrate reading habits, speech defects, singing voice or vocal skill, special speeches, and the like.

Appendix C

EXTENDED BIBLIOGRAPHY ON PARENT-TEACHER CONFERENCES

1. Abrams, J. C. "Parental Dynamics: Their Role in Learning Disabilities." *The Reading Teacher.* May 1970. 23:751-55.

2. Barrins, P. C. "Drug Abuse: the Newest and Most Dangerous Challenge to School Boards." *Education Digest.* January 1970. 35:24-26.

3. Bienvenu, M. J. and S. McClain. "Parent-Adolescent Communication and Self-Esteem." *Journal of Home Economics.* May 1970. 62:344-45.

4. Bromberg, Susan L. "A Beginning Teacher Works with Parents." *Young Children.* December 1968. 24:75-80.

5. Bronfield, F. "Brain-Injured Child: the Parent's Role." *New York Society for the Experimental Study of Education.* Yearbook. 1967. 183-85.

6. Cawelti, Donald G. "Creative Evaluation Through Parent Conferences." *Elementary School Journal.* March 1966. 66:293-97.

7. Christensen, Anne L. "How Children Feel About Reporting." *National Elementary Principal.* May 1966. 45:17-20.

8. Crocker, Eleanor C. "Depth Consultation with Parents." *Young Children.* November 1964. 20:91-99

9. Davis, S. E. "Parents and School Should Share." *The Reading Teacher.* May 1970. 23:707-10.

10. Demsch, B. "Understanding What Parents do not Tell You." *School and Community.* February 1970. 56:7.

11. Dunfee, Maxine. "What Do Parents Need to Know?" *Educational Leadership.* December 1964. 22:160-63.

12. Essex, E. "Getting Through to the Establishment." *Education Digest.* January 1970. 35:42-44.

13. Felsenthal, H. "Role of the School Psychologist in Counseling Parents of the Mentally Retarded." *Training School Bulletin.* May 1968. 65:29-35.

14. Firester, L. and J. Firester. "Wanted: Rx for the Equitable Management of Parent-School Conflict." *Education Digest.* April 1970. 35:5-7.

15. Fulton, G. B. "Sex Education: Some Issues and Answers." *Journal of School Health.* May 1970. 40:263-68.

16. Harper, M. A. "Home and School Associations; Facing the Bar of Judgment." *Momentum.* February 1970. 1:30-3.

17. Hollister, William G. "The Behavior-Guidance Tools of the Classroom Teacher." *Virginia Journal of Education.* May 1966.

18. Johnson, B. "Taping Parent Opinion; Stanley School, Tacoma, Washington." *Instructor.* March 1970. 79:144-45.

19. King, Charlyce R. "The Parent as Counselor to His Child." *Adult Leadership.* January 1967. 15:231-46.

20. Kirk, E. C. "Mobility Evaluation Report for Parents; Blind Children." *Exceptional Children.* September 1968. 35:57-62.

21. Kunruether, S. C. "Black Mothers Speak and a White Teacher Listens." *Children.* May 1970. 17:91-96.

22. Ling, A. H. "Advice for Parents of Young Deaf Children: How to Begin." *Volta Review.* May 1968. 70:316-19.

23. Lowery, L. F. "Study of the Attitudes of Parents Toward Teachers." *Journal of Educational Research.* January 1969. 62:227-30.

24. Luckey, E. B. "Sex Education: Why?" *CTA Journal.* January 1969. 65:9-11.

25. Martyn, Kenneth A. and Harold J. Bienvenu. "The Parent Conference—Progress Report, not Psycho-therapy." *Elementary School Journal.* October 1956. 57:42-44.

26. Maves, Harold J. "Contrasting Levels of Performance in Parent-Teacher Conferences." *Elementary School Journal.* January 1958. 58:219-24.

27. Medinnus, G. R., *et al.* "Parental Perceptions of Kindergarten Children." *Journal of Educational Research.* April 1970. 63:379-81.

28. Millar, T. P. "When Parents Talk to Teachers." *Elementary School Journal.* May 1969. 33:241-45.

29. Mullen, Frances A. "The Teacher Works with the Parent of the Exceptional Child." *Education.* February 1960. 80:329-32.

30. McConnell, Gaither, "What Do Parents Want to Know?" *Elementary School Journal.* November 1957. 58:83-87.

31. Niedermeyer, F. C. "Parents Teach Kindergarten Reading at Home." *Elementary School Journal.* May 1970. 70:438-45.

32. Pollock, S. E. "Parent-Student Panels." *Today's Education.* December 1969. 58:54.

33. Radin, N. "Impact of a Kindergarten Home Counseling Program." *Exceptional Children.* December 1969. 36:251-56.

34. Reszke, Luise. "The Parent-Teacher Conference—A Cooperative Plan." *The National Elementary Principal.* June 1952. 31:39-46.

35. Rice, Joseph P., Jr. "The Importance of Parent-Teacher Conferences." *Education.* September 1962. 83:43-45.

36. Romano, Louis. "Finding Out What Parents Want to Know." *Elementary School Journal.* November 1957. 58:88-90.

37. Rothney, John W. M. "Improving Reports to Parents." *The National Elementary Principal.* May 1966. 45:51-53.

38. Saxe, R. W. "Unstudied Problem: Parent Visiting." *The Educational Forum.* January 1969. 33:241-45.

39. Sharrock, A. N. "Aspects of Communication Between Schools and Parents." *Educational Research* (British). June 1970. 12:194-201.

40. Swift, M. S. "Training Poverty Mothers in Communication Skills." *The Reading Teacher.* January 1970. 23:360-67.

41. Tantum, Anna R. "Planning for Child Growth Thru Parent-Teacher Conferences." *The National Elementary Principal.* June 1952. 31:34-38.

42. Tarjan, C. "Handicapped Children in School: Reflections of a Psychiatrist." *NCEA Bulletin.* No. 65. August 1968. Pp. 170-76.

Appendix D

ORIGINAL RESEARCH

A major portion of the contents of this book has come from the original research of the writer. These documents were:

Bradley, R. C. "The Parent-Teacher Conference as a Method of Reporting Pupil Progress in Selected Elementary Public Schools in the State of Missouri." Unpublished *Educational Specialist* Thesis, Central Missouri State College, Warrensburg, Missouri, 1962.

Bradley, R. C. "Teacher Practices in Parent-Teacher Conferences as Compared With the Judgment of a Panel of Selected Educators." Unpublished doctoral dissertation, University of Missouri, Columbia, Missouri, 1963.

The members of the Panel of Selected Educators mentioned above were:

Dr. Edwin Brown, Chairman, Department of Education. University of Santa Clara, California. Co-author of the textbook, *Managing the Classroom* (New York: The Ronald Press Company, 1961).

Dr. Ruth Strang, Professor of Education, University of Arizona, Tucson. Author of "Reporting to Parents," *Practical Suggestions for Teaching.* Hollis Caswell, ed. (New York: Bureau of Publications, Teachers College, Columbia University, 1952).

Dr. Fred McKinney, Professor of Psychology, University of Missouri, Columbia. His extensive practical background in teaching of the several areas of child growth and development was of importance to the purposes of the study.

Dr. Frank Heagerty, Professor of Education, and Director of University Laboratory School and Student Teaching, University of Missouri, Columbia. He not only deals with day-by-day conference situations in the University Laboratory School, but directs special seminars and meetings relative to parent-teacher conference experiences for student teachers.

Dr. Lois Knowles, Professor of Education, University of Missouri, Columbia. Co-author of Scott, Foresman's new *Seeing Through Arithmetic* for Grades 3-6. She conducts teacher-training classes among which are "Techniques of Teaching in the Elementary Schools," and "Arithmetic for Teachers."

Dr. James Craigmile, Professor of Education, University of Missouri, Columbia, conducts courses in elementary school organization, methods, and techniques of teaching. His direct communication with elementary principals and teachers in the field has been instrumental in improving the effectiveness of their reporting practices.

The dissertation project itself was directed by the author's graduate advisor, Dr. A. Sterl Artley, Professor of Education, University of Missouri, Columbia, the nationally known reading specialist. From among his many professional writings his publication of *Your Child Learns to Read* (Dallas: Scott, Foresman and Company, 1953) deals specifically with helping parents gain a clear understanding of the kinds of problems faced in teaching children to read and of the role that parents can play in helping their children. Dr. Artley is also co-author of the Scott, Foresman and Company basal reading series for children.

Subject Index